"This is a first-class, up-to-date introduction to, and broad commentary on, the Four Gospels. The treatment combines all four Gospels into a single, running account, with comments on all important passages and issues . . . Years of experience have enabled Father Vawter to offer countless insights into thorny sections of the Gospels . . . It has immense academic value, but it also contains countless illustrations of Christian living." *The Critic*

"Vawter has succeeded admirably in the goal he set himself: to supply his readers with the information needed for a basic understanding of the Gospel texts and to whet their appetites for the more substantial fare afforded by good commentaries on the individual Gospels. The Christian who is looking for a sure guide to the study of the Gospels, which makes available in simple style and clear language the conclusions of sound New Testament scholarship, will find the object of his search in *The Four Gospels*." *The Catholic Biblical Quarterly*

"Father Vawter's commentary blends smooth, clear prose with great technical expertise. The author has a flair for explaining the very things a non-specialist needs to know . . . No review can do justice to a book which, to be fully appreciated, ought to be read in harmony with the Four Gospels, pondered, talked about, prayed over—for a long, long time." *The Sign*

"/THE FOUR GOSPELS/ does everything it was claimed to do, in a superlative way. The Rev. Bruce Vawter . . . continues for the four Gospels his tradition of a solid, positive analysis; not so scholarly as to be dry with tedious detail, yet not so superficial that the reader learns little new . . . All in all, this book seems to be a worthy result of the most genuine and most precious thrusts of Catholic scriptural study . . . The other excellences of this book must be experienced in order to be relished." *The New World*

THE FOUR GOSPELS

An Introduction

THE
FOUR
GOSPELS

An Introduction

Volume I

Bruce Vawter, C.M.

IMAGE BOOKS

A Division of Doubleday & Company, Inc.

Garden City, New York

Image Books edition 1969

by special arrangement with
Doubleday & Company, Inc.

Image Books edition published February 1969

Imprimatur: ✠ Joseph Cardinal Ritter
Archdiocese of St. Louis
September 20, 1966

*To the Fathers and Brothers of
the Congregation of the Mission
in Their 150th Year in America
1816–1966*

FOREWORD

Some years ago I wrote a book entitled *A Popular Explanation of the Four Gospels.* It achieved a measure of success, was reprinted, and went into a second and revised edition. It is now out of print and properly so, since it no longer represents what a popularization is supposed to be, namely, an impression for the general reader of what is present-day informed and professional thinking on its subject. This present book does, I hope, offer something of the kind. It is entirely new both in content and in format, though I have kept some of the chapter headings that I used before and, here and there, a sentence or two.

This is less a commentary on the Gospels than it is an explanation of what they are about. My intention throughout has been to let the Gospels tell their own story to the extent possible, and what comments I have added have been designed to assist the reader in hearing their story more clearly and with fewer distractions. Exegesis in the technical sense of the word is rare in this book, and still less often have I taken up the challenge of the many theological issues to which the Gospels give rise especially in our times. For these, the reader will have to be referred to the commentaries and special studies of every kind which are now available to him in abundance. If this book succeeds in its purpose he will want to move on to this other literature in any case.

This is an introduction to the Gospels through a reading of the Gospels. For reasons that I trust are justified in my first chapter, I intend that the Gospels be read concurrently. For this purpose, although it is not absolutely necessary, a "harmony" of the four Gospels should prove to be most useful. My arrangement of the text has mainly followed— though not rigidly—Kurt Aland's *Synopsis Quattuor Evangeliorum* of the Greek New Testament (second edition, 1964). There are many English harmonies on the market, practically any of which should be equally adaptable to the design of this book. I have deliberately avoided using any single one of the standard English translations of the Gospels for my citations of the text. The reader may choose the one he likes best. It is obviously indispensable, however, that he have some sort of biblical text before him as he reads.

For reasons that I judge adequate I have abandoned an earlier intention of including reading lists to assist in a continuing study of the Gospels. Continuing study will imply various things to various people. It might be thought useful, however, to mention here a few of the kind of books presupposed by an introductory volume like this, which deal not abstrusely but in detail with topics that evidently deserve more than the few lines that we have often been able to give them.

The whole gamut of contemporary Gospel study—the Synoptic and Johannine questions, form criticism, the processes and the theologies of the several evangelists, and the rest—is run in works like *New Testament Introduction* by Alfred Wikenhauser (Herder and Herder, 1958) or Robert-Feuillet's *Introduction to the New Testament* (Desclée, 1965). The sometimes fascinating story of the making of the Gospels and the New Testament, the historical tensions of which they are the product and the textual traditions which are their witnesses, can be read in Bruce Metzger's *The Text of the New Testament* (Oxford University Press, 1964) and *The Birth of the New Testament* by C. F. D. Moule

(Harper and Row, 1962). The specifics of the Gospel tradition that are the raw material of form criticism are ably
presented by Vincent Taylor in his *The Formation of the
Gospel Tradition* (Macmillan, 1933); and in this connection Catholic readers will be well advised to consult the
1964 Instruction of the Pontifical Biblical Commission, presented with a commentary by Joseph A. Fitzmyer, S.J., in
The Historical Truth of the Gospels (Paulist Press, 1965).
The intricacies of New Testament christology may be ex-
plored from many angles. This writer has been especially
indebted to Vincent Taylor, *The Names of Jesus* (Mac-
millan, 1962); Oscar Cullmann, *The Christology of the New
Testament* (SCM Press, 1959); E. M. Sidebottom, *The
Christ of the Fourth Gospel* (SPCK Press, 1961); and
Asher Finkel, *The Pharisees and the Teacher of Nazareth*
(Leiden: Brill, 1964).

At the end of this book the reader will find indexes of the
Gospel passages and of subjects treated. The two maps
should be adequate for his present purposes, though he
would find it useful to have at hand a standard Bible atlas
such as the *Westminster Historical Atlas to the Bible* or
Grollenberg's *Atlas of the Bible*. To most of the questions
which already exist in his mind or to which this reading
may give rise, at least a preliminary answer can be found in
a reference like *The Interpreter's Dictionary of the Bible,
The Encyclopedic Dictionary of the Bible,* or the *Dictionary
of the Bible* by John L. McKenzie, S.J., one of which should
be in the library of everyone who is seriously concerned
with the Gospels.

19 July 1966
Feast of St. Vincent de Paul

CONTENTS

Volume I

ABBREVIATIONS OF BIBLICAL REFERENCES

Gen	Genesis	Wis	Wisdom of Solomon
Ex	Exodus	Sir	Sirach (Ecclesiasticus)
Lev	Leviticus	Is	Isaiah
Num	Numbers	Jer	Jeremiah
Deut	Deuteronomy	Lam	Lamentations
Jos	Joshua	Bar	Baruch
Jgs	Judges	Ezek	Ezekiel
1–2 Sam	1–2 Samuel	Dan	Daniel
1–2 Kgs	1–2 Kings	Hos	Hosea
1–2 Chron	1–2 Chronicles	Joel	Joel
Ezra	Ezra	Amos	Amos
Neh	Nehemiah	Mi	Micah
Tob	Tobit	Hab	Habakkuk
Job	Job	Zeph	Zephaniah
Ps(s)	Psalm(s)	Zech	Zechariah
Prov	Proverbs	Mal	Malachi
Eccl	Ecclesiastes	1–2 Macc	1–2 Maccabees
Cant	Song of Songs		

4 Ezra	The apocryphal book of 4 Ezra, also called 2 Esdras
1 QS	The *Serek* ("Manual of Discipline") of the Qumran sectaries

Mt	Matthew	Col	Colossians
Mk	Mark	1–2 Thes	1–2 Thessalonians
Lk	Luke	1–2 Tim	1–2 Timothy
Jn	John	Tit	Titus
Acts	Acts of the Apostles	Phlm	Philemon
Rom	Romans	Heb	Hebrews
1–2 Cor	1–2 Corinthians	Jas	James
Gal	Galatians	1–2 Pt	1–2 Peter
Eph	Ephesians	1–2 Jn	1–2 John
Phil	Philippians	Apo	The Apocalypse or Revelation

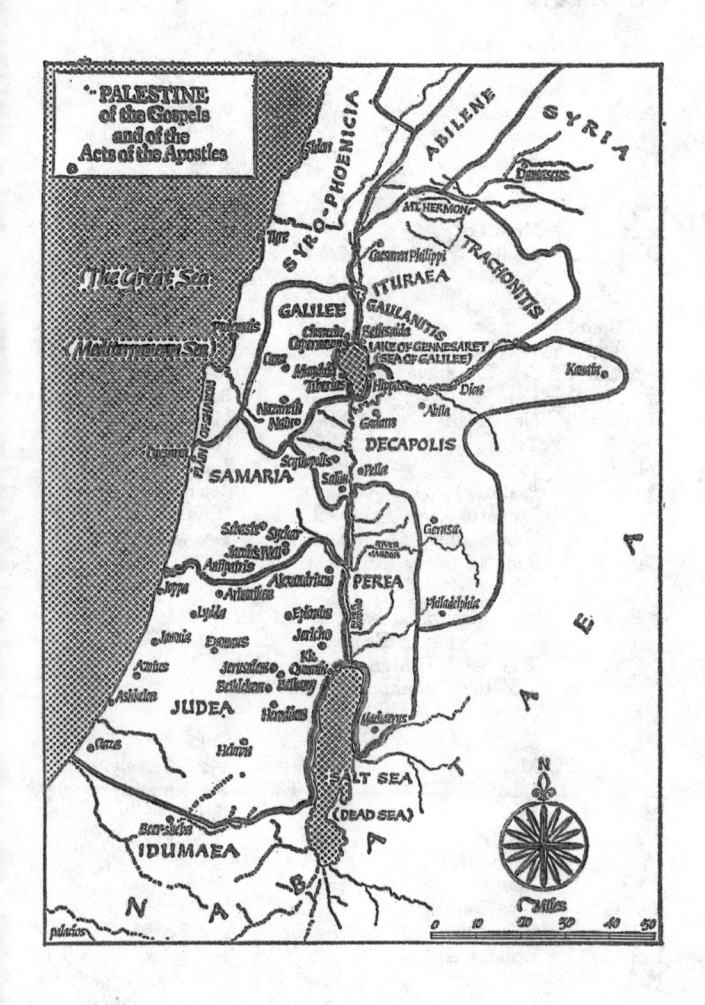

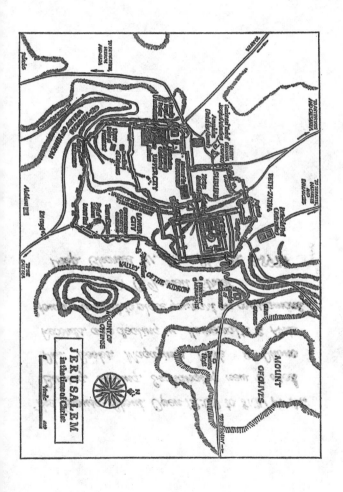

The Brouse-About. Open 12:00 to 8:30 P. M.

Buying, Selling, Exchanging new & used

Pkt. Books, Magazines Comic & Phono

Records. also dealing in Homecrafts & Arts

You are invited to place your art on consignment.

491 O'Farrell Street

Prop. Charles W. Mew Ph. Or. 3-8974

1. SOME PRELIMINARIES

When Tatian produced his *Diatessaron* sometime in the latter part of the second Christian century, he probably continued rather than began a tradition of reading the four Gospels in harmony, the tradition that justifies the arrangement of this present book. Whether or not Tatian's work was the first of its kind, it was certainly one of the most successful. For several centuries it was only in this form that the Gospels were known to a sizable part of Oriental Christianity.

There was and is both good and bad in the *Diatessaron* and in the innumerable "harmonies" that have followed in its wake. On the debit side, such works have encouraged a simplistic view of the Gospels that has given a bad name to the term harmonization. This was especially true of the *Diatessaron* and its imitators, which coalesced the four Gospels into a single narrative, forming an eclectic text for which none of the evangelists was really responsible and suppressing in the process those very signs of individual genius which are the stamp of the inspired authors chosen by the Spirit of God. However ancient this kind of harmony may be, even at its best it settles for a very superficial reading of the Gospels in which matter is preferred to form, flesh to spirit. At its worst it masks a fundamental misconception of what the Gospels are all about.

To read the Gospels in concert, on the other hand, is simply to respond to the invitation the Gospels themselves offer—the first three of them, at any rate. The kind of harmony which arranges the Gospels in parallel columns to show both their similarities and differences affords us an added dimension for the understanding of each individual Gospel. The Gospels were not written in isolation from one another, at least not from the common tradition to which they all witness, and therefore they should not be read in isolation. True, they must also be read as the distinct creations of distinct authors; however, a harmony of the Gospels, if it is rightly used, can only constantly remind us of what is unique about each of the parallels.

Four Gospels or a Life of Christ? A remaining objection that may be lodged against the simultaneous treatment of the Gospels, especially when this includes the Gospel of John, is that it may seek to pursue the outmoded approach to the Gospels that is summed up in the title "the Life of Christ." The countless volumes that bear this title or its equivalent (those who regarded themselves as disinterested historical critics preferred to write a *Life of Jesus*), mainly from the latter part of the past century and the first quarter of the present, are a monument to an age of Gospel study that was not without value but was certainly misdirected. The Gospels are not a Life of Christ, for two very good reasons. Firstly, they do not provide even the minimal amount of material that is required to write the Life of anyone. Oddly enough, most of those who set about writing the Lives admitted this from the outset. Secondly, and more importantly, the Gospels were not composed, nor were their sources formed, from any such biographical intention.

Whether by believer or unbeliever, the classic *Life of Jesus* was the product of what has been variously termed rationalism, historical positivism, or historicism. Born of the Enlightenment and of modern critical historical method, "the quest of the historical Jesus," as the process has been called, was the attempt to reconstruct from the Gospels what could be certainly known of Jesus by means of the scientific methods of the historian. The unbeliever, who began the process, not surprisingly found the Gospels to have been written in total disregard of modern historical canons. As a result, he concluded that little if anything could be said about Jesus scientifically. This in itself would not have been so bad, of course. What proved to be bad was his reluctance to leave the matter there. Instead, he tended to supply for a Gospel picture which by his lights could not be historical with a highly unscientific series of reconstructions which owed more to his sense of the fitness of things than to historical evidence. "The so-called historical Jesus of the nineteenth-century biographies," Albert Schweitzer wrote in 1906, "is really a modernization, in which Jesus is painted in the colours of modern bourgeois respectability and neo-Kantian moralism."

The believing Christian who wrote his *Life of Christ* in opposition to all this usually tried to show that the Gospels were, after all, the kind of history that the unbeliever said they were not. Very often he could not do this in any very convincing way, but he felt it to be necessary if he was to use the Gospels to set forth the historical person and message of Jesus Christ. Both believer and unbeliever found it quite natural, in other words, to measure the Gospels against a concept and standards of history writing that are really not more than a couple of centuries old. Both were wrong.

That the Gospels are historical documents of a high order, the writer firmly believes. They are the work of men who were rooted in history, who were themselves products of the history they wrote, a history that was the very breath of their being. But the Gospels are not the self-authenticating history desiderated by the modern historian. They do not appeal to disinterested witnesses to establish as factual anything they record. They were not written to prove that

certain events had really taken place; they were written
to explain what those events meant and what they continue
to mean. They begin by taking for granted what the modern
historian considers it to be the function of his craft to
demonstrate, and they immediately intrude into areas from
which he feels himself debarred. In his sense of the word,
they are not at all objective. They mingle narration of fact
with interpretation of fact, eyewitness record with hearsay
report, statistical data with theological speculation.

The Gospels acknowledge few of the conventions that the
modern historian regards as essential. The exact determination of dates, places, persons, circumstances, the proper
sequence of events—all this is the lifeblood of history as we
have been taught to know it, and yet the Gospels can be
utterly casual about any or all of it. Of such stuff as are the
Gospels, biographies are not made.

Synoptic   Historical records though they be, the Gospels
Gospels   were never intended to form the source material for a Life of Jesus. This is not to say
that they were not interested in his life, which of course they
were. They were interested in it, however, not as a past
event but as an enduring reality—this, as a matter of fact, is
what the authors of the Gospels would have understood as
the meaning of history. The Gospels contain, therefore, little
if anything that is of purely biographical interest. It is true,
they present Jesus of Nazareth as he was known to the
original eyewitnesses of the Gospel (Lk 1:2); but this Jesus
is at one and the same time the Christ encountered by faith
living and acting in his Church, and it is this Christ who
is the Jesus of the Gospels.

For a long time it has been customary to refer to the first
three Gospels as Synoptic because of the common view
(*synopsis*) they assume in narrating the Gospel story. They
follow basically the same order, contain roughly the same
material, and obviously have some kind of literary affinity
one with another. In all these respects they differ quite

sharply from the Gospel of John, which goes its own distinctive way in order, content, vocabulary, and viewpoints.

The tradition to which the Synoptic Gospels have given literary fixation rose from the apostolic *kerygma* of the primitive Church, the "message of good news" by which the divine work of salvation achieved in Jesus Christ was proclaimed to the world by the first Christian witnesses. It is this character, in fact, which has given us our word Gospel (Anglo-Saxon *god spel*, good tidings), a literal translation of the Greek *euangelion*, Latinized as *evangelium*, from which we derive our "evangelist." The concept of salvation as the proclamation of good news which was likewise a summons to faith was already ancient in biblical tradition (see especially Is 40:1–11; 52:7–10; 61:1–3, passages which have considerably influenced the New Testament and its authors). A good summary of the apostolic *kerygma* can be found in Acts 10:37–43, the sermon of St. Peter to the Gentiles. The attentive reader will note how this sermon is arranged according to the basic outline followed by the Synoptics: baptism by John the Baptist, the Galilean ministry, a journey to Jerusalem, and the narrative of Christ's suffering, crucifixion, and resurrection. In essence, too, the content of the Synoptic tradition is described in the few lines of this sermon.

The Synoptic Gospels are not, however, the *kerygma* itself but a development of it. The *kerygma* was and is the proclamation of revelation for acceptance in faith, the word of Christ which awakens faith (Rom 10:17). It addresses itself to those who do not yet believe. The Gospels, on the contrary, were written for believers, for Christians, both to deepen a faith that already existed and, even more importantly, to draw out for the reader all the implications of the words and deeds of Christ which formed the object of his faith (Lk 1:4; Jn 20:31). We might describe the difference by calling the *kerygma* preaching and the Gospels teaching, though of course the two are not always perfectly distinguished.

Why were the Gospels written? The answer to this question is not quite as obvious as it might seem. The Church, after all, got along without a written Gospel during the entirety of its first long generation, a generation that was also doubtless its most important from the standpoint of formation and development. The letters of St. Paul, without which a theology of the New Testament would hardly be thinkable, were all written before the emergence of the Gospels. Paul, too, and with him most of the other New Testament writers who were his contemporaries, shows what initially seems to be a surprising lack of interest in many of the things with which the Gospels are most concerned. He refers in passing to Jesus' birth and also to his death, burial, and resurrection and his institution of the Eucharist; but otherwise he hardly ever adverts to Jesus' earthly life. Never does he mention the Galilean ministry, which occupies a place of major stress in the Synoptic Gospels. It is at least conceivable, therefore, that subsequent generations of Christians could have continued like the first, without a written record of the Gospel stories that now mean so much to us.

As it happens, however, we possess the Gospels as a heritage from apostolic Christianity, a real testament and legacy of the first generation of the Church. The first Christians lived within an apostolic tradition that was not only preservative but also constitutive and creative (Acts 2:42; 1 Cor 11:23; Eph 3:3; 2 Thes 2:15; Jn 14:26; etc.). With the passing away of the apostolic age, however, it was recognized then as it is now that an era never to be recovered now belonged to history; the Church, so to speak, was now "on its own." Falling back upon the strong historical tradition to which they belonged, the evangelists therefore produced the Gospels as a permanent record for all time of the good news of the Christ-event as the apostolic Church had come to know it in its witness and experience, in its preaching and teaching, and in its meditation and contemplation of it in the light of the Holy Spirit. It was probably inevitable that the first Gospels should have followed the outline of the apostolic *kerygma*, the summary form in which the message of the good news had been preached during this long generation. Neither was it accidental that they should lay such stress on the earthly career of Jesus, on the events that had given rise to the faith and liturgy, the life and hope of the Church. The first heresies were already appearing, of a Gnostic and Docetist stamp, which would reduce Christianity to a mere philosophy by denying or declaring irrelevant its roots in history (see 1 Jn 4:1-3; 5:6; 2 Jn 7, etc.).

Form Criticism   Before we discuss briefly the separate characters of the several Gospels that were produced toward the end of the apostolic age, we must pause to consider the role played by the apostolic Church in forming the materials that have gone into these written Gospels. This is the dimension of New Testament study that nowadays goes by the general name of "form criticism."

Anyone who has read the Synoptic Gospels even casually, or who is familiar with them from their use as liturgical readings, cannot fail to have observed how easily they may be divided into short, self-contained units of narrative or discourse, each of which can make its own point or points often quite independently of its immediate context. The fact becomes even more obvious when the Gospels are read in parallel, and it can be seen that the same episode has often been assigned to different contexts, sometimes thereby taking on a different specific application. This phenomenon demands an explanation, which it is not hard to give. The Synoptic tradition on which our Gospels have drawn and which used the apostolic *kerygma* for its model was itself composed of many prior traditions: its components were originally independent elements of the tradition—written or oral—which had handed on the memory of the words and deeds of the Master.

These components are the "forms" with which form criticism deals. They are called this because they tend to fall into a certain limited number of categories which can be distinguished one from another. One common form, for example, is the "conflict story." In the conflict story Jesus is pictured in controversy with one or another of the groups which the Gospels represent as his habitual opponents, usually designated as the scribes and/or Pharisees or the chief priests of Jerusalem. The point at issue is some action or word of Jesus or of those identified with him—his claim to forgive sins, his attitude toward the Sabbath or the Law of Moses, his disciples' violation of Pharisaical ideas of propriety, and the like. Encapsulated in each conflict story is a pronouncement of the Lord which appears as its climax and gives the "moral" of the story. The stories are brief and to the point; details that could detract from the main issue have been pared away. This pattern is repeated time and time again throughout the Gospels. A series of five such conflict stories can be found gathered together in Mk 2:1–3:6, paralleled by Lk 5:18–6:11 and by Mt 9:1–17, 12:1–14, where they have been separated into two groups of three and two respectively.

The isolation and determination of the forms immediately leads to other questions. Why the preference for certain forms rather than for others? What do the forms themselves tell us with regard to the Church that transmitted the Gospel tradition? And, if we can answer these questions satisfactorily, what do we thereby conclude in respect to the historical origin of the recorded event and its significance for the evangelist and the tradition on which he drew? To consider these questions is the real task of form criticism, whose scope is better expressed by a more literal translation of the German term (*Formgeschichte*) of which it is the equivalent: "the history of the forms."

The prevalence of the conflict story involving the Jewish leadership of Jesus' day, to continue with the example taken above, can hardly be dissociated from the history of the apostolic Church as we know it from Acts and especially the Pauline epistles. This was, by and large, a history of conflict with Jews, both with Jews who refused to accept Christ and with those Jewish Christians who would have so identified the Church with its Jewish origins that the death and resurrection of Christ would have been made void. To all extents and purposes, the only opposition experienced by the Church during its formative years was Jewish. Only toward the very end of this period did the great secular power of the age, the Roman empire, begin to move against a Christianity in which it now dimly recognized a threat to its omnipotent sway over men's minds. (Characteristically, the later Apocalypse of John identifies the Antichrist with the Roman emperor, whereas the Johannine epistles consider every apostate and schismatic to be an Antichrist, and an anti-Roman bias is utterly lacking in the Gospels.) It was only to be expected that this history of Jewish controversy should have affected the transmission of the Gospel materials. Throughout this entire period the Church searched its memory for precedents, for instances in the life of its Master which paralleled its own concerns, when answers had been given in principle to what had become the burning issues of Christian survival. How better to refute the Jewish adversaries of Christianity than by appealing to what Jesus himself had done and said in analogous circumstances?

The other forms of the Gospel materials have a similar explanation. The pastoral, catechetical, apologetical, and liturgical uses of the Church have all had a considerable influence on the development of these forms. The very passages which we find it convenient to cite in making a point or teaching a lesson were, in other words, first employed by the apostolic Church for these same purposes, and it is this early Christian use that has imprinted itself on the tradition. Form critical study is, therefore, a modern approach to the ancient principle that it was the Church that produced the New Testament and that the Gospels ought not to be interpreted apart from the Church's life and belief. It will be our duty to refer to this principle often in the course of this book.

Some of the form critics, to be sure, have drawn unwarranted conclusions from their studies. Simply because it can be seen that a given passage had a role to play in the life of the Church, what the form critics call its *Sitz im Leben,* its "setting in life," is no reason to call its historical reality into question. Those critics who maintain that the

Church simply invented such a passage to justify its belief or practice do so from no evidence supplied by form criticism but on the grounds of skeptical principles they have inherited from other sources. That the Gospel has an authentic *Sitz im Leben* of the primitive Church does not mean that it does not have an equally authentic *Sitz im Leben* of Jesus himself. It must be studied in both dimensions, and also, of course, in the dimension of the individual evangelist who is involved as author. While warning against exaggerations, therefore, in an historic instruction dated April 21, 1964, the Pontifical Biblical Commission wisely commended the use of form criticism to Catholic interpreters of the Gospels, and even insisted on it as necessary for a full understanding of their meaning. The substance of this instruction has been incorporated by the Fathers of the Second Vatican Council into their dogmatic constitution on Divine Revelation.

The Gospel of Mark   We should now turn to a consideration, however brief, of the specific characteristics of the four Gospels with which we shall be dealing in this book. We have already seen that the Synoptic Gospels grew out of the apostolic *kerygma*. Perhaps we can now be more precise. As far as we know, of the four Gospels that we possess, the one we know as the Gospel of Mark was the first to be written, sometime between the years 60 to 70 of the Christian era. "As far as we know," and "of the four Gospels that we possess": as we shall see, there is a possibility that there was an even earlier Gospel of Matthew, which, however, is not the work that has been preserved as our first Gospel.

The determination of the priority of Mark is very much bound up with the solution of the "Synoptic question," that is, the explanation of what seems to be an undeniable literary connection between the three Synoptic Gospels. That this connection was indeed literary and not merely the result of dependence on a common tradition is obvious to most scholars. It is not only that the three Gospels follow broadly the same outline and contain essentially the same traditional materials; they also sometimes agree word for word sentence after sentence, and in the process they manage at times to use the same unusual Greek words (in some instances, words that are found nowhere else in all Greek literature). Particularly striking is their manner of citing the Old Testament. More than once they agree verbally on a quotation that represents a version all their own, corresponding precisely neither to the Hebrew text nor to the standard Greek translation of the Old Testament (the Septuagint). The conclusion seems to be inescapable either that they have all drawn on the same literary source or that they have a literary dependence one on another.

The explanation that appears to accord best both with the phenomenology of the Synoptic situation and with ancient Christian tradition concerning the Gospels is that Mark has been used as a literary source by both Matthew and Luke. When the three Gospels are read in parallel attentively, it will be seen that while Mark has practically nothing that is not also in Matthew or Luke or both, almost invariably it is his version of the events that is the lengthiest, the most circumstanced and detailed, the closest to the eyewitness record from which it ultimately derives. Not everyone will agree that this is so—there have been literally hundreds of theories proposed to solve the Synoptic problem. But nowadays probably most scholars would agree that one of the sources used by the Gospels of Matthew and Luke was the Gospel of Mark. Or, if not the canonical Gospel in the form we have it, at least a document that was almost precisely identical with it. The attempt to explain Mark as dependent on either Matthew or Luke, on the other hand, has been singularly unconvincing.

There is no serious reason to doubt the consistent Christian tradition which has identified as the author of this Gospel the New Testament personage known to Peter and Paul as Mark (Col 4:10; Phlm 24; 2 Tim 4:11; 1 Pt 5:13) and called John Mark in the Acts of the Apostles (12:12, 25, 13:13, 15:37). For one thing, his relative obscurity in the early Church is warrant enough for the reliability of the tradition.

Mark was not one of the apostles or leaders in the Church. He was a cousin of Paul's associate Barnabas; at various times he was the companion of both Peter and Paul, with whom he had at least a temporary falling out. He was doubtless a Jew from Jerusalem, where his mother maintained what was evidently a substantial household.

Neither is there any reason to question the tradition, first related by Papias, the Bishop of Hierapolis (about A.D. 130), that the basis of Mark's Gospel was the *kerygma* as preached by Peter in Rome. Another tradition, preserved by Irenaeus of Lyons (about A.D. 190), which places the composition of the Gospel in Rome after Peter's death, is doubtless also correct. There can be no doubt that Mark's Gospel is heavily in debt to an eyewitness account which from internal considerations can hardly be other than Peter's. Furthermore, though Mark's Greek is greatly influenced by Semitisms— turns of phrase that show him to have been more at home with Palestinian Aramaic than with the Greek of the Gentile world—it also contains a surprising number of Latinisms— Latin words used in preference to Greek—which suggests that the Gospel was written in an environment where Latin was spoken.

We are not to suppose that Mark's dependence on Peter was such that he merely wrote down a Gospel of which Peter was the real author. As we have already seen, the written Gospels are an outgrowth of the *kerygma,* not the *kerygma* itself. Mark had at his disposal the materials of which we have spoken above in discussing form criticism, the written and oral forms in which the traditions about Jesus had been handed down in the apostolic Church, some still preserving their Palestinian primitiveness, others marked by the now generally Gentile character of Christianity. These he combined with Peter's testimony and worked into an art form distinctively his own, for Mark was a true author.

Mark's Gospel has suffered in comparison with those of Matthew and Luke. It has even been called simply "a passion story with an introduction." This is to do less than justice to Mark's artistry. It is true that his style tends to be laconic and unpolished, that he has expressed his own personality relatively little, that he has "done" less with the Gospel form than either Matthew or Luke. However, there is far more subtlety to Mark than appears on the surface, and there is a great deal of theology in this Gospel, as we shall have occasion to see. One of Mark's unique contributions to the Gospel record is the so-called "messianic secret," of which we shall speak later.

The Gospel of Luke   Scholars may disagree as to whether Luke's or Matthew's Gospel is the older, but probably the majority would give the priority to Luke. As indicated above, one of its main sources has been the Gospel of Mark; this source accounts for about one third of Luke's Gospel. Another major source unknown to Mark has been used by both Matthew and Luke: it is this that accounts for the special correspondence of these two Gospels within the Synoptic tradition. For many reasons that will be made plain in the commentary, however, it appears that the two Gospels were composed quite independently of each other. That is to say, while they both depend on Mark and the other common source, there is no mutual dependence.

Like Mark, Luke was a relatively obscure figure in the early Church, and we have therefore all the more reason to accept the second-century tradition which names him the author of the Third Gospel. He is the one New Testament writer whom we can identify with almost utter certainty as a non-Jew; this is the obvious sense of Col 4:14, in which Paul distinguishes Luke from Jews like Mark and Jesus Justus. In this same verse Luke is called by Paul an *iatros*. The word means "physician," but whether it was intended as a literal or a figurative designation may be debated. On the supposition that it does refer to Luke's profession, many authors have felt that a medical background may be discerned in his work (see, for example, the commentary on Lk 8:43). However this may be, it is certain that Luke was a man of some education and cultivation. He seems to have joined St. Paul during his "second missionary journey" (is

Luke the Macedonian of Acts 16:9 f. who appeared to call
Paul from Asia into Europe?); thereafter he became his in-
separable companion.

The provenance of Luke's Gospel is something of an
enigma. He was with St. Paul in Rome during the apostle's
imprisonment there (about A.D. 61–63), where he could have
become acquainted with Mark's Gospel or its prototype. He
was also with him in Caesarea of Palestine (A.D. 59–60)
where he would have had a unique opportunity to follow
up the traditions handed down by the original eyewitnesses
and servants of the Gospel (Lk 1:2). Again, he spent several
years with Paul in Ephesus (A.D. 54–57), the home of the
Johannine school of the New Testament: of all the Synoptic
Gospels, Luke's has the greatest affinity for the Gospel of
John. Yet nowhere within or without the Gospel are we given
a hint of its place of origin. Perhaps this is part of its genius.
Of all the Gospels, Luke's may be considered the most "catho-
lic," the least identified with anything regional or partisan in
Christianity. It is the Gospel of a Church that had become
Catholic in fact as well as in principle.

Part of Luke's Catholicity is evidenced in his unique conception of the Gospel as the first half of a two-part work
which is concluded in the Acts of the Apostles. The Acts,
which has aptly been called "the Gospel of the Holy Spirit,"
underlines Luke's leitmotiv, which is the universality of salvation. In Acts the witness to the good news first proclaimed in
the villages of Galilee is dramatically portrayed as extending
to all the known world (the theme of Acts 1:8), while mean-
time every class of person is seen to have been embraced
by Christianity: Jews both Hebrew and Hellenist, Samaritans, proselytes, Gentiles. Because the period covered by Acts
ends with Paul's Roman imprisonment unresolved, it was once
thought that Acts, and therefore the Gospel which preceded
it, could be dated no later than A.D. 63, since otherwise Luke
would have been able to describe Paul's subsequent fate.
It is now recognized that this was to underrate Luke's imagination. Acts ends precisely where he intended it to end,
with the Church planted at the center of the Roman world,

looking forward to the limitless future that is the final stage in the history of salvation. Because Lk 19:43 f. and 21:20, 24 make it appear that the author had actually seen the destruction of Jerusalem (in A.D. 70) foretold by Jesus, most critics nowadays would date the Gospel of Luke around A.D. 80 or so.

Luke's Gospel is a production of high literary quality which tells us a great deal about the author. It has been cast in one of the literary forms then current, something like a travelogue: he represents Jesus' ministry as a long journey from Galilee, where all things begin, to Jerusalem, where they are consummated. (The same travelogue device is employed in Acts.) After the fashion of contemporary Gentile writing he has prefaced to his work a dedication and declaration of intention. He has imitated the existing "lives" of great men by including stories of Jesus' birth and pre-ministerial career and by collating the Gospel events to some extent with the chronology of profane history. In developing the theme of John the Baptist as forerunner of Jesus, he was not content simply to state the fact, but he has carefully paralleled the annunciation, birth, and early history of the Baptist ("the last prophet of the Old Testament") with those of Jesus ("the prophet of the New Testament") in a masterful development wherein the Baptist gradually recedes from the forefront, leaving the stage to Jesus.

In his use of the Marcan material, Luke has omitted narrations or details which would be misunderstood or unappreciated by Gentiles; he has either omitted or translated Semitic words or concepts into the Greek equivalents. His tendency throughout has been to smooth away difficulties—sometimes, it must be admitted, by the adoption of somewhat simplistic interpretations of words or events. In the passion narrative, on the other hand, he follows a version of the events which sometimes differs from that of Mark (who is followed by Matthew) and often offers a more realistic picture, as we shall see.

Together with Matthew and John, though not always in the same way or in the same passages, Luke has "actualized" the Gospel narrative far more than Mark has done. That is to say, he has related the words or deeds of Jesus in a way calculated to apply to the later times of the Church in which he lived.

The Gospel of Matthew When we turn to the Gospel of Matthew we are immediately presented with a whole series of problems. First of all, who is the author of this Gospel? Constant tradition, beginning with the Papias whom we mentioned in connection with Mark, has identified him with Matthew the apostle, also known as Levi, one of the Twelve who lived intimately with Jesus and who were the eyewitnesses to whom Luke appeals in his prologue. However, it is evident to almost everyone that the Gospel of Matthew has used Mark as one of its main sources. Why should one who had been an eyewitness to the Gospel events employ the work of another who had not been, whose acquaintance with them had been only indirect, through another apostle? Furthermore, both Papias and Irenaeus relate that Matthew wrote his Gospel in "Hebrew," by which they doubtless meant the Aramaic language spoken by the Jews of Palestine ("Hebrew" is used in this sense in Acts 21:40). Our canonical Gospel of Matthew, however, as those who have studied its Greek will testify to a man, is not the translation of anything, Aramaic or otherwise. It is a work that was composed originally in Greek, often enough employing plays on words that make sense only in that language. It contains rather fewer Semitisms than Mark.

On the other hand, there are numerous traits to Matthew's Gospel which characterize it as Jewish. For one thing, it cites the Old Testament almost as many times as all the other Gospels combined, and in its independent use of these texts it appears to have made its own translation of the Hebrew original. It has preserved peculiarly Jewish manners of expression which the other Gospels have not (e.g., "kingdom of heaven" in place of "kingdom of God"), along with peculiarly Semitic literary or rhetorical forms like "inclusion." ("Inclusion" is the device whereby the same catch phrase is used to introduce and to conclude a theme. Note the repeated "by their fruits you will know them" in Mt 7:16–20, and contrast the parallel in Lk 6:43–45.) Frequently enough a passage paralleled in Mark or Luke will have signs of an added Jewish influence in the Matthaean version. (See, for example, the commentary on Mt 19:3–9.)

The Jewishness of Matthew's Gospel not surprisingly has given rise to a popular idea that it was written for Jewish Christians in contrast to Luke's, which is obviously Gentile in its orientation. This idea, however, can hardly be correct. When Matthew is read in the whole, it is clear enough that for its author the period of Jewish Christianity now belongs to the past. Not only is the Church destined to embrace all mankind (Mt 28:19), this Gospel goes out of its way to insist that the Church is now properly Gentile rather than Jewish (cf. 8:11 f., 21:43 f., etc.). It is no accident that Matthew, of all the Gospels, gives the greatest space to the relations between Jesus and scribal Judaism: the author stands in the greatest possible opposition to the Judaizing tendencies of Jewish Christianity. There are even some passages in the Gospel which in the view of some prove that the author could not possibly have been a Jew (see the commentary on Mt 12:11, 21:5).

To explain all these paradoxes is not easy. Nevertheless, there are certain facts which can be reasonably connected in order to give at least a partial solution. The common source besides Mark that has been used by the Gospels of Matthew and Luke (called Q by the critics, from the German *Quelle*, source), may very well have been the original Aramaic Gospel written by the apostle Matthew and later translated into Greek. It is interesting to note that Papias referred to this Aramaic work as the "sayings" (*logia*) of Jesus, and that the Q material of Matthew and Luke does largely consist of discourses, whereas Mark is almost exclusively narrative, recording the Lord's words only where they occur as pronouncements in forms like the conflict stories. This Aramaic work, which would have been treasured as an early apostolic witness, may have been circulated in various forms throughout the Church. If we may imagine the use made of it by the First Gospel as much more extensive and more literal than that of Luke, we may have the explanation both of Matthew's Jewish coloration and the persistent ascription of this Gospel to the apostle Matthew.

However, the inspired author of our Gospel of Matthew—for it is the Greek Gospel as we possess it that has been declared canonical by the Church—is a later writer who, like Luke, has made use of Mark, of Q, and other sources proper to himself, to produce this testament of apostolic Christianity. Who he was, we do not know. The internal evidence would indicate that the Gospel was written no earlier than that of Luke; but whether by a Jewish Christian or a Gentile, may be debated. Its early use by St. Ignatius of Antioch has suggested to many that its place of composition was Syria, and doubtless it did emanate from such an ancient, non-Jewish center of Christianity as this.

The signs of Matthew's mixed origins are plentiful. We have already noted some indications of its Jewish background, and we shall have occasion to note various others. The fact that Jesus' teaching appears in the Gospel divided into five long discourses is probably one of these: it is the new Torah. Corresponding to this is Matthew's portrayal of Jesus on the Mountain as a new Moses once more revealing the Law to Israel. The Gospel displays a predilection for the number seven and other combinations reminiscent of the Old Testament. However, far more important in determining the distinctive qualities of this Gospel have been the developments within the Church that produced it and the consequent concerns of those for whom it was written.

Matthew's is, in point of fact, the Gospel of the Church par excellence. It is the only Gospel in which the word "Church" is actually used. None of the other Gospels has treated of the Church so systematically—of its Old Testament roots, of the spirit of its law, of its structure, its sacraments, its hierarchy, and its eschatology. It is this and other associated qualities that give it a perennial relevance that may be seen reflected in its customary use as the "standard" Gospel.

The Gospel No one can think of the relevance of the
of John Gospel message, however, or of the discourses
of Jesus, without immediately taking cognizance of the Gospel of John. We can go further than this.
Despite all their several virtues and their indispensable contributions, the Synoptic Gospels alone could never have
transmitted the fullness of the heritage of apostolic Christianity. For this, in God's providence, we have been given
the Fourth Gospel.

Since the second century, Christian tradition has placed
the origin of this Gospel in Ephesus, the work of John the
apostle, the son of Zebedee (mentioned as such by all the
Synoptic Gospels, but never by John!). The Gospel itself
claims to rest on the authority of an eyewitness who was an
immediate disciple of Jesus, and by a process of elimination
this unnamed disciple may be reasonably identified with
John the apostle. It displays a familiarity with the Palestinian
scene that often surpasses that of the Synoptic Gospels, and
in much of its language it betrays the influence of Aramaic,
the speech of a Palestinian Jew.

If there is good reason to ascribe the Gospel to the apostolic
authority of John, however, there is equally good reason to
suppose that he is not the literary author of the Gospel as
we have it. The literary author would be, rather, a disciple
of the apostle or, perhaps more precisely, a school of disciples
(see especially Jn 21:24). There are various reasons for this
judgment. One is the fact, recognized also from quite early
Christian times, that the same person could not have been
the literary author of works as diverse in style and content
as the Gospel, the three Johannine epistles, and the Apocalypse—all of which, however, have been confidently ascribed
to the same apostle. Even more important is the evidence
which the Gospel itself gives of having been composed in
stages, often with the use of variant versions of the same
material. The most natural accounting for this phenomenon
is the supposition that the Gospel was dictated in snatches
over a considerable period of time, sometimes repetitiously,
and that only after the removal of its author, presumably by

death, was it put together by those who were no longer sure of the intended order or sequence. As we shall see, this supposition goes far toward explaining away what would otherwise be some insurmountable difficulties encountered in this Gospel. What is most certain, however, needs no explaining away—and that is, that this Gospel is throughout the product of a single mind that has authored its distinctive concepts and contributed to it all that makes it uniquely the Gospel of John.

It has always been generally taken for granted that John's is a "late" Gospel. Early Christian tradition regarded it as a work of the apostle's old age, a final testament intended to supplement and complete the work of the Synoptics. Led by considerations of style and of the presumed development of doctrine within Christianity itself, critics of the past century very commonly tended to make it quite late indeed, from sometime well into the second Christian century. Most of the reasons on which such judgments were grounded are no longer accorded much weight by present-day students of the Gospel and its background. Strictly speaking, there is no reason why John could not be as old as the Synoptic Gospels. Its admittedly distinctive language that sets it apart from the Synoptics is, nevertheless, just as authentically Palestinian: the so-called Dead Sea Scrolls first discovered in 1947 have helped to make this clear. The fact that we now possess a manuscript fragment of the Gospel of John (the Rylands Papyrus) that cannot be more recent than about A.D. 130–50 confirms the tradition sufficiently that would set its origins in the last decades of the first century.

The many contrasts between John and the Synoptic Gospels go to make up what has been posed as "the Johannine question." Only rarely does John coincide with the Synoptics in relating the same event or saying of Jesus, and even in these rare instances of agreement the order, lesson, or application may still be diverse. Much less obvious instances of correspondence occur in which there may be a genuine parallel between the two traditions as respects one or several events, which, however, are likely to appear as a unit in the Synoptic Gospels and as dispersed episodes in John, or vice versa. The chronology and the geographical emphases of John are quite out of harmony with those of the Synoptic Gospels. Most importantly however, the picture of the Johannine Christ does seem to differ radically from that of the Snyoptic Jesus. In the Synoptic Gospels Jesus appears in the recognizable role of a Palestinian teacher, speaking in parables and in the easy language of the people, and working miracles of healing and of exorcism. In John there are few miracles, no exorcisms, and no parables—and the Christ who speaks does so in magisterial tones and in a language that is typical of the Johannine epistles as well as of the Gospel, but not at all of the Synoptic Gospels.

That this situation should have been characterized as a Johannine question involves in part a kind of prejudgment. There is, after all, no particular reason why John should be measured against the standard of the Synoptic Gospels rather than the other way round. In the past, however, it was often taken for granted that while the Synoptics had confined themselves more or less to the actual historical conditions of the life and teaching of Jesus, John had disregarded them in the interests of his advanced theology and had transmuted Jesus' words into the language of later Christianity. As already indicated, this simple view can no longer be maintained. Both in the Synoptics and in John, Jesus speaks as a Palestinian Jew, and while some explanation must be given of the respective emphases, neither is antecedently more or less "historical" than the other. The same kind of judgment must be made concerning the other discrepancies between John and the Synoptics.

It is far more likely, for example, that Jesus paid multiple visits to Jerusalem, as John tells the story, than that he should have come only the one time mentioned in the Synoptic outline. Here and elsewhere the kerygmatic framework adopted by the Synoptics has doubtless synthesized, telescoped, and assimilated the historical facts in the interest of a topical and logical rather than a chronological order. In one sense the Synoptics are "timeless": from them alone we could not determine whether Jesus' ministry lasted a year or several or perhaps only a few months. John, on the other hand, probably does intend to give us a chronology of the ministry, at least in a limited way. We must insist that it is only in a limited way, because for John as well as for the Synoptics chronology and such matters are always subordinated to deeper concerns. Once and for all, let it be noted that in arranging the Gospel passages as we have in this book, relating the Synoptic material to John and John to the Synoptics, we do not intend to make the chronology any more precise than the Gospels themselves intended. Sometimes it is altogether impossible to "harmonize" the two blocs of tradition—just as it is sometimes impossible to reconcile the Synoptics completely among themselves—for the very good reason that the materials with which we deal were not designed with any such end in view.

When all is said and done, the basic difference between John and the Synoptic Gospels is that while the latter are an outgrowth of the standard apostolic *kerygma* the Fourth Gospel has developed independently of it. This is not to say that it is unaware of the Synoptic tradition; on the contrary, it seems to presuppose it on any number of occasions. Whether there has been any dependence of the written Gospel of John on the written Synoptic Gospels may be disputed. Probably the majority view would have it that John has been written with advertence to the Gospel of Mark, but there does not appear to be any conclusive evidence to link it to the other Synoptics. The undoubted affinity of John for Luke, as was suggested above, may very well be accounted for by Luke's knowledge of the Johannine tradition.

Developed apart from the Synoptic outline and perspective, the Gospel of John is uniquely the witness of its apostolic author. It is the fruit of a lifetime of meditation on the enduring historical significance of Jesus' words and deeds in which the three Gospel "depths" of which we spoke above tend to merge and unite. In it we hear speaking at one and the same time the Jesus of history, the Jesus living in his Church through the grace and enlightenment of the Holy

Spirit, and the Jesus known through his prophet John. No other Gospel so much repays careful reading as does this one. Its special characteristics we can best see in the commentary, but suffice it to say for the present that it was not for nothing that the early Fathers called this the "spiritual" Gospel and spoke of its author as the Theologian.

Roman   Having made some necessary observations on
Palestine   the nature of the literature with which we shall be concerned in this book, we should also say a few words about the world in which it grew up and with which it deals. It was, of course, a Roman world. The Gospels emerged from important centers of the worldwide Roman empire: Ephesus, Antioch, Rome itself. They appeared in the Greek language which was official throughout the Empire. Their setting is Roman Palestine, a tiny and, from the Roman point of view, quite insignificant outpost of this empire. They are at one and the same time, therefore, both the products of their age and in the most profound contradiction to it.

The Gospels testify to realities that were to have no part to play in the official Roman scheme of things for a couple of centuries. What that scheme of things had to do with the Gospel realities, we can readily see in the few scant references to Jesus which occur in contemporary non-Christian literature. The Jewish historian Flavius Josephus (A.D. 37–105 more or less) mentioned Jesus in his *Jewish Antiquities* (XVIII. 63 f.). Unfortunately, the text as we have it today has been tampered with by Christian interpolators; all that can be concluded with certainty is that Josephus knew of Jesus as a Jew put to death under Pontius Pilate from whom had derived "the race of Christians." The younger Pliny, writing in A.D. 112, noted merely that the Christians known to him worshiped Christ "as a God" (*Epistles* X. 96). Cornelius Tacitus (A.D. 54–119), recording the persecution of the Christians under Nero, knew that Christ had been put to death by Pilate during the reign of Tiberius (*Annals* XV. 44); Christianity itself Tacitus regarded as a "most mischie-

vous superstition." Finally, Suetonius (A.D. 75–160) refers
to Christ, if he refers to him at all, only as a name, the
meaning of which he had misunderstood (*Life of Claudius*
XXV. 4).

The map on page 18 will give us a picture of the Palestine
that signified so little in Roman eyes. During the ministry
of Jesus it was divided into two political units, each of which
has a certain significance for the Gospel narrative. Judea and
Samaria formed one unit which was ruled directly by a
Roman governor whose headquarters were in Caesarea. The
governor who has become best known in history because of
his involvement in the crucifixion of Jesus was Pontius Pilate,
who administered Roman rule from A.D. 26–36. It is customary to refer to these Roman governors as "the Procurators";
however, this title was not actually used till after Christ's
death. In his own day, Pilate was styled "Prefect of Judea."
Technically speaking, Judea was not important enough to be
a full-fledged province in the Roman civil service. It was
subject to the Legate of Syria, who was expected to render
military help as needed. Practically, however, it ranked as
an imperial (as distinct from a senatorial) province, that is,
a district in which the populace was regarded as hostile and
in which repressive measures could be taken with a mini-
mum of formalities when rebellion was threatened.

Direct Roman involvement in Palestinian affairs dated from
63 B.C., when the Jewish commonwealth, torn by civil war
resulting from rival claims to the throne and the high priesthood, had been annexed to the Province of Syria as a solution
of *pax romana*. From 40–4 B.C. the entire land had been
ruled by that extraordinary adventurer, half genius half
madman, with whom we are so familiar from the story of
Christ's birth, Herod the Great. Herod, a non-Jew who had
married into the royal Hasmonaean house whose intrigues
had hastened the intervention of the Romans, obtained the
title "king" from the Roman Senate. His kingdom embraced
almost everything that appears on the map of Palestine except
the Decapolis, a nearly totally pagan region that always remained directly subject to the Legate of Syria. On Herod's

death, however, the kingdom was dismembered. Judea and Samaria, after a brief interlude, assumed the provincial status described above. The extreme northeastern portion (Ituraea, Trachonitis, etc.), also mainly pagan, came under the government of Philip, apparently the most capable of all Herod's sons. Like the Decapolis, this region has only a minor role to play in the Gospel story.

The other major political unit of Roman Palestine in the days of Jesus was made up of Galilee and Perea. Perea does not figure largely in the Gospels, but Galilee was Jesus' homeland, the scene of the greater part of his public ministry, and the region from which he drew his first disciples. After the death of Herod the Great, Galilee and Perea had fallen to the lot of another of his sons, Herod Antipas. Antipas, like Philip, was never permitted by the Romans to allow himself a more imposing title than "tetrarch" (originally, this referred to someone who ruled the fourth part of some province); however, popularly he was regarded as king and is so called in the Gospels.

Common subjection to the Legate of Syria and Roman standardization worked toward a sameness of political institutions throughout Palestine. The hated taxgathering system (the "publicans" of the Gospels), all-important to the Roman administration, was a continuous source of friction and a case of conscience for pious Jews (cf. Mt 22:15–22). By Roman lights, the Jews were treated leniently and given extraordinary privileges. They were not required to serve in the army, and officially every effort was made to respect their religious scruples. Within limits, they were permitted to govern themselves by their own laws. Nevertheless, Roman administration in this provincial outpost was inclined to be clumsy, inept, and corrupt, and the tension between Jew and Roman is very apparent in the Gospel story. The Roman governors continually intervened in the appointment and deposition of the high priests and in many other ways never permitted the Jews to forget that they were a subject people. Presaged by uprisings recorded in part by the New Testament, the endemic hatred of Roman rule finally led to the great revolt of A.D. 66, the end of which was the destruction of Herod's great temple and, eventually, of Jewish Palestine itself.

Jewish   From the Jewish point of view, the map of
Palestine   Palestine would have been drawn quite differ-
                ently from the lines laid down by the Romans.
The chief city for the Jews was not, of course, the administrative center of Caesarea, but Jerusalem, the ancient holy city of David and the site of Solomon's temple. The temple which now stood there was one of the wonders of the contemporary world, shrewdly built by the great Herod at the outset of his reign in order to assure Jewish allegiance. In Jerusalem sat the Sanhedrin, the great council of the Jewish nation and its highest court, presided over by the high priest and composed of members drawn from the chief priestly and lay families and from the scribal profession. Jerusalem, and Judea because of it, was the spiritual and intellectual heartland of Judaism, the goal of its pilgrimages and the norm of its observance even for the vastly greater number of Jews who lived outside Palestine, in the Diaspora.

In Jewish eyes, Samaria was no part of Judea but a foreign country inhabited by foreigners. In point of fact the Samaritans, descendants of northern Israelites who had intermarried with Gentile settlers in the land, were ethnically little different, if at all, from the Jews of Judea. Their religion, too, a selective form of Judaism, was probably closer in doctrine and practice to what would have been considered normative than was the religion of many Judean Jews. However, a long history of mutual antagonism and hatred sundered the two peoples utterly. (See Sir 50:25 f., where the Samaritans are equated with the Edomites and the Philistines: the Samaritans are "the degenerate folk who dwell in Shechem.") It was this Jewish attitude toward the Samaritans that contributes the special poignancy to Jesus' parable of "the good Samaritan."

Toward the Galileans, the Judeans adopted a somewhat different attitude. As L. E. Elliott-Binns has said, "The

Jews [that is, the Judeans] hated the Samaritans; the Galileans they merely despised." Evidence of this Judean attitude toward Galileans can be seen in Jn 1:46, 7:52. The reasons for this feeling were manifold, but chiefly derived from the Galileans' involvement with the Gentiles. The very name of Galilee proclaimed this involvement: it was the "circuit [*galil*] of the Gentiles" (Is 8:23; Mt 4:15), surrounded by Gentiles and heavily infiltrated by them. Jews who lived in Galilee simply could not adopt the attitude of exclusion with regard to Gentiles and Gentile ways that was possible in Judea. Inevitably different customs and observances grew up, encouraged by Galilee's relative isolation from the Judean center. The educated Galilean Jew probably spoke the Greek of the Gentiles as well as Palestinian Aramaic. It has even been suggested, though with less probability, that Greek was more common than Aramaic as the language used by the Jews among themselves. There were, in any case, Greek-language synagogues, especially for those Jews who had come out of the Diaspora; there was even at least one of these in Jerusalem itself. For whatever causes, the Galileans spoke a dialect that readily distinguished them from the Judeans (cf. Mt 26:73).

Together with an openness toward religious doctrine and a lack of rigor in its observance the Galileans combined a fierce Jewish nationalism, not unusual in the provincial population of any ethnic group. Revolts against foreign domination were quite as likely to begin in Galilee as in Judea. The combination of these qualities could readily account for "sons of thunder" (Mk 3:17) whose laxity with regard to Jewish observances repeatedly scandalized the more literalminded doctors of the Law.

Cutting across geographical differences were the "denominational" divergences that distinguished one Jew's religion from another. The reader may be initially surprised to learn of such differences—some of which were rather important—since the orthodox Judaism of post-Christian times has generally presented such a monolithic structure. For all

practical purposes only one form of Judaism, that of the
Pharisees, survived the Roman repressions of A.D. 70 and
135 that followed the major and final Jewish revolts in Palestine. In the time of Jesus, however, the religion of Judaism
was by no means as standardized as it became through the
talmudic legislation of Christian times.

In one sense of the word, it is probably not correct to
regard Pharisaism as a denomination or sect. It was, as it
remained after the destruction of Jerusalem, by and large
the normative religion of most of Palestine and the Diaspora,
the religion taught in the synagogues and professed by the
greatest number of the scribes (who would later be known
as the rabbis). It was, in broad outline, the religion as
practiced by Jesus and the early Jewish Christians; St.
Paul considered it a point of honor to identify himself as a
Pharisee (Phil 3:5). Much of Jesus' teaching was echoed by
the best of Pharisaical Judaism. It represented the progressive
tradition of Old Testament religion, a religion of the spirit
rather than of the letter, which allowed for development and
accommodation. In practice, Pharisaism was normative to
some extent even for those who rejected it in principle. The
Jerusalem priesthood, for example, was obliged to follow the
Pharisaical interpretation of the liturgical law.

Why is it that the Gospels so often give the impression
that Jesus and the Pharisees were in essential opposition, if
indeed he actually practiced Pharisaical religion? Several
observations are in order. Firstly, when we say that Pharisaism was normative Judaism, we are speaking of it in its
non-professional sense, as the normal development of Old
Testament religion. Jesus, like the average Jew of his day,
could practice this religion without being a professional
Pharisee. The professional Pharisee, as a matter of fact,
would not have conceded that the average Jew practiced
his religion at all. Pharisaism in the professional sense descended to many particulars which were the practice of only
a few: in this sense Pharisaism was, indeed, a faction. From
the rest of the Jews, "this accursed crowd which knows not

the Law" (Jn 7:49), the Pharisee considered himself separated by his superior knowledge and consequent observance ("Pharisee" probably means "separated"). Secondly, while Pharisaism was born of a progressive tendency, it also had a built-in proclivity for the type of legalistic formalism with which it is frequently identified in the Gospels. The selfsame tradition that sought the spirit in the letter could, in the wrong hands, become a soulless literalism in its own right—conservatism is the liberalism of the past generation. It was this kind of Pharisaism that Christ condemned (cf. Mk 7:1–13). It is only fair to add that it was likewise condemned by some of the Pharisaical scribes who stood in the tradition of Hillel and Gamaliel, in whose school St. Paul studied (Acts 22:3). Finally, as we saw above in the discussion of form criticism, the Gospels had cause to lay stress on the opposition between Jesus and the leaders of Judaism rather than to emphasize their points of agreement.

The chief rivals to the Pharisees mentioned in the Gospels were the Sadducees; the meaning of this term is unknown, but it is usually thought to have had some relation to the Zadokite priesthood. The Sadducees were truly a sect who had very little following among the people but included most of the priestly aristocracy. They rejected such Pharisaical developments in doctrine as a belief in the resurrection of the body (probably also, therefore, a belief in personal immortality) and a world of angels and spirits (cf. Acts 23:8); like the Samaritans, they may have rejected as canonical Scripture anything beyond the Torah of Moses. In their legal interpretations they were more rigorous than the Pharisees, adhering to the letter of the law to the disregard of any subsequent developments or the need of adaptation. With this religious fundamentalism they combined a spirit of conciliation with the Romans that made their patriotism suspect in the eyes of many Jews. This latter attitude was doubtless dictated by their economic status more than by anything else. At all events, Sadduceeism did not possess the vigor to survive the fall of Jerusalem.

A third division of Jews which, curiously enough, is never mentioned in the Gospels—unless, indeed, it is taken for granted more often than we realize—until fairly recently was known only from the somewhat conflicting accounts of Josephus and Philo of Alexandria (approximately 20 B.C.–A.D. 45). This was the Essenes, a name for which no satisfactory explanation has yet been given. Because the sectaries of Qumran, the people who produced the so-called Dead Sea Scrolls, have been rather convincingly identified as Essenes, we now know a great deal more about the peculiarities of this sect.

In the commentary we shall have occasion to refer to Qumran people and their literature, hence only a few general observations are necessary at this time. There seems to be no doubt that Essenian Judaism exercised some influence on the beginnings of Christianity, and it is even likely that there were disciples of Jesus who had first been Essenes. This is hardly surprising: those Jews who embraced Christianity could have come from Essenism as easily as from Pharisaism or another form of Judaism. Despite a number of incidental correspondences from this direction, however, it is certain that Jesus and the writers of the New Testament were far more indebted to normative Judaism than to Essenism.

The Essenes were a "withdrawal" sect: even those who did not, as the Qumran people did, live a quasi-monastic existence, considered themselves to be completely separated from conventional Jewish life. In some respects they appear to have been super-Pharisees, but in others they differed quite radically from the normal tradition of Judaism. They rejected the Jerusalem temple and followed their own liturgical calendar. Their religion was highly eschatological; they were expecting an imminent end of the world as we know it, and like all sects of their kind they regarded themselves as the only elect which would be spared in the general conflagration: they were the only true Israel. It is likely enough that there were other sects of the same kind throughout Palestine; the times, as we shall see, were ripe for them. The Essenes, too, were unable to survive when the Roman fist at last closed inexorably on Palestinian Jewry.

It was into this kind of world that the Gospels were born. They are at once a clarion of their age and the knell of the coming age that would transform it utterly.

2. THE WORD MADE FLESH

Jn 1:1–2   The Prologue to John, the passage which forms the subject matter of this chapter, is a formidable enough beginning for any study of the Gospels. Volumes have been written on it, and on individual parts of it, without pretending to do more than scratch the surface of its meaning.

It may be thought that its high theological content might require it to be deferred for later consideration, after some of the (deceptively) simpler presentations of the Synoptic Gospels. However, since the Gospels are an expression of Christian faith in Christ, it is well to begin where John did, with the origins of the Christ-event where Christian faith had learnt to place them, anterior even to the nativity stories recorded by Matthew and Luke. Though the doctrine of the pre-existence of Christ is never dealt with explicitly in the Synoptic Gospels, it was part of the faith that produced them; it is found in the writings of Paul, and enunciated by him in the words of even older Christian confessions (Phil 2:6–8; Col 1:15–17, etc.).

Is the Prologue of John itself such a confession, a hymn, possibly of liturgical origin, that has been used by the evangelist to introduce his Gospel? Many authors think so, for reasons that are deserving of consideration. Such a question we cannot and need not answer here, however. The Prologue is, in any case, an integral part of the Gospel, whatever may have been its ultimate origin. It is, in a way, a summary of the entire Gospel.

John writes *In the beginning,* making a pointed allusion to the first verse of Genesis: just as the Old Testament began with the story of God's creation of the universe and world of man, the Johannine version of the New Testament now begins to tell the story of the new creation that has taken place in Jesus Christ. (The concept of the redemptive Christ-event as a new creation was also a common Christian idea; it can be found explicit in 1 Cor 15:45–49, for example.) Jesus himself is the creative *Word* of God.

For the uniquely Johannine conception of Christ as the Word (*logos*) we probably do not have to go outside the thought forms of the Old Testament, though *logos* also had an analogous usage in the popular Hellenistic philosophy of the time. God's word is his utterance of himself in power, manifestation, revelation. It is creative: "By the word of the Lord the heavens were made" (Ps 33:6); similarly, in verse 3 John says that without the Word nothing was made. In a pre-eminent way it is through the prophets that God's word became known. Judaism exalted the Torah as the word of God par excellence and Moses, therefore, as the greatest of the prophets. Christ, however, has revealed God much more excellently than Moses and the prophets (note vss. 17 f. and cf. Heb 1:1–4). This he has done because he himself is the very Word of God indeed, God incarnate, manifest, visible (so also Col 1:15–20).

John says that in the beginning the Word already *was.* The evangelist knew how to take full advantage of the popular Greek in which he wrote, which was able to distinguish various aspects of being. Here and elsewhere in the Prologue when referring to the Word he uses the imperfect tense, signifying continuous existence without reference to beginning or ending: the Word has the timelessness of God himself. On the contrary, when he wants to speak of past events that have occurred at determined times (as in vss.

3, 6, 14, creation, the appearance of the Baptist, the incarnation), he uses the aorist tense. There was nothing particularly startling about this language, as far as Jewish tradition was concerned. The wisdom of God, identified with his word, had long been personified and represented as present with God from the beginning of creation (see, for example, Prov 3:19, 8:22–31). Neither, therefore, was there anything extraordinary about speaking of the Word as *with God*, or more accurately, *in God's presence* (literally, "towards God"). A distinction is thereby drawn between the Word and the personal God (determined by the definite article in the Greek). This would have been perfectly comprehensible to a Jew but definitely puzzling to a pantheistic Hellenist for whom *logos* meant simply a divine emanation.

The Word was God. Here, on the contrary, John says something that the Hellenist would think he understood but which a Jew could hardly say. Judaism could personify the wisdom or word of God and represent it as the first of God's creatures, present with him from the beginning, but it could not identify it with God. This its conception of monotheism would not allow. Already, therefore, while using traditional language, John has introduced uniquely Christian ideas that give new meaning to the words with which he had to work. Here "God" is used predicatively, without the article: the Word, whom he has just distinguished from the Person of God, is nevertheless a divine being in his own right. We immediately see, therefore, that the Word of which he is speaking is a "he" and not an "it."

Jn 1:3a   This being so, when he now speaks explicitly of the Word as creative, he says more than the traditional language of itself might signify. As the following verses show, he is already associating in his mind the new creation of Christ with the first creation of all things. On the surface, he repeats the thought of Ben Sira: "At God's word were his works brought into being" (Sir 42:15); so also Is 48:13 (both texts merely paraphrase Gen 1:3). There is an even more striking parallel in one of the Qumran scrolls:

"Through his knowledge all things have come to be, and everything that is is ordained by his thought; and without him nothing is made" (1 QS 11:11). The Word of John, however, is a Person of mind and will who has himself entered into the first creative act as surely as he did into the work of redemption. Nevertheless, John never explicitly calls Christ the Creator. Later Christian theology, too, while considering every external work of God as done by all three divine Persons, has continued the biblical tradition of "attributing" the work of creation to God the Father only.

The better punctuation of the text, as attested both by manuscript evidence and the earliest Christian tradition, is the following: "(3a) . . . without him nothing came to be. (3b) What came to be (4) in him was life . . ."

Jn 1:3b–5   This further statement in no way merely repeats the thought of the preceding. In the first place, John is now speaking of the life of men, something quite different from the mere existence of all things. Secondly, in the Johannine writings "life" never means simple existence. This is one of the key words of John's Gospel, a word by which he designates that gift of God by which he has brought man into his own sphere of existence, which a later theology would call "sanctifying grace."

What came to be in him was life. Some of the Greek manuscripts have *is life;* both readings can be defended. By some this is taken to mean that whatever came to be (in the context, only men are meant) found its life, and could find its life, in the Word only. This, of course, is certainly John's thought. However, it is probable that he means much more than this. The "what came to be" is the life itself, which in turn is *the light of men.* Just as John did not speak of the Word as Creator but rather as having a role in creation, so he does with regard to the communication of life to man. If the Word is God, as John has said, then of course he is also Author of this life as well as the means by which it is communicated. But John is not writing a treatise on the metaphysical nature of divine Persons. He is writing a Gospel,

which is a history of salvation. And in the divine economy
of salvation life "came to be" in Christ that he might dispense
it to mankind: "As the Father has life in himself, so he has
given to the Son to have life in himself" (Jn 5:26f.;
note also 3:35f.). "I have life because of the Father," Jesus
says, and correspondingly, whoever communicates with
Christ "will have life because of me" (Jn 6:57). The New
Testament consistently describes salvation as a work of God
accomplished through Jesus Christ: it "attributes" it to
God the Father working through the Son.

It will be observed that John makes no conscious effort to
distinguish between the Word as timeless and pre-existent
and as incarnate and encountered in history—this despite the
fact that only in verse 14 does he refer explicitly to the
incarnation. Some of what he says applies properly only to
the one or the other condition, but it is we, not he, who
feel the need to make the distinction. This is perfectly in
line with the rest of New Testament christology, which is
first and foremost a soteriology. That is to say, it deals with
Christ in his existential character as divine Savior without
attempting to isolate his divine nature for separate consideration. The time was as yet far distant when the theology
of Christ's personality and the relation between his divine
and human natures would have to be thoroughly elaborated
in the Church, following on the christological heresies of the
fourth and subsequent centuries.

"Light" is another favorite Johannine word. As the term
itself might suggest, it means enlightenment: God's manifestation of himself to men. This it is, however, in no merely
intellectual sense. Through his Word God manifests himself
as he really is; as Jesus says, God's manifestation of himself
consists in his coming and dwelling with the one whom he
loves (Jn 14:22f.). When John speaks, as he so often does,
of our "knowing" God, he does not mean that we know
something about God; he means that we know God himself,
as a man knows his friend, as a husband knows his wife:
there is a shared existence, a community of being. So
much we understand by the life of grace. That is why

life can be equated here with light. That is why primitive
Christianity spoke of the baptism that summons men into
the new life of God's grace an "enlightenment," a passing
from darkness into light (see also 1 Pt 2:9).

The light shines in the darkness probably represents
John's judgment on the entire history of God's revelation, not
just the ministry of Jesus. "Darkness" is, obviously, the
opposite of light. By this term John designates the world
of man which is desperately in need of divine enlightenment. This world is not evil, for God loves it (Jn 3:16); it
is only when men prefer their miserable state of darkness to
the light that evil becomes manifest (Jn 3:19): then occurs
"the power of darkness" (Lk 22:53), the reign of evil. Faith,
the acceptance of God as he has revealed himself, casts out
darkness (Jn 12:46). The light-darkness dichotomy, fairly
common elsewhere in the New Testament, was also employed by the Qumran sectaries.

The final words of this section can be translated *the darkness did not comprehend it* or *the darkness did not overcome it*. If the first, the author thinks of the long history of
revelation, culminating in Jesus Christ, which has also been
so often a history of rejection and unbelief. If the second, he
testifies to the power of divine grace, continuing through
the prophets to the One greater than the prophets. Or perhaps he intends the reader to take both meanings: multiple
levels of meaning are far from unusual in John.

Jn 1:6–8 Almost casually, the person of John the Baptist
              is introduced into the text. John follows the
standard Gospel outline to the extent of beginning with the
ministry of the Baptist (vss. 19 ff.), and the fact that here
and in verse 15 the Baptist is apparently intruded into this
paean on the Word by the use of verses borrowed from the
later narrative is evidence to many that the Prologue has
been adapted by John from an earlier text (note how vs.
9 logically follows on vs. 5, and vs. 16 on vs. 14). This may
be. However, it is also typical of John to interlock the

various parts of his Gospel by anticipations and back-references.

This man came as a witness. "Witness" is another of John's key ideas, which we can better appreciate when it is formally introduced in the story of the ministry of the Baptist. It is well to note here, however, that by introducing at this time the idea of the Baptist as witness to the Word—the incarnate Word, of course—John confirms what was said above, that throughout this entire passage, and not just from verse 14 on, he is thinking of the Word both as eternally with God and as incarnate in the person of Christ. In insisting on the Baptist as a witness to the light and not the light itself, John reflects the mild but persistent "polemics" waged throughout the Gospels in respect to the Baptist. It is not that the Gospels intended to minimize his importance; as we shall see, this is far from the case. There were contemporary with the Church, however, various Baptist sects, composed of those who had taken the preaching of the kingdom by John the Baptist as itself the fulfillment of prophetic expectation rather than what the Baptist himself proclaimed it to be, the final prophetic voice heralding the fulfillment in Jesus Christ (see Acts 19:1–7). The Gospels sought to show this, therefore, from the Baptist's own life and words. Here we have another example of the formative influences that have been brought to bear on the Gospel materials.

Jn 1:9–13 John says of the Word that *he was the true light that enlightens every man.* All the way through this Gospel we hear this adjective "true." Jesus is the "true" vine, he gives "true" life, and so on. Probably this exemplifies the evangelist's ability to turn to good account for the mainly Gentile Christianity for which he wrote a usage that had been authentically Christ's. For the Jew, all that was "true" pertained pre-eminently to God (cf. Jn 7:28), and was thus distinguished from the "vanity" that is the lot of every merely human act or device (cf. Eccl 1:2–8 and *passim*). In the popular Hellenistic philosophy of the

Roman world there was an analogous usage. The "true" designated the reality that was judged to be only partially reflected in what was visible and tangible in the world of man. The *coming into the world* of this verse probably goes with "the true light" rather than with "every man"; however, little difference is made in the sense of the passage in either case.

The "world" of which John speaks, as we noted above, is the world of man and his affairs, not of itself evil, but *de facto* prone to the control of darkness because of sin. As John has already intimated, the entire history of God's invasion of this world through his word has been one of man's refusal to know God: "know," we are reminded, is not merely to acknowledge theoretically, but to experience practically. St. Paul also indicts the world for refusing to acknowledge the God who had revealed himself to it by his creative word (Rom 1:18-23). By *his own* John singles out particularly the Old Testament people of God, Israel, whose fault was the greater for the special intimacy into which God had drawn it with himself especially through the prophetic word. Refusal to heed this word is the burden of the prophets' constant complaint against Israel (cf. Is 6:9 f.; Jer 1:18 f.; Ezek 2:3-6; Amos 4:6-11; Acts 7:51-53, etc.). The major theme of the entire first half of John's Gospel is that of the light shining in darkness and the rejection of Jesus the Word by his own.

Still, though unbelief has been far too often the rule, it was never total. At all times during the history of salvation there have been those who accepted God's word and thus were made the recipients of his extraordinary grace by which they were made *sons of God* (see Deut 14:1; Ex 4:22; Hos 1:10). So it has proved to be with the Word incarnate, and to this the Gospel is testimony. The Gospels and the rest of the New Testament use many different terms to express the mysterious and wonderful relationship with God into which man is brought through divine grace. John has already spoken of "life" and "light." Here he speaks of divine sonship, emphasizing in verse 13 that nothing less than a genuine rebirth of man is involved which cannot be effected by man's unaided power, generative or otherwise; the notion of this heavenly birth will be the special theme of John's chapter 3. He also says that this new birth takes place in *those who believe in his name*. Faith is the response to God revealing himself, the acceptance of his word. It is not merely a condition for the divine action to work in man; it is itself concretely the transforming power of God constituting men his children, since no one can believe unless he be drawn by God (Jn 6:44). In the New Testament faith hardly ever means belief in some*thing*; almost invariably it signifies belief in some*one*, namely God, the state of man's being which is both the result and the constitutive element of a total commitment of his person to the Other, a commitment in turn which implies a community of life with the Other. In Semitic usage the "name" is the person himself, the person, that is, as he can be known and experienced by others. The Jews often referred to God simply as "the Name."

John says he gave men *power to become sons of God*. The choice of words is not casual. John's is a Gospel of vitality, of dynamism. For all his stress on faith, one may be at first surprised to learn that the word "faith" never occurs in the Gospel of John. But again, this is a studied procedure. John always uses the verb, "believe," for he wants to insist that faith is an active thing that involves man's whole life and being, not simply a passive state of mind. Similarly Paul speaks of faith as a "work" (1 Thes 1:3). In the same way, to become a son of God is not just a once-for-all experience which man passively undergoes. It is a lifelong engagement on which he embarks through faith, which must continually find expression in his every thought and deed.

Jn 1:14   So habituated are Christians to the concept of the incarnation, it is difficult for them to appreciate how startling to men of the first Christian century, how shocking to their sensibilities, was John's climactic statement: *The Word became flesh*. Both to Jew and Gentile an assertion of this kind had to run the inevitable risk of being taken as patent and calculated absurdity, as in fact it has so often been taken by Jew and Gentile thereafter.

Latent in popular Hellenistic thought was the conviction that man's body, the flesh, was evil, entirely antithetic to anything divine. The Platonic aphorism is famous: *sōma sēma*, "the body is a prison." The real being of man was his spirit, which was encased in the flesh that restricted and shamed it. The Greeks burnt the bodies of the dead that the spirit might be fully and finally released from the imprisoning flesh. It might be thought paradoxical that men could think this way and yet so often adopt hedonism as their philosophy of life, making the pleasures of the flesh their paramount aim. The paradox, however, is only apparent —if the flesh were indeed opposed to man's "real" existence, what was done in the flesh could be considered morally irrelevant. This pernicious conception of man's corporeal nature entered Christianity early as a heresy (cf. 1 Cor 6:12–20) and has dogged its footsteps through all subsequent generations, sometimes appearing as a distorted and un-Christian approach to asceticism.

There was no room in the healthy materialism of Jewish thought for such ideas. As God's creation, the flesh was good. There precisely, however, was the rub: "flesh" implied all that was created, therefore passing and transitory, not antithetic to but certainly incompatible with the divine Creator. "All flesh is grass," wrote the prophet, thus characterizing the contingency of man. "Their glory is like the flower of the field. The grass withers, the flower wilts . . . but the word of our God stands forever" (Is 40:6–8). Here, as we readily see, the strongest possible contrast is drawn between flesh and the word of God. Yet John says that the Word became flesh. He has deliberately chosen the most uncompromising word that was available to him in order to express the reality of the incarnation. This is an habitual stress in the Gospels. The christological heresy that offered the greatest challenge to Christian orthodoxy in its earliest period was not denial of Christ's divinity; such a denial would be reserved for a later age, not for one in which "divine saviors" were commonplace. The danger was rather that of Docetism: the tendency to deny or at least to mitigate the reality of the humanity of Christ and all that it implied.

John's Gospel is apostolic testimony that the Word become flesh *dwelt among us.* This is another starkly realistic statement, the literal, or etymological meaning of which is: "he pitched his tent among us." It is not unlikely that John was thinking of the etymology, for the Greek verb (*skēnoun*) had long been used by preference as the equivalent of the Old Testament Hebrew expression (*šākan*) by which the presence of the Lord was designated, especially his presence in visible "glory" at the Tent of Meeting (cf. Ex 40:34–38). We have even more grounds for this understanding of John's meaning when we see that he goes on to say: *We saw his glory.* Throughout the Old Testament the "glory" of God refers especially to his visible presence, made manifest in smoke, fire, or some other medium. It refers as well and specifically to God's manifestation of his saving presence (Is 60:1; Hab 2:14; etc.). Under both these aspects this is also the meaning that John attaches to the word as it relates to Christ. We shall understand this better as we see the term in actual use throughout the Gospel. It will suffice to say now that by "glory" John means the entire Christ-event, in which the saving presence of God has been visibly manifested.

Glory of an only-begotten Son from the Father. This specification of the glory proper to the Word will be the principal theme of the second half of John's Gospel, beginning with chapter 13. Now that John has definitely spoken of the Word become flesh he abandons the more generic term and refers to him in his character in salvation history as Son; in verse 17 he will use for the first time his historical name. To speak of this glory as *rich in grace and truth* is to identify it further as the salvific work of God. "Grace and truth" represents the Old Testament hendiadys *hesed we'ĕmet* (see especially Ex 34:6, where the expression ap-

pears practically as a descriptive definition of God), the
sense of which is "loving-kindness and constancy" or perhaps "utter steadfast love." This loving protection of a God
faithful to his promises was, concretely, the salvation for
which the Israelite looked: it was the grace of God's saving
presence.

Jn 1:15–18   After another parenthetical reference to the
witness of the Baptist, a text which we shall
later see verbatim in its proper context, John continues and
concludes his theological introduction. *Of his riches* of grace
and truth *we have all received*. As before, John's treatment
of the Word who is Son of God concentrates on his mission
as Savior. *Grace after grace* doubtless means that the saving
mission of Christ and the Christian life which is its result
are grace-ful throughout: first, last, and always they are
purely a divine gift. To the Jew the greatest of God's gifts
was the Torah which epitomized his religion; here was, indeed, truth and salvation. Not to minimize the Old Testament
revelation, but to put it in perspective, John says that *the
Law was given through Moses*, but *grace and truth came
through Jesus Christ*. The Law was grace and truth—John
would hardly have denied this—but in the fullest sense, grace
and truth are the exclusive revelation of Christ; similarly,
the author of Heb 1:1–4 contrasts the diversity and fragmen-
tation of prophetic revelation with the true image of God
that has been seen in his Son.

Probably the same contrast is uppermost in John's mind
when he adds that *no one has ever seen God*. Here the Old
Testament tradition on which he depended was varied and
seemingly contradictory. The Bible certainly does relate often
enough that this or that person was granted a vision of God
(see Ex 24:9–11, for example). The Jews of John's time,
however, were sophisticated enough to understand these simple stories in the spirit in which they had been written. They
knew that the God of heaven had nothing about him that
was literally palpable to mortal eyes. Another of the naïve
biblical stories tried to express this truth by the assertion that

even Moses, who was closer to God than any other man and
spoke to him "face to face" (Ex 33:11; Num 12:8; Deut
34:10), nevertheless was not permitted to see God's "glory"
but only his "back" (Ex 33:18–23). Thus, though God has
indeed made himself known, he stands *revealed,* in the prophets and especially in Moses—his moral will and nature, his
words and deeds of love, mercy, fidelity, salvation—still,
only in the Christ-event has this revelation become complete.
Only one who is *in the bosom of the Father,* who himself
lives and shares the divine life as no merely human prophet
could, could be the instrument of this revelation. For he alone
is *God the only-begotten* (this reading of the text is prefera-
ble to "the only-begotten Son" which appears in most of
the manuscripts); in this Man alone has God appeared whole
and entire, incarnate in his very flesh.

With this John brings his magnificent Prologue to a close.
His Gospel is to be the record of how and in what ways
the Only-begotten has revealed the glory of the saving God.
In their own manner and after their own proper viewpoints,
as we shall see, the Synoptic Gospels are also a record of
this selfsame revelation. It is to them that we now turn.

3. THE TERM OF PROPHECY

Lk 1:1–4   From the sublimity of the Johannine prologue we now turn to the comparatively matter-of-fact prose of the Synoptic Gospels. Of the Synoptics, only Luke has given us an introduction to the Gospel message. In doing so, he conformed to the literary conventions of his time, which required a dedication and a statement of purpose. He also did it in the grand style: these verses are written not in the vulgar Greek that we otherwise expect in the Gospels, but rather in the language of the classical Greek authors.

Was *Theophilus* (God's friend) an historical personage, or is this simply Luke's name for the Christian reader for whom the Gospel was written? The same dedication appears at the beginning of the Acts of the Apostles, introducing the second volume of Luke's work in his tripartite view of the record of salvation history—the era of Israel (the Old Testament), the era of Jesus (the Gospel), the era of the Spirit (Acts). Most commentators seem to be of the mind that Theophilus was, indeed, a real person. The question is of no great importance, however, since in any case it is evident that Luke did not write for Theophilus alone, and Theophilus' condition is precisely that of the entire Christian world, ourselves included, which forms Luke's wider audience.

Luke, of course, did not invent the Gospel form which he used so effectively and artistically. Not only is it practically certain that he had the Gospel of Mark before him as he wrote, as we saw in Chapter 1 the Synoptic tradition which he mainly reproduces itself grew out of the *kerygma* of the primitive Church. Luke tells us this. He writes that Theophilus *may understand the certainty of the things in which you were catechized.* Luke's situation was that of Theophilus. He had received the same catechesis *regarding the things that have been brought to fulfillment among us,* that is, in the Church, from the same source of tradition: *as the original eyewitnesses and servants of the word handed them down to us.* Moreover, Luke takes his place within a succession of those who had attempted to articulate the Gospel message as he was now doing. *Many have undertaken to draw up an account,* he says. He does not tell us how many of these undertakings he regarded as successful or whether he made use of any or all of them in preparing his own Gospel.

He does tell us, however, at least some of the special qualities he ascribes to his Gospel, qualities which justify and even necessitate his taking pen in hand. For one thing, he has *followed up all things carefully from the very first,* verifying, checking, striving to make his Gospel as accurate and as instructive as possible. In Chapter 1, we discussed some of the means that were available to Luke to do this. Commentators would generally agree that he has succeeded admirably in this intention. Again, he has constructed his Gospel as an *orderly account.* By this he does not necessarily mean chronological order. In fact, as we have already seen, precise chronology is not a characteristic of the Gospels, for many reasons. An orderly account, rather, in Luke's sense is one that follows a logical pattern, a literary form, by which the writer functions not as a mere chronicler of events but as an interpreter of history, showing the relation of one fact to another, bringing out the inner meaning of events, a meaning that is seen through the eye of faith. One does not read very far in Luke's Gospel without perceiving the order that he has followed.

Lk 1:5-7 The beginning of Luke's order immediately becomes apparent in the passage that opens before us. In company with Matthew and in contrast to Mark and John, Luke prefaces to the Gospel proper—that is, the history of the ministry of salvation that begins with the preaching of John the Baptist—a section which we customarily regard as a narrative of Jesus' infancy. Actually, this is probably not too accurate a description of what Luke intended to give us. That is to say, it is doubtful that there existed in the Church of Luke's time a literary form that could properly be called "narrative of the Lord's birth and childhood," that there was, in other words, an interest in such biographical details for their own sake. It is true that such an interest did develop somewhat later on; it is very much reflected in the apocryphal gospels, the greater number of them of heretical origin, which are filled with biographical details, most of them legendary and some downright grotesque and pernicious, attempting to supply for the "deficiencies" of the canonical Gospels. The apostolic Church that produced the Gospel materials, however, hardly could afford the "luxury" of mere biography, even biography of Jesus. Its conservation of the tradition and its literary use of the tradition were strongly determined throughout by the practical demands of its life in the world, its pastoral ministry, catechetics, apologetics, polemics. Ordinarily only what was directly relevant to these ends passed into the *kerygma* and from the *kerygma* into the Gospel. We have already noted how that busy pastor St. Paul corroborates all this, how the Gospel that he preached in his letters has taken so little cognizance of the earthly life of Jesus. There is something of a parallel in the "holy places" of Palestine, the sites associated with this or that event in the life of Jesus. For most of these there is no authentic tradition that can be traced back beyond the fourth or fifth Christian century, for

the simple reason that the earliest Christian community there
was in no position to cherish these places and so establish a
tradition.

This is not to say that Luke does not give us true information about the birth of Christ or that this has nothing
to do with his Gospel. Far from it. Indeed, that is the point
that we should now make: that for both Matthew and Luke
what we term their infancy narratives are in actuality components in the strictest sense of the word of their record
of the Gospel, the good news of the salvation achieved in
Jesus Christ and perpetuated in his Church. They are not
introductions to or preparations for the Gospel story as told
by these two evangelists, but integral parts of it. This is
the main reason for the divergences between the two narratives, quite apart from the fact that the data which the
evangelists share in common had reached them through different and independent streams of tradition.

In Luke's Gospel the infancy narrative is an elaborate
expansion of the teaching common to all the Gospels, that
the Baptist is the last divinely sent prophetic witness to the
coming Christ. There is a systematic paralleling throughout
these two chapters between the Baptist and Jesus, in which
annunciation corresponds to annunciation, birth to birth, hidden life to hidden life, and in which the Baptist gradually
recedes from prominence and Jesus comes to the fore (cf.
Jn 3:30). Linking the two parallel developments are the two
mothers, their relationship and association, and the prophetic
theme is constantly maintained through countless allusions
to the Old Testament. The language also changes. Beginning
with 1:5 the classicism of the introduction is dropped
abruptly and Luke begins to write Greek that has a strong
Semitic flavor. The Semitisms, however, are not those of
Palestinian Aramaic, as in Mark and John, but biblical Hebrew. This fact has led many to the conclusion that Luke's
source for these chapters was a primitive Christian composition in Hebrew, later translated into Greek. There is much to
be said for such a theory; Luke certainly did use sources,
and the Qumran literature has shown that Hebrew was still

a living language, at least for literary purposes, at the beginning of the Christian era. On the other hand, however, Luke is a superb enough artist to have deliberately imitated here the "translation Greek" of the Septuagint, the Old Testament of the nascent Church. John the Baptist is the "last man of the Old Testament" (cf. Lk 7:28) who gives way to Jesus Christ, the "first man of the New Testament.

Luke begins with lines reminiscent of 1 Sam 1:1 f., introducing a theme that will be further pursued in these narratives. *Herod* was *king of Judea*—the title conferred on him by the Roman Senate, understanding broadly all of Jewish Palestine—officially from 40 B.C. The character of this king, Idumaean and Arabian by birth, is known to us chiefly from the writings of Flavius Josephus and is corroborated by the picture drawn of him by Matthew; Luke, however, mentions him only to give a general chronological indication.

It will be noted that Luke stresses the completely priestly ancestry of John the Baptist. *Zechariah* was a priest of the Jerusalem temple, *of the division* of the priesthood *called after Abijah* (cf. 1 Chron 24:10), that is, belonging to the eighth of twenty-four divisions of the Jewish priesthood which officiated in turn at the temple. Traditionally, all these were descended from Aaron, the Mosaic high priest (cf. Ex 28:1 ff.). *Elizabeth,* too, was *of the daughters of Aaron.* John the Baptist, therefore, is eminently a priestly as well as a prophetic figure. In Jewish messianic thinking a priest often accompanied the Messiah as forerunner and anointer (cf. Zech 3:6–9, 4:1–3, 11–14; etc.).

Lk 1:8–12   John the Baptist was a child of promise born to aged parents, like Isaac (Gen 17:15–21), like Samson (Jgs 13:2–7), like Samuel (1 Sam 1:3–18). In this section Luke has already begun to employ a literary form which contributes a deep theological content to his narrative and which must by no means be overlooked through any misconception of the author as a "factual" historian. This form consists in the systematic exploitation of Old

Testament stories, language, events, figures, all of which are woven into the tissue and fabric of which the Gospel account is composed. So systematic is the construction, we can take note only of the more important allusions. This literary form is sometimes called *midrash*, a late Jewish term for a scriptural commentary that draws out and applies to contemporary life the historical or moral implications of the sacred text. The second half of the Book of Wisdom (chs. 11–19) is a good example of *midrash*, where the author retells the Pentateuchal story of Israel's oppression in Egypt and the Exodus, systematically applying the older history to the circumstances of his own time, when God's people was once more being persecuted by Egyptians. This type of *midrash*, called by them *pesher*, was much in vogue among the people of Qumran. Strictly speaking, Luke is not so much commenting on the Old Testament as he is using it to clothe and describe New Testament events. *Midrash*, therefore, may not be the precise term for his literary form. In any case, it is an exemplification in narrative of the conviction that the events of the Old Testament foreshadowed those of the New (cf. 1 Cor 10:11), that the God who had revealed himself fully in Jesus Christ had not done so without showing himself in many types beforehand (cf. Heb 1:1 f.).

We should not misunderstand the purpose of this literary form, nor the intentions of those who have attempted to define it through their studies. The agreement of the independent Gospels of Matthew and Luke testifies to the core of essential historical fact that had been handed down by the tradition. The no less obvious diversity between them indicates what pertains to literary artistry and interpretation. Most of what is contained in these chapters could have been described in a variety of other ways without impairing its historical affirmation in the least. Some of what is related is, in fact, ineffable and incapable of ever being adequately captured in human speech and narration. We have, for example, annunciations, revelations to men of the mind and intentions of God. How precisely do such things occur? Prophets and mystics through the centuries have complained over the impossibility of their explaining to others exactly what had been the circumstances of their experiences. Luke, or his source, has chosen to narrate them in a way that was meaningful to the Christians of the first century, in the terms of familiar Old Testament types. These stories are not the statistical reports of uncommitted observers but the interpretation known through faith and given in the language of faith to certain events that took place during the reign of the man whom history knows as Herod the Great. Apart from the Christian faith that perceived the true meaning of these events, they would have meant nothing to history.

One of the Old Testament types of which Luke has made considerable use in this section is the vision of the seventy weeks (of years) in the ninth chapter of the Book of Daniel. Zechariah was *officiating as priest before God* at the time of the annunciation of the Baptist's birth. It was *his lot to enter the temple of the Lord to burn incense*. The daily morning and evening sacrifices of animals were performed on the altar of holocausts in the temple courtyard, but the conclusion of the rite was the scattering of incense on the altar within the holy place of the temple, which only the officiating priest could enter. Even with the priesthood distributed into twenty-four divisions, they were in such numbers that the performance of this highly coveted function had to be determined by lot. Now it was also at the hour of the evening sacrifice that Daniel received his vision of the seventy weeks (Dan 9:21), and from Gabriel, the angel of Zechariah's vision (cf. Lk 1:19); nowhere else in the Bible is there mention of an angel Gabriel. Daniel's vision was an apocalyptic reinterpretation of Jeremiah's prophecy of the seventy years of exile (Jer 25:11, 29:10) uttered in 605 B.C.; according to Daniel the end of the exile would be really consummated after seventy *weeks* of years, that is, 490 years after Jeremiah's prophecy (for both Jeremiah and Daniel these numbers are schematic and approximative). Then would occur the banishment of iniquity, the beginning of the reign of righteousness, and

the anointing of a Most Holy (Dan 9:24). For the author
of Daniel, this meant the reconsecration of the temple in
165 B.C. (the age in which he was living), after the successful rebellion of Judah the Maccabee against the Seleucid
king Antiochus IV Epiphanes who had erected there the
"horrible abomination," the statue of Zeus Olympios (Dan
9:27; 2 Macc 6:2): the feast to commemorate this Dedication (cf. Jn 10:22), in Hebrew *Hanukkah*, is still celebrated
by Jews to this day. It will be noted that Luke counts
seventy weeks (490 days, cf. Lk 1:26, 56f., 2:21f.; Lev
12:2–6) from the annunciation of Gabriel to the presentation
of Jesus in the temple: he knows of a Most Holy and of
a reign of righteousness that far transcend anything Daniel
dreamt of.

Luke is not simply being clever; by this device he begins
to convey a profound theological teaching. What the temple
of Jerusalem was, pre-eminently the house of God, Christ
is in a far more excellent way. Jesus replaces the temple
(cf. Jn 2:19–21, 4:20–24), Jesus and the Church which
is the body of Christ (cf. 1 Cor 3:16f.). This explains
the significance of the temple in the Lucan outline: the
Gospel which begins in the temple as a place of Jewish
sacrifice ends in the temple that has become a place of
Christian prayer (Lk 24:53); again, the Gospel of the
Spirit, the Acts of the Apostles, shows the movement of
Christianity from the temple (Acts 3:1) into the entire
world which will henceforth be its home.

Lk 1:13–20   Not only does Luke parallel the Baptist with
                   Jesus, for the reasons already indicated, he
also parallels strikingly the details of the stories. The annunciations to Zechariah and Mary (cf. Lk 1:26–38) follow a common pattern. After the introduction of the persons
involved there is the description of the appearance of the
angel, an appearance which excites fear and awe. The angel
immediately proceeds to words of comfort, then announces
the coming birth and the name of the child together with
the office that he will fill in the saving economy of God.

To the objection that is now made by the recipient of the annunciation the angel replies with a reiteration that the divine power will effect what it has announced, and a probative sign is added (Zechariah's dumbness, Elizabeth's pregnancy as a sign to Mary).

The pattern has been modeled on the narratives of classic annunciations in the Old Testament: the birth of Isaac (Gen 17–18), the mission of Moses (Ex 3–4), the mission of Gideon (Jgs 6:11–24), the birth of Samson (Jgs 13). An examination of these Old Testament passages will make clear as well the provenance of some of the phraseology employed by the Gospel.

The name *John* (and also that of Jesus) was quite as common in those days as it is in these. The Bible, however, always takes careful note of the meaning of names, to which far more significance was attached by the ancients than by us. John (Hebrew *Yohanan*) means "Yahweh has bestowed grace": a name eminently suited to the precursor of the Lord. His prophetic character is now underlined. Like Jeremiah (cf. Jer 1:5) *he will be filled with a holy spirit from his mother's womb,* given a prophetic call even before his birth. Like Elijah he will be the messenger of reconciliation (Mal 3:23 f., cf. 3:1). And like Samuel and Samson he will be a perpetual Nazirite (cf. Num 6:1–8), consecrated to a penitential life that will foreshadow the Life of sacrificial obedience by which the world's salvation has been assured (cf. Phil 2:8–11).

Lk 1:21–25   Like others who have received the revelation of God, Zechariah's eventual appearance was something of a consternation to the people who awaited him (cf. Ex 32:1, 34:29 f.); they recognized that something had taken place that was beyond their ken. As officiating priest he was supposed to give the final benediction, which, however, he could not do, but only *make signs to them.*

After the completion of the tour of duty of Zechariah's division, he returned *to his own house* in the Judean highlands (cf. Lk 1:39). Tradition has usually and most consistently identified this site with Ain Karim, a village in the southwestern suburb of Jerusalem. Elizabeth's reaction to the long-hoped-for conception of a child was to echo the words of Rachel (cf. Gen 30:23).

Lk 1:26–33 And now we read the beautiful story of the annunciation to Mary, *in the sixth month* of Elizabeth's pregnancy. This took place in a little *town of Galilee called Nazareth,* a village little esteemed in a countryside that was little esteemed (see the remarks on Galilee in Chapter 1). Nazareth is never mentioned in the Old Testament and very little outside it; even by the later Christians it was held in little veneration until a relatively tardy period. Its sole claim to fame in history is as the residence of the Holy Family.

In keeping with the marriage customs of the time, Mary was doubtless a girl of some fourteen or fifteen at the time of the annunciation. Her home was probably like most in this poor village, a cave dug into the side of a hill with perhaps a small extension on the front. There would have been a single door to the house, with a small opening on the side for ventilation. Light came from the open door or from a lamp consisting of a saucer of oil in which floated a wick. On the floor were perhaps a few mats, perhaps not even that. The floor itself was simply clay beaten hard by the many footsteps of the family.

Mary was *a virgin betrothed to a man named Joseph.* The virgin birth of our Lord is one of the historical facts on which the independent narratives of Luke and Matthew are agreed. In view of what has already been said of the literary form of these narratives it might be well to note —even though in this book we are concerned with biblical exposition rather than the justification of Christian belief —that in their transmission of this tradition the evangelists have neither imitated nor even paralleled any of the various wonder-legends that have become associated with the births of other famous men. Such parallels have often been claimed: Sargon of Akkad, Buddha, and the emperor Augustus are among the names most frequently cited. However, in the analysis, the Gospel story of divine annunciation accompanied by virginal conception remains unique. The chief inspiration for the narratives of both Matthew and Luke has been the Old Testament; but in the Old Testament, too, any real precedent for this account is entirely lacking.

Again in connection with the literary form in which Luke has clothed this narrative, it should be observed that he never really describes the vision of an angel, whatever have been the echoes of his story in Christian art. His emphasis is entirely on words of revelation. Mary is greeted in the language with which the prophets had apostrophized the eschatological Jerusalem about to receive its Redeemer (compare the words of the annunciation with Zeph 3:14–17; Zech 9:9 f.; Joel 2:21–27). Once more Luke is not merely playing with words: in his Gospel and in John's especially our Lady has a truly ecclesial character, herself the first of the redeemed figuring the whole people of God who are the recipients of God's beneficent grace and mercy. Hence the traditional translation *full of grace* (literally, "most favored one"), while it has taken on a depth of meaning for later Christian theology that transcends (without contradicting) the intention of the evangelist, nevertheless does accurately portray his thought. To the full, above and before all other creatures, has Mary been favored by God.

Jesus himself is designated as the Messiah of the Davidic line, one of the principal figures in which the salvation hopes of the Old Testament were crystallized; thus, as scion of *David his father,* he *shall be called Son of the Most High* (cf. 2 Sam 7:12–16; Pss 89:20–38, 132:11 f.). In verse 27 *of the house of David* doubtless refers to Joseph rather than to Mary, though Mary may also have been of Davidic descent as well as having some relationship to the priestly line of Aaron (vs. 36). Both Matthew and Luke trace Jesus' earthly ancestry through Joseph, his legal father, as a matter of course. Jesus' Davidic descent was part of the primitive Christian *kerygma* (cf. Rom 1:3), denoting one of the es-

sential links in the continuity of salvation history. As will be
seen, however, his fulfillment of the Davidic expectation was
also uniquely his own.

Lk 1:34–38   Mary's question, unlike Zechariah's, does not
                   express doubt, but it does reflect wonder-
ment: *How will this be, since I do not know man?* Many
have taken this to mean that Mary had already consecrated herself to a life of virginity, that her words indicate
more than simply a present situation of fact. Otherwise,
they say, her question would have been pointless, since in
the normal course of events her marriage with Joseph would
have soon been consummated and thus the child foretold by
the angel would be conceived.

It is not, of course, impossible that our Lady should have
resolved on a celibate life, unusual though this was in the
Jewish tradition. Quite apart from the fact that she was
something more than an "average" Jewish girl, celibacy was
not without precedent among the Jews, even in Old Testament times (cf. Jer 16:2), and it was certainly practiced
at the beginning of the Christian era by some of the Essenes. However, it is doubtful that any such conclusion can
be drawn from Luke's narrative. In the pattern of the annunciation story the question is merely that of a virgin avow-
ing her purity in the face of an enigmatic statement which
implied that she would bear a child while she was yet un-
married. It serves to introduce the angelic explanation that
the conception of the child will be virginal, achieved through
the power of God and not of man.

In the angel's reply another Old Testament type is introduced to identify further Mary's character: she is a new
Ark of the Covenant which God has made with his people
(cf. Ex 25:10–16, 37:1–9). The Ark of the Covenant had
been the abiding symbol of God's presence; in the Tent of
Meeting and in Solomon's temple it was regarded as God's
throne and footstool (cf. Is 6:1; Pss 99:5, 132:7; 1 Chron
28:2), the special residence of his "glory" (see above on
Jn 1:14). As it once had done to the Ark (see Ex

40:34 f.), *the power of the Most High will overshadow* Mary. This parallels the words, *Holy Spirit will come upon you:* the creative spirit of God (Gen 1:2) will bring to pass what has been promised. As we shall see, Luke continues the theme of Mary the Ark of the Covenant in his story of her visitation of Elizabeth.

All good mariology, the biblical included, must be at the same time good christology: the mystery of the Mother of God is seen properly only when it is viewed as one aspect of the greater mystery of her Son as the saving power of God. If Mary is the Ark of the Covenant, the tabernacle of the divine presence, what of Jesus? He is this divine presence. *Therefore the Holy that is to be born shall be called Son of God.* Luke has, literally, "the holy thing to be born": there is an allusion to Dan 9:24 (see the comment above on vss. 8–12). In Jewish ears, "son of God" could have various particular meanings but always one central and pervading significance. The king of Israel was God's son (cf. 2 Sam 7:14) because he epitomized in his person the promised saving presence of God whose instrument he was, or was supposed to be. The Messiah, the eschatological king par excellence, would be son of God in this same way. All Israel, God's people chosen and saved by him, could be called "sons of the living God" (Hos 2:1), just as we have already seen John speak of all believers in the Word as God's sons (Jn 1:12).

In the context of this narrative, and even more in the full context of the Gospel, it is plain that Luke knows Jesus to be Son of God in a way that transcends all these others without contradicting them. Jesus himself, as we shall see, probably proclaimed himself as Son of God uniquely. The recognition of the full meaning of this proclamation, however, is part of the Easter and Pentecostal faith of the Church, enlightened by the Spirit which has also inspired the Gospels. It is no derogation from Mary's signal privileges, then, to conclude that she, too, at the time of the annunciation was unaware of the magnitude of what had been revealed to her. In this as in all else she is typical of the

Church which first received the Word, then was led by
the Spirit of God into the fullness of truth (Jn 16:13).

Mary's response was wholly in keeping with her character
as model for all the faithful. *Behold the slave-girl of the
Lord:* what she has always been she wills to continue to be,
completely at the disposal of the divine pleasure wherever
it may lead her. It is evidently Luke's meaning that at this
moment the incarnation took place. This he describes as he
does everything else, with the utmost delicacy and tact.

Lk 1:39–55 Elizabeth's pregnancy in advanced age had
been offered to Mary as a sign of the divine
power, and now *with haste* Mary goes *into the hill country*
about Jerusalem, to the *town of Judah* where Zechariah and
Elizabeth had their residence, to visit her favored kins-
woman. Jesus has already begun his life pilgrimage that
will end in Jerusalem. Also, the Precursor while yet unborn
begins his work of announcing the Savior.

The stirring of a child within the womb is a normal
enough occurrence, but to those deep in biblical history such
things would be recognized as portents: Luke uses the same
verb found in the description of a similar happening in
Gen 25:22. Elizabeth was thereupon inspired to recognize
Mary as the most favored of all women because of the child
she was to bear, the identity of whom was made known to
her. Elizabeth's salutation of Mary together with the angel's
make up the first part of the Hail Mary! *How has this been
granted to me that the mother of my Lord should come to
me?* echoes the words of David to the Ark of the Lord,
following which it remained in the house of Obed-edom
for three months (2 Sam 6:9–11). *Blessed is she who has
believed* praises Mary's unshakable trust in God and expresses
Elizabeth's share in it.

Some manuscripts place the famous Magnificat which follows on Elizabeth's lips rather than Mary's. The reason for
this is not hard to find. The resemblance of the Magnificat to
the Song of Hannah (1 Sam 2:1–10) was not lost to early
readers of the New Testament, and it is Elizabeth rather

than Mary who is likened to Hannah in the Gospel. However, there is scarcely any doubt that the great majority of the manuscripts have correctly ascribed the words to Mary, as Luke intended. Luke's use of his Old Testament types is imaginative, never mechanical.

The canticles of the Gospel, here the Magnificat, the Benedictus in verses 68–79, the Nunc Dimittis in 2:29–32, somewhat parallel the sermons of Acts which are ascribed variously to Peter, Stephen, Paul, and others. They are, of course, free compositions of the author and his sources, employing the same vocabulary and style. No one has ever been under the illusion that they could have been drawn from the stenographic reports of eyewitnesses. Nevertheless, just as scholars will agree that the sermons of Acts in a general way authentically reflect the settings and personalities with which they are associated, something similar can be said of the canticles. They are in no way anachronistic, but rather highly accurate portrayals of the most elevated kind of Jewish messianic expectation, done exclusively in Old Testament terms. They are, in fact, mainly mosaics of Old Testament texts. The Magnificat itself has this character to a degree that almost amounts to a *tour de force*. If the reader would test this, let him read it in conjunction with the following texts, read in order: 1 Sam 2:1, 1:11; Gen 30:13; Deut 10:21; Pss 111:9, 103:17, 89:11; Job 12:19, 5:11; 1 Sam 2:7; Ps 107:9; Is 41:8; Ps 98:3; Mi 7:20; 2 Sam 22:51. As the Qumran literature has shown, impromptu compositions of this kind would have presented no difficulty to pious Jews immersed in the Old Testament.

The Magnificat is less a prayer than it is a meditation on the goodness of God and his saving deeds of mercy toward his people throughout history. There is very little of a personal note in it. However, the connection with Mary is definite enough. It is to *the lowly* and *the hungry* that the mercy of God has been shown; these were by now consecrated terms for the faithful clients of the Lord in whom the people of God could be epitomized (cf. Mt 5:3–10; Lk 6:20–26). Among these Mary takes a chief and culminating place: *he has regarded the lowliness of his handmaid. Hence-forth,* with Elizabeth's salutation as the norm, *all generations will call me blessed.*

Lk 1:56–79   It is evidently Luke's thought that Mary re-mained with Elizabeth until the time of the Baptist's birth, even though he makes no mention of Mary in the succeeding narrative. It is in accordance with his no-tion of an "orderly account" to finish one story, once he has begun it, before embarking on another. The end of the story of the visitation is that after three months' time Mary *returned to her own house.*

After the birth of John the Baptist he was circumcised, in accordance with the Mosaic law, eight days later, at which time it was also customary to bestow on the child his name. *They were going to call him by his father's name:* this was not a common practice. It is not clear whether Elizabeth had learnt from Zechariah that his name should be John or whether she had arrived at it through inde-pendent inspiration. At any rate, Elizabeth's relatives and friends *all marveled* when Zechariah (who appears to have been struck deaf as well as dumb) confirmed her choice: either because of the amazing coincidence or because the parents were resolved on a name that was not "in the family." One gets the impression that the relatives and friends were disposed to be busybodies as well as goodhearted people rejoicing with the aged couple.

Zechariah's regaining his faculties was one more circum-stance surrounding the birth of this child that convinced the neighbors that *the hand of the Lord was with him.* When Luke says that *all these things were spoken abroad in the hill country of Judea* and that *all who heard of them laid them up in their hearts,* he is doubtless indicat-ing in a general way the source of his information and its reliability, in accord with his claim in his prologue. He makes similar statements later on concerning our Lady.

Zechariah's recovered speech is immediately put to in-spired use in the utterance of the magnificent hymn we know as the Benedictus. Like the Magnificat, it has been woven out of Old Testament texts. The reader can "find" it in the following, read in order: Pss 41:14, 72:18, 106:48, 111:9, 132:17; Ezek 29:21; 1 Sam 2:10; Ps 106:10; Mi 7:20; Ps 106:45; Ex 2:24; Jer 11:5; Ps 105:8 f.; Mal 3:1; Is 40:3, 42:7, 9:1; Ps 107:10. While the Magnificat extols the beneficent acts of God in history, however, the Benedictus tends to advert to the culmination of the divine plan in the present events. The *horn of salvation for us in the house of David his servant* refers, obviously, to the yet unborn Jesus, present, nevertheless, in the body of his mother who was doubtless standing by. Zechariah's own child is addressed as *prophet of the Most High,* as having the character of Elijah ascribed to him in the angelic annunciation.

Lk 1:80 Having paralleled the annunciation of the Baptist and of Jesus and now having told the story of the Baptist's birth and circumcision, Luke will proceed to the complementary history of the Lord's nativity which we shall consider in our next chapter. For the moment, however, he is done with the Baptist *until the day of his manifestation to Israel* (Lk 3:2 and parallels). Hence he speedily summarizes in a few short words roughly thirty years of the Precursor's childhood and manhood.

Luke says that *he was in the deserts.* What is meant is the wilderness of Judea between Jerusalem and the Dead Sea, from time immemorial and down to the present a desolate region chosen as a place of refuge by those who have withdrawn from the world for political or religious reasons. Because this is also the region of Qumran, in recent years there has been a revival of an old theory concerning John the Baptist's penitential and meditative life of preparation, supposing it to have been spent in the bosom of some group like the Essenes. While the question cannot be settled definitely one way or the other, there is indeed something to be said for the idea that some of the contacts between Qumran and the New Testament may be explained through the Baptist. We shall see the further relevance of this hypothesis when we come to the history of Jesus' first disciples.

Mt 1:18–25 We shall conclude this chapter with a consideration of Matthew's parallel to Luke's story of the annunciation: here an annunciation made to Joseph. It will also be necessary to preface some preliminary remarks on the Matthaean form of the infancy narrative.

Matthew's "Gospel of the Infancy," the first two chapters of his work, is also very much an integral part of his whole Gospel, not something that has just been added on. It is *the book of the origin of Jesus Christ, the son of David, the son of Abraham* (Mt 1:1). Just as the Gospel as a whole falls into five major divisions of narrative and discourse, so in the Gospel of the Infancy we have five distinct narratives each built about a major prophetic text of the Old Testament. These are the annunciation to Joseph (1:18–25), Jesus' birth in Bethlehem (2:1–12), the flight into Egypt (2:13–15), the slaughter of the innocents (2:16–18), and the residence of the Holy Family at Nazareth (2:19–23); as will be seen, the genealogy with which the Gospel begins and which we shall consider later in connection with Luke's genealogy of the Savior is actually an introduction to the story of the annunciation to Joseph. This technique of exploiting Old Testament prophecy is typically Matthaean, one of the distinctive characteristics of the First Gospel.

Matthew's Gospel is pre-eminently ecclesiological: its theme first and foremost is the mystery of God's kingdom, first broached to Israel and now realized in the Church revealed to the people of God through his Messiah and chosen instrument Jesus Christ. The Gospel of the Infancy genuinely introduces this great theme by showing how in the coming of Jesus the history of Old Testament Israel has been epitomized. He who is the beginning of the new Israel, of the Church, is also the fulfillment and summation of all that has gone before. The promise was first given to Abraham and achieved in his offspring Jesus (cf. Gal 3:15–18). Christ who comes as a second—and a greater—Moses also figures in his own life Israel's call from Egypt and its exile, along with its higher destiny to be God's prophetic instrument for the salvation of the Gentiles.

Within their separate contexts, therefore, though following similar methods, the infancy narratives of Matthew and Luke go their distinct ways. They agree on the few basic affirmations about Jesus' conception and birth that were part of the heritage of Christian faith, but they have been written from independent traditions that differed in many details. If they do not contradict each other, neither do they attempt to supplement each other, and for this reason there is some difficulty in reading them as one continuous narrative. Matthew's concern throughout is with Joseph rather than Mary. He does not, as Luke does, begin the story in Nazareth; rather, he seems to presuppose that Bethlehem was the home of Mary and Joseph and that only because of special circumstances after Jesus' birth did they take up residence in Galilee. Incidentals of this kind, however, hardly affect what the evangelists considered to be the substance of their message. Given their separate aims and origins, the two accounts doubtless have a higher degree of correspondence than would have been antecedently expected.

The origin of Jesus Christ was in this way. As Matthew begins Mary is already *with child by the Holy Spirit* and the fact is known to Joseph. Matthew, too, emphasizes that Mary was *betrothed to Joseph* and that this was *before they came together,* that is, before there had been any consummation of a marriage. The virginal conception, therefore, is just as plain in Matthew's account as it is in Luke's. It may be noted how Matthew speaks of Mary and Joseph as persons already well known to his readers, needing no introduction. The narrative is quite compact, wasting no time on superfluous details.

Was Joseph aware merely that Mary was pregnant, or did he already have an intimation—from Mary herself, perhaps

—that her state was the result of a special grace of God?
Here we are confronted by a much debated interpretation
of the text. That Joseph was *a just man and unwilling to
expose her* has been held to have as its obvious meaning
that he suspected her, not unnaturally, of adultery. Though
the two were not yet officially married, nevertheless an
affianced bride was considered under Jewish law to have
both the rights and duties of a wife, and therefore co-
habitation with another man would bring with it all the
penalties of adultery. Joseph, however, a kindly man, wished
to spare Mary this obloquy, and therefore *he was minded
to put her away privately*, simply to divorce her without
giving any precise reason, as was possible according to
contemporary Jewish practice (see on Mt 19:3–12).

This is a reasonable enough understanding of the text
which may very well be correct. However, it is equally possible that it underestimates the fullness of Matthew's meaning, particularly the sense in which he speaks of Joseph as
a "just" man. A just man, after all, was a man faithful to
the law, and the law did not look kindly on a maiden who
had betrayed her troth (cf. Deut 22:23 f.). If, then, it is
Matthew's meaning that Joseph was unwilling to expose
Mary to reproach *despite* his being a just man, he may be
asking us to view the contemplated divorce in another light.
In other words, Joseph recognizing the mystery of God
at work in Mary's life may have been intending to with-
draw humbly from the scene. In this case, the subsequent
vision would have as its chief purpose to inform him of the
role he was intended to play as Mary's husband and, as
son of David, the legal father of the Savior.

At all events, *while thinking these things* it was revealed
to Joseph what he must do. As in Luke, the divine revelation takes the form of an angelic appearance, but here (and
in Mt 2:12 f., 19, 22; cf. also 27:19) the appearance
occurs in a dream, another means of divine communication
well known from the Old Testament (see especially Gen
15:12–16, 37:5–10; Num 12:6). Joseph was bidden to have
no fear about accepting Mary as his wife, since *what has*

been conceived in her is of the Holy Spirit. He is to be the father of this family, bestowing upon the child his name. The name *Jesus* (Hebrew *yᵉhôšûaʿ*, later abbreviated to *yēšûaʿ*) meant, effectively, "God saves." It was an extremely common name, both in the times of the Old Testament (Joshua, Jeshua) and the New, but the Gospel does not hesitate to underline the relevance of its etymology in the present instance: *he will save his people from their sins.*

Matthew invokes from Old Testament prophecy another name of equal relevance: this Jesus of whose birth he is speaking is the *Immanuel* of Is 7:14. This is the first of the Old Testament texts which he cites explicitly to indicate a foreshadowing pattern in the salvation history of the past. The precise historical circumstances of Isaiah's prophecy need not concern us here, as they did not concern Matthew. Isaiah had spoken of the birth of a child as the sign of God's salvation, whose very existence would be living evidence of God's saving presence: *ʿimmānû ʾēl*, "God with us." Such is Jesus. Furthermore, in the Greek text of the Old Testament which Matthew was using (though not in the original Hebrew of Isaiah's prophecy) the mother of this child was called *parthénos*, "virgin"—and Matthew, of course, was writing of a virgin birth.

The episode is brought to a rapid conclusion. Whatever the state of Joseph's mind had been, his course was now clear to him. *He took to himself his wife:* Joseph concluded his betrothal with Mary by receiving her into his home as his wife and acknowledging her child as his own. The Gospel was not written to defend the Christian tradition of Mary's perpetual virginity, but it certainly contains nothing that opposes it. *He did not know her till she brought forth* her son is Matthew's final insistence on the virginal conception of Jesus; he does not necessarily imply subsequent marital relations between Joseph and Mary (see the similar uses of "till" in Mt 12:20, 13:33, 14:22, 16:28, 22:44, 24:39). Some manuscripts (not the best ones) preface "firstborn" to "son" in this passage: see on Lk 2:7.

4. JOY TO THE WORLD

Lk 2:1-7 We resume and conclude the infancy narrative by retiring to Luke, the only evangelist who really tells the story of the nativity. He introduces this important event with another chronological indication. *Those days* refers, of course, to his previous indication (Lk 1:5), the time when Herod the Great was king (37–4 B.C.); Matthew also places the birth of Jesus within the reign of Herod. Luke now adds that these things took place during the lifetime of *Caesar Augustus* (30 B.C. to A.D. 14). Immediately we are made aware of the fact that our conventional reckoning of dates as B.C. and A.D., based on calculations made in the sixth Christian century, is in error by at least a few years. Jesus Christ was born sometime before 4 B.C.

Luke's further statistical information is subject to varying and uncertain interpretations owing to our lack of precise corroborative materials. The uncertainties concern minor matters of detail, but they do render an exact chronology impossible. There is no independent record that *a decree went forth . . . that a census of the whole world should be taken.* The "whole world" is the *oikoumenē,* the "inhabited earth," that is, the Roman empire. Various censuses, usually for taxation purposes, took place in the various parts of the

Empire during the time of Augustus, involving both Roman
citizens and those who were not. At one time or another,
doubtless the whole *oikoumenē* was included in the census.
Luke, of course, is interested in the census that affected
Palestine; but it is in keeping with his universalistic interests to fit the birth of Jesus into a context in which the
whole earth was involved.

Luke speaks of *this first census,* doubtless to distinguish
it from another, well-known census which he mentions in
Acts 5:37 (recorded also by Flavius Josephus), which took
place in A.D. 6–7. It is only this second census, as a matter of
fact, that is known to profane history as having taken place
while Quirinius was governor of Syria. Publius Sulpicius
Quirinius was certainly the Roman governor of Syria after
A.D. 6. That he served a term as governor before 4 B.C. cannot be proved, but neither can it be disproved. In any case,
Luke is mainly interested in connecting our Lord's birth
with known persons and events rather than in supplying an
exact chronology. It is known that the Romans undertook
a census in Egypt every fourteen years. If this practice held
true in the other Roman provinces, then presumably around
8 B.C. a census would have been taken in the province of
Syria, under which Palestine would have been included.
This is as close as we can come to assigning a date for
the birth of Jesus.

All were going to register, each to his own city. This was
certainly not the Roman method of taking a census, but again
we are not entirely sure of the background of the text. It is
likely enough that a Roman census of the Jews of Palestine
would have been administered by Herod, and it is equally
likely that it would have been done in the Jewish fashion, in
the places of ancestral origin, since Rome was always willing
to accommodate itself to its difficult Jewish subjects in matters that it did not consider essential. However, Luke's purpose here is to explain how it was that Jesus, of Galilean
parentage, came to be born in Bethlehem, and on any
accounting the census does not explain this, since Mary's
presence would not have been required in any case. Joseph

was of the house and family of David; Luke stresses Joseph's Davidic ancestry quite emphatically. We are half given the impression that the Holy Family had some connection with the city of David other than the casual one afforded by the census. It will be recalled that Matthew appears to take it for granted that Mary and Joseph were originally Judeans rather than Galileans. It is also to be noted that Luke still calls Mary Joseph's *betrothed* rather than his wife, though it is evident that the marriage spoken of in Mt 1:24 had by now taken place. This is Luke's delicate way of saying what Matthew said more bluntly in 1:25.

Equally delicate is Luke's description of our Lord's virginal birth, a description which stands in great contrast to the crudities of some of the apocryphal gospels. *The days of her delivery were fulfilled, and she brought forth a son, her firstborn.* "Firstborn" (Hebrew *beкôr*, Greek *prōtotokos*) was a technical term for "the child who opens the womb" (cf. Ex 13:12–15). A "firstborn" might well be an only child: a funerary inscription from Egypt of the year 5 B.C.— almost precisely contemporary with the birth of the Savior— describes the virtues of a young Jewish mother who died giving birth to her *prōtotokos.* The firstborn had special privileges and was an object of predilection; thus Israel was called the Lord's "firstborn" (Ex 4:22). *She wrapped him round and laid him in a manger:* the manger, a wooden or stone trough for the feeding of animals, may have belonged to the shepherds who appear in the next episode; it seems to be presupposed that its location was already known to them (cf. vss. 12, 15 f.). Swept clean and lined with straw it would have made a comfortable if makeshift crib for a newborn child. That the manger was in a cave as the ancient Bethlehemite tradition maintains is not at all unlikely.

There was for them no place in the inn are words that have often been misunderstood. We need not think of stony-hearted innkeepers and townspeople turning away the Holy Family and refusing them hospitality. The text seems to suppose that Mary and Joseph had already been in Bethlehem for some days, and during this time they had probably stayed at the inn. The inn, the Palestinian *khan*, which would have been outside the city near the traveled roads, was simply an enclosure in which men and cattle were bedded down for the night. Privacy, always at a premium in the Near East, would have been impossible here. Luke is undoubtedly suggesting that Mary and Joseph deliberately chose a place of seclusion for the enactment of the mystery of the Lord's birth.

Lk 2:8–20   The familiar story of the shepherds is without analogy in the parallel history of the Baptist and it has no counterpart in Old Testament events or in "hero" legends; it is part of the Bethlehemite tradition of the humble birth of Christ. This event which had first been announced to one who called herself the lowly handmaid of the Lord is now first witnessed to by other humble folk, like those who will later hear the kingdom declared their own in Jesus' proclamation of the Gospel (cf. Lk 6:20).

The story conforms to the Lucan pattern: an angelic annunciation accompanied by an injunction not to fear is followed by an explanation and a sign. There is also a canticle which anticipates the later messianic acclaim of Jesus (cf. Lk 19:38), taken as usual from Old Testament phrases (cf. Ps 118:25; Is 57:19). *On earth peace:* "peace" inadequately translates a Semitic concept which really connotes wholeness, completion, at-one-ment with God. Concretely this happy state is now present in the babe of Bethlehem; similarly St. Paul calls Christ "our peace" (Eph 2:14). *Among men of good will:* a parallel expression in the Qumran literature confirms what was always the best understanding of these words, that the "good will" in question is God's. That is to say, it is through the gratuitous act of the divine mercy that this peace has been brought to men.

Two additional words in this passage are deserving of note. In verse 11 Jesus is called for the first time in the Gospel *Savior*, a term pre-eminently reserved in the Old Testament to the God of Israel. The angelic annunciation

I bring you good news is the Greek verb corresponding to our word "Gospel." The shepherds respond to this proclamation by saying, literally, *Let us go . . . see this word which has come to pass,* and, as is the duty of all who receive the word, *they made known what had been told them,* in a sense becoming the first to preach the Gospel. Contrasting with the surprise of the villagers who heard the shepherds' testimony is the quiet Virgin who was *pondering these things in her heart.*

The episode of the shepherds who *were out in the fields in that same district* says nothing either for or against the tradition which makes December the month of the nativity. The climate of Bethlehem is temperate enough to allow for a very mild December. But in any case the traditional dating of Christmas, which probably cannot be traced back beyond the fourth Christian century, was doubtless arrived at on considerations other than those of the Gospel.

Mt 1:1–17
Lk 3:23–38
Before pursuing the infancy narratives to their conclusion, it is appropriate at this point to consider the two earthly genealogies of Jesus which appear in the Gospels in Matthew as a preface to the story of his birth and in Luke as an insertion into the introductory part of the history of the public ministry.

The reader who approaches the genealogies for the first time is initially surprised to discover the many discrepancies between them. Matthew's is more typically Jewish in maintaining the descending order from father to son; Luke's, while not without precedent in the Old Testament, adopts the less usual procedure of working back through preceding generations. In keeping with his universalistic interpretation of the Gospel, Luke not surprisingly traces Jesus' ancestry all the way to human origins; Matthew, adhering more closely to the Gospel's Jewish beginnings, shows Jesus' descent from Abraham through the royal line of David. The most obvious difference, however, is in the genealogical names from David to Joseph, which follow two quite separate traditions, including even a discrepancy in the name of Joseph's father.

We have no way of reconciling the two genealogies completely, but there is no particular reason why we should try. To a considerable extent both are artificial. Even apart from the fact that no one could trace a person's ancestry back through seventy-five names to Adam, as Luke does, it will be noted that for the names prior to David he has simply reproduced the already artificial genealogies of the Old Testament. Matthew has three series of fourteen names. The fourteen he probably derived from 1 Chron 2:1–15, which already had counted fourteen generations from Abraham to David; fourteen is also the first multiple of seven, a number favored in Matthew, and is the sum of the numerical value of the Hebrew letters of David's name (d-w-d: vowels are not written in the Hebrew alphabet). In order to preserve symmetry he has omitted the names of three of the Davidic kings on whom he concentrates in his genealogy. In both lists the names subsequent to Zerubbabel are unknown to the Old Testament. Luke has given Joseph's Davidic lineage through a certain Heli, Matthew through a man named Jacob.

Both evangelists insist on what was part of the earliest Christian confession (cf. Rom 1:3), that through Joseph, his legal father, Jesus was truly of the Davidic descent in which the messianic expectation had been fixed. It would have been by no means unusual that a Jewish carpenter would be able to vindicate such an ancestry through family traditions. Such genealogies, however, were never complete and were subject to many variations.

We have seen the universalistic note of Luke's genealogy. In its own way, Matthew's is also universalistic. Contrary to Semitic custom, it includes the names of four women, the common denominator of whom seems to be that they were all Gentiles, non-Israelites who nevertheless became part of the history of the people of God even in Old Testament times.

Lk 2:21-24   Following the story of the shepherds, Luke concludes his narrative of the nativity by telling of two events which were of importance to him. *After eight days,* in accordance with the Mosaic law, occurred *his circumcision,* the rite by which a Jewish boy was accepted into the religious society of his people. Jesus, who was "born of a woman, born under the law" (Gal 4:4), became officially subject to the law of Moses by this rite. At the same time, as we have already noted in the parallel history of the Baptist, it was customary for the child to receive his name. It is doubtless the name-giving that was chiefly of interest to Luke.

The other event occurred thirty-three days later (cf. Lev 12:1-4): the end of the period of ritual uncleanness after childbirth and the time of the mother's ceremonial purification. Luke says curiously *the time of their purification.* The plural pronoun probably is used because, although the rite of purification involved Mary alone, occasion was taken at the same time to fulfill another law that did involve Jesus and which is the real subject of this passage: *they brought him to Jerusalem to present him to the Lord.* This presentation of Jesus—which did not have to be performed in the temple—was the "redemption" of the firstborn from the Lord by the payment of five silver shekels, say three dollars in our money (cf. Num 18:15 f.). Thus, though the purification was the occasion, and the sacrifice that is mentioned is that of the purificatory rite (cf. Lev 12:6-8), what is uppermost in Luke's mind is that Jesus ("Savior") the Redeemer now appears before the Lord himself redeemed: Daniel's prophecy of the seventy weeks has now been fulfilled in the consecration of a most holy (see above on Lk 1:8-12).

Lk 2:25-38   Accompanying this event, as was most fitting, were signs like those which accompanied Jesus' annunciation and birth. In the temple were two holy people who like Elizabeth and Zechariah, Mary and

Joseph, represent the very best in the contemporary Jewish messianic expectation.

Simeon, for some reason, has often been represented in postbiblical tradition as a priest and an aged man. Luke says merely that he was *a just man and devout who was awaiting the consolation of Israel.* He was, in other words, like Mary one of the poor and humble of the Lord to whom prophecy had promised the messianic salvation (cf. Is 40:1, 49:13, 61:1 f., 66:13). This man, whom inspiration had first assured of a fulfillment of this hope in his own lifetime, was now inspired to discover its realization in the child in Mary's arms. His prayer of thanksgiving is reproduced in the canticle which we call the Nunc Dimittis, as usual an echo of prophetic themes whose universalism would have especially appealed to Luke (cf. Is 40:5, 52:10).

Simeon likewise has a prophetic blessing for Mary and her Child. It is the destiny of every prophetic word to be *a sign contradicted.* Jesus, the Word incarnate, will be no exception to this rule. Faith, the acceptance of the prophetic word of which he himself is the sign (cf. Mk 8:11 f.; Mt 16:1–4; Is 7:3–14, 8:14 f.), will determine in every case whether he shall be *for the fall or for the rise of many in Israel.* Broadly speaking, this is the teaching that is spelt out in the first half of John's Gospel. Simeon's word to Mary is also Johannine: *your own soul a sword shall pierce.* In the temple episode with which Luke will conclude his infancy narrative (Lk 2:41–52), Mary will receive a foretaste of the role which she is to play in the redemptive work of her Son. It will not be an easy role, for it will involve the same kind of renunciation of self and sacrificial obedience that are Christ's destiny. Not through the natural ties of motherhood but rather in her capacity as mother and model of the faithful will Mary accomplish what God has designed for her (see on Jn 2:1–11).

The *prophetess Anna* whom Luke introduces on this same occasion is described by him in some detail, but little is said of any prophetic function that she fulfilled. One of the devout of the Old Testament, she likewise foreshadowed the dedicated widows who were to become one of the institutions of the apostolic Church (cf. 1 Tim 5:3–8) *awaiting the redemption of Jerusalem.*

Lk 2:39–40 Having concluded his story of the nativity, Luke now takes the Holy Family back to their Galilean homeland; he has nothing further to relate concerning the circumstances of the Lord's birth. A final parallel to his story about the Precursor (cf. Lk 1:80) summarizes the "hidden life" of obscurity in which Jesus, too, was prepared for the day of his manifestation to Israel.

Mt 2:1–12 Matthew, however, who has even less to say about Jesus' actual birth than Luke does, resumes his infancy narrative at this point, *after Jesus had been born in Bethehem of Judea in the days of King Herod,* with the well-known story of the coming of the Magi, an episode designed to feature the second of his prophetic texts concerning the Messiah (see above on Mt 1:18–25). As has already been seen, there is little use in trying to relate this event chronologically to what has been described in Luke's account. The two narratives have been prepared from altogether distinct traditions which grew up without reference to each other and in which such chronological considerations played no part. In the past, commentators have spent a great deal of time quite fruitlessly debating the precise sequence of events which, it was thought, was supposed by the combined Gospel story. What is now recognized as the proper study of the Gospel is to ascertain what each evangelist intended to contribute to its message through the use which he made of traditions which were independent of another's.

There can be no doubt as to what Matthew intended to bring out in the Magi story. His is a Gospel very much intended to speak to the existing Church, a Gentile Church which had transcended the privileges of the earthly Israel. The pagan Magi who have traveled from afar to seek out the awaited king stand in glaring contrast to the king and the

wise of Jerusalem, all of whom are unaware of the great
thing that has taken place among them and some of whom
are made aware of it only to view it as an evil to be sup-
pressed: truly, even from the very beginning Jesus "did
not find faith like this in Israel" (see on Mt 8:5–13 and
parallel). As before, the Gospel narrative includes many
illusions to Old Testament prophecy and themes besides the
one explicit citation of Mi 5:1 on the Bethlehemite origin of
the Messiah. The theme of the Gentiles pilgriming to
Jerusalem in the time of redemption is to be found in such
passages as Is 60:6 and Ps 72:10 f. (a text which is doubtless
responsible for the later Christian legend which transformed
the Magi into kings). Possibly the star of the Magi is intended to evoke the star (*kôkāb*) from Jacob mentioned in
the oracle of Balaam of Num 24:17: the secular messiah
who led the second Jewish revolt against the Romans,
which culminated in A.D. 135, was known popularly as Bar
Kokeba, "son of the star." On the other hand, we may have
to look no further for an explanation of the star than to the
tradition of the Magi itself, since magi were astrologers.
But above all, in this narrative the evangelist is thinking
of Jesus in his character of a second and greater Moses—
the Moses who like Jesus was born under a tyrannous king
to the accompaniment of the slaying of innocents (Ex 1:15–
22), who had to flee to a foreign land to save his life from
the wrath of this king (Ex 2:15), the Moses who was born
to be Israel's rescuer (Ex 2:10), its ruler and judge (Ex
2:14; cf. Acts 7:35).

Confronted by such a story as that of the Magi, the
modern reader is likely to ask questions for which no answer
is provided by the evangelist or the tradition on which he
depended. *Magi from the east arrived in Jerusalem.* Elsewhere in the New Testament (e.g., Acts 13:6) a *magos* is a
practitioner of occult arts, and the word is usually employed in a pejorative sense. Traditionally *magoi* were the
astrologer priests of Persian Zoroastrianism, a monotheistic
religion of sorts which had had some influence on the development of postexilic Judaism but which certainly had

little if any acquaintance with Palestinian Jewry and did not share its messianic aspirations. That Persian priests should have been led by their astronomical calculations to discern the birth of the Jewish Messiah and that they should have journeyed from distant Persia to Herod's provincial court in Jerusalem is unlikely in the extreme. Neither this fact, however, nor the undeniably "midrashic" interpretation which the evangelist has given to the story justifies any peremptory judgment concerning the historicity of whatever real happening may lie behind the tradition. That it is symbolic in much of its detail is undeniable, but it is equally undeniable that the Gospel traditions have not in principle been concocted out of thin air. What is true is that in the form in which these traditions have reached us they are no longer a legitimate object for the microscopic investigation of historical criticism. Who the Magi really were, therefore, and what were the precise circumstances of their relation to the birth of the Savior are questions that cannot be answered from the Gospel sources, the only sources that we possess.

King Herod was troubled, and all Jerusalem with him. This perturbation, unwonted in those who should have been eagerly awaiting *the one born King of the Jews,* anticipates the consternation of Jerusalem at the time of Jesus' entry there as messianic king (cf. Mt 21:10). The messianic text from Micah is cited by Matthew not in the restricted sense of the original Hebrew prophecy, which was to celebrate the Ephrathite clan of David chosen by the Lord to be his elect dynasty, but in the sense of Christian fulfillment pointing to the Messiah's Davidic and Bethlehemite origin. Herod's duplicity continues to contrast with the simple good faith of the Magi.

The star went before them till it stopped over the place where the child lay. As it figures in the story the star of the Magi is obviously a divine portent that can find no explanation in any of the normal manifestations of celestial phenomena. *Entering the house:* in Matthew's Gospel there is nothing of the tradition of Jesus' birth as a stranger in

Bethlehem; as in 2:22 f., the evangelist takes it for granted that the Holy Family made their dwelling there. *They worshiped him:* Matthew, of course, takes the divine nature of Christ as part of the Gospel message. Whether he intends to suggest that the Magi acknowledged his divine as well as his royal character is not certain, but it is likely enough that he did. The three *gifts of gold, frankincense, and myrrh* have doubtless contributed to the idea that there were three Magi. These were traditional gifts of homage (cf. Ps 72:10, 11, 15; Is 60:6; Cant 3:6; Sir 24:20); there may be an echo of the same idea in Jn 19:39.

Mt 2:13–15   In dreams the Lord both warns the Magi not to return to the perfidious Herod with news of Christ's birth and commands Joseph to take the child and his mother into Egypt away from his cruel power. There really would have been nothing too unusual about such a journey for Palestinian Jews. There were Jewish colonies throughout this nearby country, and Alexandria was one of the largest Jewish centers of the contemporary world.

Matthew, however, finds in this event a profound prophetic significance, on a par with Jesus' Bethlehemite origin. *Out of Egypt I called my son* were the words of the prophet Hosea (Hos 11:1) referring to Israel's election by God as concretely demonstrated in the exodus from Egypt by which it passed, under Moses, from slavery into freedom. It has been Jesus' destiny to be the Savior of the new Israel by becoming the firstborn of many brethren (cf. Col 1:18), reliving Israel's history in his own to bring that history to an even more glorious fulfillment. Israel was first God's son, and now his only Son has become one of Israel that all might be called sons of God.

Mt 2:16–18   Finding himself outwitted by the Magi, Herod reacts with all the ruthlessness by which he is notorious in profane history. Bethlehem and its environs, it is true, comprised only a small town, and the evangelist therefore represents the slaughter of the innocents as of perhaps a score of children rather than of the hundreds or thousands that became the theme of later artists and liturgists. But in any case it was a savage act worthy of the world which hates Christ, whose way is death in opposition to his way of life.

To accompany this account Matthew has chosen the most poignant of his prophetic texts, that of Jeremiah (Jer 31:15) on the occasion of the captivity and exile of northern Israel centuries before. Jeremiah had represented Rachel, the mother of Benjamin and Joseph (i.e., in popular thought, the people of Ephraim), rising from her grave at Ramah to weep over the plight of her descendants. In Matthew's time, as it is today, tradition had transferred the site of Rachel's tomb to the vicinity of Bethlehem (cf. Gen 35:19), and in this circumstance the evangelist found an even more appropriate cause for Rachel's weeping. But it is not of this coincidence alone that he takes note. Jeremiah's was a prophecy of salvation after tears, of redemption that would follow suffering, of return after exile and death.

Mt 2:19–23   The last of Matthew's prophetic texts that have provided the outline for his infancy narrative remains an enigma despite all the efforts that have been made to explain it. *He shall be called a Nazarene* is the customary translation, since it is evident enough that the evangelist intends to offer a providential accounting in prophecy for the fact that Jesus, born in Bethlehem, was nevertheless known as a Galilean from the town of Nazareth, where Mary and Joseph went after their return from Egypt. Luke was at pains to explain how Jesus came to be born in Bethlehem in the first place, but Matthew, as he appears to have no knowledge that the Holy Family originated in Nazareth, must explain why they did not return to Bethlehem. This was because of *Archelaus*, he says, who despite Jewish opposition was confirmed by the Romans to succeed his father Herod in Judea after Herod's death in 4 B.C. Archelaus, who proved to be somewhat of a worse ruler than his father, if this were conceivable, governed Judea—

though not Galilee or Perea—until he finally had to be removed in A.D. 6. The Holy Family, therefore, passed into the territory of Herod Antipas, likewise a son of the great Herod, but without his father's evil reputation. *Those who sought the child's life are dead* reflects Matthew's consciousness of the parallel with Moses' life (cf. Ex 4:19).

The word that Matthew actually uses is *nazōraios,* which does not at first glance seem to be closely related to Nazareth; in point of fact, the New Testament has another word, *nazarēnos,* which is a much more obvious term for Nazarene. On the analogy with words like *pharisaios* and *saddoukaios,* we would expect *nazōraios* to come out in English something like Nazoree. It does not, because we know of no need for such a word. Nevertheless, some scholars have thought that there was such a title, of uncertain meaning, probably pejorative, applied by the Jews to Christ and the first Christians. To this day, Jews refer to Jesus in Hebrew as *Yešu han-nōṣrî* and to Christians as *han-nōṣrîm.* These terms are generally taken to mean "Nazarene(s)," but again this does not seem to have been their original sense.

If there was such a contemptuous name given to Christ and the Christians, it may be in this sense that Matthew connects it with prophecy, relating it to Nazareth by a play on words. Nazareth, we know, was an insignificant village with a low reputation (cf. Jn 1:46). Jesus, the Lord's Servant, was reputed by men as lowly and of no account, as had been written in prophecy (cf. Is 52:13–53:6). But many other correspondences to the word have been sought in the Old Testament, such as the *neṣer* (shoot) of Is 11:1, 60:21, etc., the *nōṣer* (guardian) of Is 27:3, etc., or the *nāzîr* (a consecrated person) of Jgs 13:5, etc. It would help, of course, if we knew what prophetic passage Matthew had in mind. He speaks of *what was said by the prophets* either, as St. Jerome thought, because he refers to a general prophetic idea rather than to a specific prophecy, or because he is invoking some non-canonical prophecy that is now unknown to us. The mingling of canonical with apocryphal testimonial passages appears in the literature of the Qumran sectaries.

Lk 2:41–52   On his final prophetic note, Matthew's Gospel of the Infancy concluded. Luke's infancy narrative, too, as we saw, could very well have been completed with his final parallel (in Lk 2:39 f.) linking the coming of the Savior with the Precursor, his summation of the hidden life of Jesus at Nazareth. In a sense, the story with which Luke does choose to end his narrative appears both supplementary and anticlimactic, and bears a superficial resemblance to the apocryphal gospels which abound with wonderful stories about Jesus' boyhood. However, even if Luke has included the incident as an afterthought, it is his story throughout and he has thoroughly integrated it into his Gospel. As is apparent, it parallels and complements the story of Jesus' presentation in the temple.

His parents went every year to Jerusalem for the feast of the Passover. In these days of the Diaspora even pious Jews who lived afar were not expected to keep the three pilgrimage feasts in Jerusalem (Deut 16:16), but all who could would try to be present there for the Passover, commemorating the events of Israel's exodus from Egypt. At *twelve years of age* Jesus himself was not yet *bar mitzvah* and therefore not personally obliged to the Law in any case. The story that unfolds is perfectly comprehensible in itself. *Having completed the* seven *days* of the Passover observance, Mary and Joseph begin the return journey to Galilee, are separated from each other in caravan, and only when camp is made at the end of the first day's journey do they discover that Jesus is nowhere in the company. *After three days* would indicate the morning of the day following the one spent in the return to Jerusalem. Luke undoubtedly intends to evoke the memory of the resurrection of Jesus on the third day.

The scene of the finding of Jesus in the temple precincts evokes a picture familiar to travelers in the Near East: the informal schools conducted by masters with disciples at their feet, posing and answering questions. Mary's protestation is typically a mother's, in which relief is mingled with a touch of exasperation at finding him calmly attending the discussions of the rabbis while he had been frantically sought after. But it is now that she must begin to learn her destiny, foretold years ago by Simeon. *Your father and I have sought you,* she has said. Rather, replies Jesus, *why did you not know that I would be at my Father's?* He who was in one sense Jesus' father, and in a sense certainly not to be minimized, must nevertheless soon make way for Jesus' Father above all in the public life which this Son will lead as one of sacrificial obedience which will permit no interference from earthly ties. Joseph, as a matter of fact, now unobtrusively disappears from the Gospel story. Mary his mother will remain, but, as we shall see, the Gospel will be no less clear concerning the role in which providence has cast her. Not as Mary of Nazareth, wife of the carpenter and mother of a boy Jesus, but as the first of believers and exemplar of Christians will her life find its fulfillment, even as she has already been hailed as Daughter of Zion and Ark of the Covenant. Her greater unity with her Son will be achieved through the paradox of the separating sword of renunciation.

He was subject to them. Jesus' presence in the temple is a foreshadowing of his entire life, which is that of the obedient Servant of God who has come not to be ministered to but to minister to others; this chosen role is likewise exemplified in the "hidden life." At the close of this narrative Luke again reminds us of the parallel with the history of the Baptist by a summary statement very like that of verse 40.

5. A LIGHT BEGINS TO SHINE

Lk 3:1–2   All the Gospels begin the story of the salvation wrought in Jesus Christ by recalling the proclamation of the kingdom by John the Baptist, the last in the long prophetic series that had testified to the saving design of God. Only Luke, however, as is his wont (cf. Lk 2:1 f.), has attempted to relate the kerygmatic history of the Gospel to the world history into which the New Testament was born.

The fifteenth year of Tiberius Caesar, however, is not as precise an indication as it might be, though Luke undoubtedly intended it to be so. Tiberius became emperor in his own right in A.D. 14, on the death of the emperor Augustus who was reigning at the time of Jesus' birth. He had already been accepted by Augustus as co-ruler a couple of years before this, however. Presumably Luke is counting from the beginning of Tiberius' separate reign. Presumably, too, he is counting by the Roman method of reckoning regnal years. If these assumptions are correct, he indicates a date sometime between October of A.D. 27 and September of A.D. 28. This was the beginning of the Baptist's prophetic mission: *the word of God came upon John, the son of Zechariah, in the desert;* thus he resumes the story which he broke off in 1:80. It is the evident sense of the Gospels that Jesus' own ministry did not begin long after this.

A glance at the map of Palestine in Jesus' time will make clearer the rest of the data that Luke gives. *Pontius Pilate was governor of Judea,* which included Samaria, between A.D. 26–36, the fifth to serve in that capacity after the removal of Herod's son Archelaus. The *Herod* who was *tetrarch of Galilee* and Perea was Antipas, another of Herod's sons, while still another, *Philip,* governed *Ituraea and Trachonitis,* the northern region of Herod's old kingdom, a region which scarcely enters into the Gospel picture. In mentioning *Lysanias the tetrarch of Abilene,* Luke was once thought to have made a serious historical blunder, since the only Lysanias of that description then known had been put to death by Mark Antony in 34 B.C. A contempory inscription discovered and published in 1912, however, confirmed the existence of Luke's Lysanias. Abilene does not figure in the Gospel; Luke merely notes Lysanias as a statistical fact, a ruler on a par with Antipas and Philip.

The high priesthood of Annas and Caiaphas does concern the Gospel record, and of course we shall meet these worthies again.

Lk 3:3–6 Matthew and Mark, who lack Luke's historical
Mt 3:1–6 introduction to the Gospel story, substitute for
Mk 1:1–6 it in their own ways. Matthew's *in those days* obviously has no reference to the infancy narrative which he has made the preface of his Gospel. The expression is merely conventional and somewhat mechanical, as are so many apparently statistical references in the Gospels. Mark, who is only now beginning his Gospel is, seemingly, the only evangelist to use that word for his work (of all the evangelists, only Mark and Matthew use the word *gospel* at all). Even here, however, Mark's emphasis is doubtless less on his narrative of the Gospel than on the fact of the Gospel itself, the good news of the salvation prophesied of old and now fulfilled in Jesus Christ. Similarly, his refer-

ence to *the beginning* may evoke the idea of new creation as well as entitle his work.

The Synoptic Gospels have a representation of the Baptist which partly agrees with the presentation of John and partly, as we shall see, is at variance with it. They all apply to him the words of Is 40:3, which spoke of the joyful news of coming salvation, the Lord again coming to visit his people after their exile and degradation. It is interesting to see how the several evangelists use the quotation. Mark prefaces to it lines that come from Ex 23:20 and Mal 3:1, all of which he includes as the words of *Isaiah the prophet*. One of the sources on which the evangelists drew—one of the Gospel "forms"—was testimonial collections, series of Old Testament texts of the same or similar purport which had been melded together and were cited only by a generic reference; this passage is far from being isolated in the Gospels. Matthew and Luke omit the expansion on the Isaian text here probably because they found it in a better context in the source they share independently of Mark and have therefore reproduced it elsewhere in their Gospels (Mt 11:10; Lk 7:27). Luke, on the other hand, extends the Isaian citation down to Is 40:5, undoubtedly because of the final words: *and all mankind shall see the salvation of God;* Luke rarely misses an opportunity to stress the universality of salvation.

Matthew and Mark also agree (Luke, however, does not) in recognizing in John the Baptist a second Elijah the prophet: it is for this reason that they note the Baptist's *garment of camel's hair and leather belt* (see 2 Kgs 1:8). Luke omits this description, as he does that of the Baptist's simple and penitential diet, probably because he felt that such references would be lost on his Gentile readers. *Locusts and wild honey,* that is, the sweet gums of various trees, are still eaten by the desert Arabs; the locusts are roasted and eaten whole or ground into a powder and mixed with other food.

John the Baptist was preaching a *baptism of repentance* in view of the imminent *kingdom of God* ("kingdom of

heaven" in Matthew: a Jewish paraphrase). As such, he
was continuing a venerable prophetic tradition. It is not
merely that he spoke of the coming soon of what prophets
had first enunciated and had become one of the favorite
themes of later Judaism, God's definitive breaking into man's
history, establishing for all time a reign in which his will
would be as truly done on earth as it is in heaven. This
expectation, sometimes expressed in nationalistic and partic-
ularistic terms, sometimes quite spiritually, was shared by
many in Israel, and not only by withdrawal groups like the
Essenes: the Gospels show here and elsewhere with what
enthusiasm the Baptist's preaching had been received in
Palestine. Far more important was it that John was preaching
metanoia, the word that we translate "repentance," which
means a change of mind and heart, conversion, a thorough-
going revision of one's actions and attitudes to bring them
into conformity with the will of God. This is what the
prophets had preached as the condition of God's coming:
for his kingdom God has need of men. This it is that leads to
the forgiveness of sins and the beginning of the kingdom.

As the sign of this entry into a new way of life John
baptized his disciples in water. Baptism was a rite not unknown to the Jews, and it is likely that it was practiced by
the Qumran Jews in particular; at all events, its symbolism
is obvious enough to explain its use by other religions which
have no connection with Judaism or Christianity. Because
of John's proximity to the New Testament, however, and because of the continuation that his practice was to find in the
sacramental baptism of the Church, he has been remembered in Christian tradition as the Baptizer.

Mt 3:7–10   Matthew and Luke supplement Mark's ac-
Lk 3:7–9   count from another source that they share in
             common, a passage which suggests some of
the content of the Baptist's preaching. It further explains what
was involved in the *metanoia* preached by John: it must be
a soul-searching that results in total compliance with the
grace of God, setting no reliance on any supposed auto-

matic guarantees of race or formal religion. "He is not a Jew
who is so outwardly . . . but who is so inwardly" (Rom
2:28 f.). This, too, was in the authentic prophetic tradition
(cf. Jer 31:31–34, for example). *The axe is laid to the
root of the trees* lends an expressive eschatological note to
this preaching: the kingdom is near, and the time for
repentance is short.

Brood of vipers is a surprisingly harsh judgment to encounter this early in the Gospel story, and for this reason
many are of the opinion that the tradition on which Matthew
and Luke depended has anticipated in the career of the
Baptist a situation that better fits in the ministry of Jesus
(cf. Mt 12:34, 23:33). It is a common tradition of the
Gospels, however, that John who was popularly received as
a prophet was regarded with cynical skepticism or feigned
acceptance by many within the Jewish leadership (cf. Mk
11:30–32 and parallels). It is to these latter that these
words were addressed, as is evident from Matthew's reference
to *many of the Pharisees and Sadducees*—terms which themselves are doubtless excessively generic, as we shall see. It
is Luke's casual *the crowds* which could give the impression, belied by his own context, that the Baptist's denuncia-
tion was a wholesale one. Elsewhere (cf. Lk 7:29 f.) he
clearly makes the distinction just mentioned.

Lk 3:10–14   Luke himself now expands on the story
from a source of his own to show the basic
good will of "the crowds." This evangelist rarely misses an
opportunity to "actualize" the Gospel story for his readers:
what the Baptist indicated as the conditions necessary for
reception of the kingdom could serve as guidelines for the
members of the kingdom-Church.

The Baptist's injunctions reiterate the essentials of the
prophetic conception of true religion: justice and charity
proved by deeds (cf. Jas 1:27, 2:16 f.). *The taxgatherers*
of our text were the famous "publicans," Jews who collected
the taxes farmed out by the Roman authorities, men who
were in an easy position for extortion and for victimizing

their fellow Jews who excommunicated them for their service of a heathen oppressor. Probably in much the same position were the *soldiers*, military police in the hire of the Romans who in a police state could often wield a terrible and arbitrary power. Like the prophets and like Jesus himself (cf. Mt 22:15–22), John refrains from any sociological comment on these existing political institutions; his attention is wholly directed to the people who are involved in the institutions.

Lk 3:15   Luke alone of the Synoptic writers goes on
Jn 1:19–24   to say that so great was the enthusiasm that
                was engendered by the Baptist's preaching, and so much in tune was his proclamation with popular anticipation, that the question began to be asked whether he might be the Messiah, the long awaited one who would redeem Israel for God. In this he agrees with John, who now begins his version of the Gospel story with the account of a mission to the Baptist from the Jewish leadership in Jerusalem.

This is John's witness. The significance of "witness" in the Fourth Gospel we have already seen anticipated in the Prologue, Jn 1:7, 15. The witness of the Baptist consists in testifying to what he, John, is not, then to what Jesus is; this witness to the truth of God's word will be continued throughout by the protagonists of the Gospel as the fulfillment of the prophetic witness of the Old Testament and the beginning of the new prophetic witness of the Church inspired by the Spirit of truth. *The Jews* in John's Gospel usually designates the official leadership of Judaism in Jerusalem, though sometimes the term is more general or neutral. Because these persons, who historically were Jews, epitomize for John the unbelieving world which will not accept Christ, "the Jews" is more often than not a pejorative expression in the Fourth Gospel. It is not, however, a term of opprobrium in itself for an author who himself was doubtless a Jew. John says that the delegation to the Baptist was composed of *priests and Levites* (this combination only here in the Gospels), those who were empowered by the Mosaic law to judge in religious matters; in verse 24 he says they were *of the Pharisees*. The association of priests and Pharisees is unlikely, and the unlikelihood is only increased if we read in verse 24 with some manuscripts that the priests had been sent *by* the Pharisees. Either these terms are being used somewhat indifferently for readers for whom the exact distinctions in Judaism were no longer of concern, a situation which seems to be verified elsewhere in the Gospels, or, as is equally likely, John has summarized in one account various embassies that had gone out to the Baptist.

I am not the Messiah. Jesus' habitual identification of himself in John's Gospel is "I am," the full significance of which we shall see later; the Baptist's negative confession thus prepares the way for the revelation of the Word. *Elijah . . . I am not:* as we have already seen, Matthew and Mark see in John the Baptist a fulfillment of the Jewish expectation that the prophet Elijah would return to inaugurate the kingdom of God (Mal 3:23; Sir 48:4–12). The Baptist, however, refuses the identification. The Gospel of John, too, doubtless prefers to find the Elijah-figure realized in Jesus himself: this probably represents an earlier stage of Christian thinking, a vestige of which can also be found in the Synoptic tradition (see on Lk 7:11–17). Allied with this is the Baptist's denial that he is *the prophet*. The prophet in question is the eschatological prophet-like-Moses who appears in some Jewish messianic speculation, and sometimes identified with the eschatological Elijah, as the one sent by God to reveal the kingdom; the speculation resulted from a reinterpretation of Deut 18:18 concerning the prophetic succession in Israel. Throughout the New Testament, and especially in John's Gospel, the prophetic character of Jesus is stressed, often in connection with this messianic idea (cf. Jn 6:14, 7:40; Acts 7:37). The Baptist identifies himself only with the disembodied prophetic voice of Is 40:3, as already seen in the Synoptic Gospels.

Jn 1:25–27   Why, then, was John baptizing for the king-
Mk 1:7–8   dom of God if, seemingly, he had dissociated
Mt 3:11–12   himself from any active part in the kingdom?
Lk 3:16–17   All the Gospels address themselves to this
                question, which was obviously an important
one for them. The Baptist had been an extremely popular
preacher who had attracted many disciples, and in the
mind of many his relation to the Church was ambiguous
or confused. In apostolic times there were groups which
traced their origin to the Baptist, which however maintained
their separate existence apart from the Christian community
(cf. Acts 19:1–7). It was necessary to show from the Baptist's
own testimony that his role had been fulfilled in immediately prophesying the Christ.

The Baptist characterizes himself with extreme humility in
relation to the coming one, in whose presence he is not even
worthy of the slave's task of removing his master's sandals.
As for his baptism (mentioned by John only in vs. 33), it is
only a foreshadowing of greater things to come. *He will
baptize with Holy Spirit:* what John's baptism only announces will become a reality in the coming kingdom. The
holy spirit of God as the principle of the divine power in its
dealings with man (the prophetic spirit, etc.; cf. especially
Is 11:2) was already a familiar concept from the Old
Testament. Christian revelation was to make known the
personality of the Spirit in a way as yet unknown by the
Baptist. Matthew and Luke add *and with fire.* Fire, too, was
a frequent Old Testament representation of the divine
presence (Ex 3:2, 19:18; Ezek 1:4, etc.), and it was
particularly associated with the coming of God's purificatory
judgment (cf. Mal 3:2; Is 1:25; Zech 13:9). It is doubtless
in this sense that fire is mentioned here, as is further exemplified in the figure of the *winnowing* that is soon to take
place: the judgment and election of God that will come to
term in the response evoked by the kingdom. The evangelists
themselves doubtless expect their Christian readers to reflect
even more concretely on the sacramental baptism of the

Church and the Pentecostal fire that had launched it in the world as the continuing presence of the Spirit.

Lk 3:18–20   Luke alone now proceeds to do something that initially seems quite strange and unworkmanlike, interrupting the flow of the Gospel narrative. Before going on with the story, he gives in summary form the account found elsewhere in Matthew and Mark (Mt 14:3–5; Mk 6:17–20) of the Baptist's imprisonment by Herod Antipas. This, however, is Luke's method: he likes to finish a story once he has begun it (cf. also Lk 1:80, 2:40, 52). Having given samples of the Baptist's preaching, he states that it continued for some time, and then explains what brought it to a halt.

Lk 3:21—22   All the Gospels knew as an historical fact
Mk 1:9–11   that Jesus had received baptism at the hands
Mt 3:13–17   of John the Baptist; even John, who omits this narrative for his own reasons, was aware that it had taken place. Whereas Mark simply tells the story as a matter of fact, however, the later Gospels seem to be sensitive to its implications. Why should he who was sinless have submitted to a baptism of repentance for the forgiveness of sins? Luke hurriedly deals with the actual baptism almost as an aside, using only three words, and devotes his attention to what follows. Matthew shows the most concern. Not only has he introduced a dialogue between Jesus and the Baptist that explained the proceedings, probably for the same reason in his earlier description of the Baptist's baptism he did not characterize it, as did Mark and Luke, as one "of repentance for the forgiveness of sins" (compare Mt 3:1 f. with Mk 1:4 and Lk 3:3).

Mark, serenely unconcerned with the tradition he was reporting, also makes no effort to show any further connection between Jesus and the Baptist; he now without further ado introduces Jesus for the first time (according to Lk 3:23 he was "about thirty years of age") *coming from Nazareth of Galilee to be baptized by John in the Jordan.*

In Mark there is no testimony of the Baptist that Jesus was the one for whose coming he had been preparing. Neither does such a testimony appear in Luke, though Luke has shown very well in his Gospel of the Infancy the intimate association that he ascribes to Jesus and the Baptist; he is the only evangelist who tells us that the two were blood relatives. Perhaps by adding "bodily" to his description of the descent of the Holy Spirit upon Jesus (vs. 22), Luke intends to suggest that the vision was also perceptible to the Baptist and therefore a subject for his testimony. To this extent he would be in line with the more explicit portrayal of John's Gospel. Matthew may have a similar intention in changing the declaration of the heavenly voice from the second to the third person (vs. 17, "This is my beloved Son"); and certainly the dialogue between the Baptist and Jesus presupposes some understanding on the former's part of the latter's character.

At first glance Jesus' reassurance to the humble Baptist protesting the incongruity of this baptism does not explain a great deal. *It is proper for us to fulfill all justice* means little more than "it is necessary to do God's will"; by "justice" (cf. also Mt 5:6, 10, 20, 6:1, 33, 21:32) is meant the rightdoing which consists in submission to and furtherance of the will of God. An examination of the details of the theophany which follows, however, explains the meaning further. Rising from the water of the baptism in which he had humbled himself, Jesus sees *the heavens opened above him* (Mark says he saw them "split open") and *the Spirit of God descending as a dove upon him,* and in this moment he is proclaimed the Servant of the Lord. The theophany, therefore, which doubtless had a trinitarian meaning for the evangelists, is also a portrayal of the doctrine contained in the ancient christological hymn in Phil 2:6–11. In a fashion it sums up the whole significance of Jesus' life, a life of abasement from which emerges a glorified Savior: cf. Lk 12:50, etc., in which Jesus refers to his sacrificial death as his "baptism." *You are my beloved son, with whom I am well pleased* evokes most clearly the Servant canticles of

Is 42:1, 44:2. An important variant in the text of Luke replaces these words with those of Ps 2:7: a more "routine" messianic text.

In the intention of the Gospels this scene represents the divine proclamation of Jesus' salvific character, and, with the qualifications noted above, it is to be noted that it is a proclamation made to Jesus himself. The Gospels do not concern themselves with the question of a prior "messianic consciousness" on his part, though perhaps passages like Lk 2:40, 49, 52 are intended as hints in that direction.

Mk 1:12–13   The Synoptic Gospels follow the story of
Lk 4:1–2   Jesus' baptism with an account of his temp-
Mt 4:1–2   tation in the wilderness (Luke inserts be-
                 tween the two his version of Jesus' geneal-
ogy, which we have already seen). Probably there was a catechetical purpose in this ordering of events: the newly baptized Christian would be reminded that, despite the presence of the Spirit which he had received, he was still subject to the wiles of Satan in the wilderness of this world. There is also an evocation of the salvation history of the Old Testament: the forty years of desert wandering during which Israel, after passing through the waters of liberation (Ex 14:19–31), was prepared to receive the kingdom which the Lord had promised it. It may be for this reason that Mark notes that Jesus was *with the wild beasts* (cf. Num 21:6–9; Deut 8:15).

Above all, however, the evangelists see here the beginning of Jesus' prophetic role, the activity of a man *filled with Holy Spirit*—Mark says expressively that *the Spirit drove him into the desert.* The narrative of the forty days fast recalls the history of the prophet Elijah, as does Mark's statement that *the angels ministered to him* (cf. 1 Kgs 19:4–8).

Lk 4:3–13   Moreover, in the extended narrative of the
Mt 4:3–11   temptation contained in Matthew and Luke
                we are given a much deeper insight into the
kind of prophet Jesus is to be, how, in other words, he will

reveal God. The narrative has been drawn by these evangelists from a common source and slightly modified by each; the
most obvious change is Luke's revision of the order of events,
a device which permits him to give his customary emphasis
to the Jerusalem temple (see on Lk 1:8–12). It is a master-
piece of biblical storytelling consisting in a deft use of
allusion in which far more is implied than appears on the
surface. Again Jesus relives the experience of Israel, but
whereas Israel succumbed to temptation in the desert, he
triumphs over it. Undoubtedly this is the dramatization of
spiritual experiences at various times and places to which
Jesus, as one of us, was always subject (Heb 2:18, 4:15);
the Gospels themselves give hints of other such occasions.
What was offered to Jesus, and what he emphatically rejected, was the opportunity to become a Jewish Messiah in
the vulgar sense.

The note that *he was hungry* after his fast serves to introduce the first phase of the temptation: *If you are the Son of
God, command these stones to become bread.* Similarly in
the wilderness Israel had been tempted through hunger and
had given way to the temptation, rebelling against the divine
will (Num 11:5–20). Jesus has just been declared God's
Son: may not God's Son exercise his right to be fed by the
use of divine power? Miraculous abundance of food was one
of the characteristics popularly ascribed to the messianic age.
Jesus counters with the words of Deut 8:3, referring to the
lesson that Israel should have learnt from its hunger in the
desert but had not. His appearance in the world as God's
Son is not for his personal advantage but for obedient service
in God's designs on his people (cf. Jn 4:34).

The tempter returns to the attack, this time showing that
he too can cite the Scripture (Ps 91:11 f.). Belief in the
protecting agency of angels was widespread, and who should
have a better right to this protection than the Son of God?
To test this, why should Jesus not cast himself from the highest pinnacle of the temple compound so that all Jerusalem
might see how God takes care of his Son? It was frequently
believed that the Messiah would perform all kinds of won-

ders like this. Again Jesus cites Deuteronomy, and again in reference to a failing of Israel (Deut 6:16). Not even the Son of God—or, especially not the Son of God—can presume to act as an autonomous agent and continue to rely on the divine protection. Divine protection and obedience to the divine will go hand in hand.

The final presentation of the temptation is the most significant. *All these [kingdoms of the world] I will give you if you fall down and do me homage.* We must not, of course, see in this an invitation to a crude diabolism. Rather, Jesus is being confronted with the option of pursuing his ends by the use of political power, in the manner that the Jewish Messiah was expected to; this is precisely the temptation which Jn 6:15 says was offered to Jesus by the enthusiastic crowds. Satan is the ruler of this world (Jn 12:31; cf. vs. 6 in Luke), not in the sense that the world is irremediably evil, but in the sense that by sin the world and its ways have become subject to his direction. Whoever chooses as his own the route of worldly wisdom to the ends foreordained by God has thereby chosen the false gods of this world, as Paul protested to the Corinthians (cf. 1 Cor 2:6–16). What Israel had not always succeeded in avoiding, and what many Christians at various times have found an irresistible temptation, Jesus utterly rejects as a satanic intimation, citing Deuteronomy for the third and final time: *the Lord your God shall you adore and him only shall you serve* (Deut 5:7–9, 6:13, 10:20).

Matthew concludes his narrative by repeating Mark's words about the ministering angels. More significantly, perhaps, Luke says that *the devil departed from him till a more opportune time.* It is not of the human condition to be forever free of temptation.

Jn 1:28–34   The Synoptic Gospels now begin their second major division, the story of the Galilean ministry. John, too, as we shall soon see, also takes Jesus into Galilee, but with a quite different version of the events; the points of contact between the two traditions become very

rare indeed. It is impossible to work out a convincing harmonization from the standpoint of chronology, and chronology
is far from being the only note of discord. While nothing
is ever said in either tradition that excludes the other as an
impossibility, neither one has supplied us with sufficient statistical data to make a positive conciliation possible. Each
will have to be examined separately for its own particular
contributions.

As he often does, John makes more precise something that
is said in more general terms in the Synoptic Gospels: *These
things took place in Bethany beyond the Jordan where John
was baptizing;* the site of this Bethany, however, is otherwise
unknown. *The following day.* John says nothing of the baptism and temptation of Jesus. Rather, he continues and concludes the theme he has begun, of the witness of the Baptist
to the Word. Just as he began his Gospel with a treatment
of the creative Word of God in evident allusion to the Genesis
creation story (see Chapter 2), he now commences an artificial seven-day unfolding of the new creation, culminating
in 2:11 with the first manifestation of Jesus' "glory" (see on
Jn 1:14). The seven-day sequence, counting from the beginning of the Baptist's witness, can be seen indicated in 1:29,
35, 40–42, 43, 2:1. That 2:1 introduces something that takes
place "on the third day" is additionally significant, recalling
the resurrection through which Christ became "life-giving
Spirit" (1 Cor 15:45).

The artificiality of "the next day" immediately becomes
apparent. Though John does not mention Jesus' baptism in
so many words, he evidently supposes it, for the Baptist's
testimony, previously negative and generic, is now positive
and precise in virtue of a revelation given him at that time.
He can now point to Jesus as *the lamb of God who takes
away the world's sin.* From what we know of the Gospels,
there can hardly be any doubt that the evangelist understands, and expects his readers to understand, a reference in
these words to the suffering Servant of the Lord of Is
53:7–12. From what we otherwise know of the Baptist,
however, it would be difficult to believe that he could have

had in mind at this time a notion of the redemptive value of the sacrificial life of Christ (see on Mt 11:1–6; Lk 7:18–23). Nevertheless, he could have had a revelation of Jesus' character as God's Servant, in the same sense that we find it revealed in the Synoptic story of the baptism, namely the figure of Is 42:1 ff. upon whom the Lord has put his Spirit (cf. vs. 32 below) and who will "establish justice in the earth." This is rendered the more probable when it is realized that in the Aramaic which the baptist spoke the same expression means "lamb of God" and "servant of God."

But the Baptist also says of Jesus that *he existed before me*. Does this not presuppose a knowledge of the fullness of Jesus' character, the pre-existent Word of God? For the evangelist again, that is doubtless what these words signify. The Baptist, however, if he thought of this Person as a returned Elijah (see above on vs. 21), could have intended something much more prosaic. The Baptist proceeds to explain that this knowledge had been revealed to him through a prearranged sign, verified at the time of Jesus' baptism (already intimated, we have seen, in Matthew's version of the story). *The Spirit descended and remained upon him* (Is 42:1), and thus he recognized in him *God's chosen one* (this is the better reading of the manuscripts): another reference to Is 42:1.

Jn 1:35–42   From the witness of the Baptist the Fourth Gospel now turns to that of Jesus' first disciples, whom we discover to have been first the disciples of John the Baptist. There is nothing of this in the Synoptic Gospels, which place the call of these same disciples in Galilee rather than Judea. It is most likely that in this instance John's version of the events is to be preferred as closest to the historical happenings. It is antecedently likely, given the common tradition of the association of Jesus and the Baptist, that there would have been some such connection as this rising from the earliest sources of the tradition. It has been suggested, too, that in this fact we may have an explanation of the influence, linguistic and otherwise, that seems to have been exercised on the Gospel tradition by a Judean group like that of Qumran. From where John was baptizing by the Jordan it was only a few miles to Qumran; and, according to Luke, his entire youth had been spent in this neighborhood. The suggestion is not at all unreasonable that there was some connection between the Baptist who preached the coming kingdom of God and the Essene community which had retired to the same desert in which he preached to prepare for the kingdom's imminent arrival. If some of Jesus' first disciples came to him from the Baptist, the route of Qumran influence into the formation of the New Testament tradition should not be too hard to trace.

The first two disciples are introduced to Jesus by the Baptist himself, repeating the designation he made in verse 29; they are *Andrew the brother of Simon Peter* (the two are usually mentioned together in the Synoptic Gospels) and an unnamed disciple who may himself be the John of the Fourth Gospel. A progressive development is shown in the recognition of the disciples, who first give Jesus the courtesy title *Rabbi,* then, after spending the day and night with him, name him *Messiah.* The reference to *the tenth hour,* that is, late afternoon, is doubtless intended to situate the subsequent action on the following day; it is even likely that verse 41 originally read "early next morning" (*prōi*) rather than "first of all" (*prōton*).

The special importance of Peter among the original group of disciples is brought out by the change of his name, a sign of entry into a new way of life (cf. Apo 3:12). *Cephas* is the Grecianized form of the Aramaic *kêphā,* "rock," which has also been translated by the Greek word *petros=*our "Peter." Mk 3:16 also notes that Jesus made this change of names, while Mt 16:18 associates it with Peter's great confession (the equivalent of this appears in Jn 6:68 f.) and his being accorded primatial status (cf. Jn 21:15–19). Again it is probable that John retains a more accurate historical recollection of events that happened separately and that Matthew's version has put them together for topical reasons.

Jn 1:43–51   As already noted, John's chronology is symbolic, and it is not certain whether he intends to situate this entire scene in Judea. It is likely enough that *Philip*, at least, is presented by him as another disciple of the Baptist; *Nathanael*, however, may have been found by Philip in Galilee. *Bethsaida*, here called Galilean, was technically in the adjoining territory of Gaulanitis; for some reason John says that it was *the city of Andrew and Peter*, though the Synoptic Gospels identify them as residents of Capernaum. Nathanael (the name is found only in John) is usually identified with the Bartholomew of the Synoptic Gospels, but the equation is not certain.

The witness to Jesus' character continues to become more precise. Philip speaks to Nathanael of *him of whom Moses wrote in the Law and the prophets as well,* that is, the eschatological prophet of Deut 18:18 and the Davidic Messiah. Nathanael, despite his initial skepticism—*what good can possibly come from Nazareth?* indicates both the insignificance of Nazareth and a Galilean inferiority complex concerning God's salvific plans (cf. Jn 7:41)—concedes, on the basis of Jesus' prophetic knowledge of some fact otherwise known only to himself, that he must indeed be *the Son of God,* the Messiah (Jn 11:27; cf. 2 Sam 7:14; Pss 2:7, 89:26 ff.), *the king of Israel* (Jn 12:13; cf. Zeph 3:15). But this is not enough, says Jesus; Nathanael will yet see *far greater things* as the object of his faith, and in these know Jesus as he truly is.

The far greater things which Nathanael will see are already intimated in the name given him by Christ, the *true Israelite:* by popular etymology "Israel" was taken to mean "one who sees God." Unlike the original guileful Israel (Jacob) who also saw God (Gen 28:10–17), Nathanael is *without guile. You shall see heaven opened and the angels of God ascending and descending upon the Son of Man:* referring to Jacob's vision, Jesus says that the true Israelite will see the far greater thing of the divine presence made manifest in himself (cf. Jn 1:14, 2:11). The Son of Man, in John as in the Synoptic Gospels, is the title which Jesus uses by preference for himself. Its full implications we shall see as the Gospel story progresses.

It is quite evident that here as elsewhere there is a marked difference between the Johannine portrayal of Christ and the Synoptics' representation of a Jesus reticent in the extreme concerning his messianic character. From a strictly historical point of view, there is no doubt that we must prefer the Synoptic picture of a gradual and implied revelation. Whereas Peter's confession of Jesus' messiahship comes as a grand climax in Mark's Gospel to a slow and patient awakening of faith (Mk 8:27–30), in these few verses of John's first chapter virtually every messianic title has already been applied to Jesus and taken almost as a matter of course! But John, who presupposes the Synoptic tradition, likewise takes the fullness of Christian faith in Jesus for granted. His purpose in retelling the Gospel story is to bring out its implications for the Christian here and now. We see this immediately in the next episode in which he shows how the disciples, true Israelites all, actually beheld the glory of the Word made man.

Jn 2:1–11   *On the third day* (see above on vs. 29) after Jesus' promise to Nathanael we find him at *a wedding feast in Cana of Galilee* (probably the present-day Khirbet Qana, a ruin nearby the village of Kefr Kenna, the "traditional" site of Cana). Despite the Synoptics' interest in the Galilean ministry, neither this event nor Cana itself is ever mentioned in the other Gospels. Such a story as this, however, would not have been easily adaptable to the kerygmatic outline which lies behind the Synoptic Gospels, whereas it is eminently suited to the symbolic treatment in which John delights. In it John has found an illustration of one of his favorite themes: the presence of the historical Christ in the faith of the Church. The story also establishes a pattern which John repeats often in his Gospel.

The mother of Jesus was there. As becomes quickly apparent, the mother of Jesus who is mentioned by John always in this way, has a spiritual as well as an historical significance in the Fourth Gospel paralleling the portrayal of Mary in Luke's Gospel of the Infancy; her other most significant appearance is in Jn 19:25–28 at the end of Jesus' public life. In this episode she assumes a dominant role as the member of the family who had been primarily invited, presumably as having some special connection with the anonymous wedding couple. Jesus' *disciples* evidently include the five thus far mentioned and possibly others; there is no further explanation in John concerning the gathering of the remainder of the Twelve (Jn 6:67). The story that unfolds involves all of these as principals.

Mary's simple statement, *they have no wine*, is the equivalent of a request, as is shown by her subsequent instructions to the servants. *What to me and to you?*, to cite the Lord's reply quite literally, is a biblical idiom (cf. Jgs 11:12; 2 Sam 16:10; 1 Kgs 17:18; 2 Kgs 3:3; 2 Chron 35:21; Mk 5:7) which verbally is a rejection of Mary's request on the grounds that she has no claim on Jesus. The sense in which it is and is not a rejection in fact is made plain in the continuation of the story. Pertinent here is the title of address, *woman*, and Jesus' explanation that *my hour has not yet come*.

To insist, as is often done, that "woman" was an ordinary term of address implying neither coldness nor disrespect (cf. Jn 4:21), is valid but somewhat pointless. It is worse than pointless to paraphrase it, as some translations have done, with some such expression as "mother." It is precisely not as his mother, in the merely natural sense of the word, that Jesus now speaks to Mary. The unusual title cannot be dissociated from its other appearance in Jn 19:25–28, where it becomes even more apparent that for John, just as for Luke, Mary is a figure of the whole people of God, the Church. As such she is the woman, the new Eve, mother of all the living (Gen 3:20; cf. Apo 12:1–6). She has this character, however, only in virtue of her Son who has come to bring new life, and he is only now beginning his work. In John, the "hour" of Jesus refers to his glorification, that is, to his salvific death and resurrection (cf. Jn 7:30, 8:20, 12:23, 27, 13:1, 17:1). Until this work is accomplished, the woman has no title to what she requests. Nor may she request it under another title. Simeon had already spoken to her of the role in which she had been cast in the history of salvation, a providential role quite transcending the ties of natural relationship (Lk 2:35; see also on Lk 2:49 and Mk 3:31–35 and parallels).

Nevertheless, the hour which has not yet come can be anticipated in Jesus' "signs." *Do whatever he commands you to do:* Mary's instruction shows that she has understood Jesus' intention; John expects his readers to recognize such implications without being told. The rest of the story mainly consists of lifelike detail, though John also intends us to take a second look at some of what he says. The *six stone water jars* dramatize the magnitude of Jesus' act: the amount of liquid involved would have been in the neighborhood of 150 gallons! That they were there *for the Jewish purifications,* that is, the ritual washings to which the Jews were attentive before and after meals, both explains the presence of such a large quantity of water and forms part of the Johannine pattern in these stories. Time after time in the narratives that follow some life-medium (frequently enough water) or some other good identified with Judaism is seen to be replaced with a better good that comes from Jesus, who is life in truth. The familiarity with which *the headwaiter* addresses the bridegroom in the denouement of the story suggests that the custom was being followed of electing one of the invited guests to serve as the master of the banquet.

This Jesus did as the first of his signs. For John the "signs" are pre-eminently those things which Jesus did—or rather, which he now does—in which the eye of faith may perceive the saving act of God, in which he is, therefore, pre-eminently the Word of God. Thus John says that *he revealed his glory.* The continuing episodes of this Gospel detail many similar signs. *His disciples believed in him:* Jesus has now fulfilled his promise to Nathanael, though as yet admittedly in an obscure way. The story of the "new creation" has concluded with a wonder of creation that will in turn be the beginning of a series of life-giving acts in which the Life of the world reveals himself as an object of faith greater than anything the Old Testament could encompass. With the same eye of faith, John suggests to his Christian reader, this same glory is yet to be seen in the Church, in the signs by which the life-giving Christ continues his saving work. There can hardly be any doubt that in telling the story of the water made wine John intends for us to recognize in a special way the significance of the sacrament of the Eucharist.

6. LIVING WATER

Jn 2:12 In this chapter we shall mainly pursue John's Gospel, seeing how some of the themes which he has once begun to draw out continue to be reasserted. John makes only a cursory mention of Jesus' stay in Capernaum, agreeing with the Synoptic Gospels to the extent that the ministry there was of brief duration. However, there is a Synoptic emphasis on Capernaum that is quite lacking in John, as we shall see. If the shortest reading in the manuscripts of this text is the original one, Jesus' companions at this time are listed merely as *his mother and his brethren.* In this case, "brethren" would doubtless refer to his disciples rather than, as later and usually in the Gospels (Jn 7:3, etc.), to the members of his family.

Jn 2:13–17
Mt 21:12–13
Mk 11:15–17
Lk 19:45–46

John immediately takes Jesus back to Jerusalem on the occasion of a *Jewish Passover.* The festivals of Judaism are emphasized by John as part of his way of showing how Jesus has fulfilled the hopes of which they were the sign. This is only the first of several Passovers which John places within the period of Jesus' public life. The following episode is also recorded by the Synoptic Gospels as taking place at a Passover season, the only Passover with which they deal, at the end rather than at the beginning of Jesus' ministry; and even then, the Synoptics do not agree on which day of the week the event took place. The chronology is obviously not to be pressed on either side; if a point had to be made of it, we would probably have to agree that the Synoptics' is more likely. We treat the matter now, however, because of the close relation it has to John's theological development.

The versions of the story, of which Luke's is by far the briefest, agree on the essentials. *Entering the temple*, that is, the outer courtyards surrounding the holy places, Jesus drives out of the precincts the buyers and sellers of the animals used in sacrifice and the animals themselves (John alone speaks of him using a *whip of cords*); he also overturns the banking tables used by the money-changers. The animals, of course, were bought and sold for the convenience of pilgrims, who could hardly have been expected to bring them along with them. Similarly, money-changing was a necessity for foreigners as well as to provide acceptable, "non-idolatrous" money, money that did not bear pagan inscriptions or images. Though there may have been some incidental chicanery involved in all this, still the enterprises of themselves were perfectly legitimate. To what, then, was Jesus objecting?

The answer is given in his accusation, given by the Synoptics as *you have made it*, the temple, *a robbers' den*. This is a citation of Jer 7:11, just as his preceding words concerning the temple as *a house of prayer* are a citation of Is 56:7; Jesus is not, therefore, necessarily passing judgment on the personal honesty of those whom he was confronting, but he is repeating a prophetic judgment on the inviolable sanctity of God's house. The sense of his gesture becomes more explicit in the Johannine version of his command: *Don't turn my Father's house into a market place*. Jewish custom forbade the use of the temple grounds for profane purposes, even for such an innocent one as a convenient meeting place for friends. The custom was now being flagrantly violated. Consistent with his action in expelling the buyers and sellers, according to Mark Jesus *would not allow anyone to carry anything through the sacred place,* to use it, in other words, as a shortcut from one place to another.

Jesus' action was understood by his disciples as a sign of messianic fulfillment (cf. Zech 14:21), and according to John they applied to him in this connection the words of Ps 69:10, a psalm used very often in the New Testament in a messianic sense. His zeal for the holiness of the temple contrasted strongly with the laxity of the temple personnel, in whose charge the temple was. This episode is at least a partial explanation of the hostility shown to Jesus by the Jerusalem priesthood.

Jn 2:18–22 Representatives of this group, as usual called by John simply *the Jews,* now come forward to demand by what authority he has done what they have neglected to do. They ask for *a sign:* this demand for a supernatural intervention was constantly being made of Jesus (cf. Mk 8:11, etc.), who consistently refused to comply with it. His signs were never given indiscriminately or for the ill-disposed; they were signs of faith, to awaken it or to deepen it. This is brought out by John, who now indicates the full significance that he saw in the episode he has just related: *Destroy this temple and in three days I will raise it up . . . he spoke of the temple of his body.* The resurrection is the great and adequate sign for all believers. The temple, holy though it was, has now been replaced by a holier temple, the resurrected Christ, and by the Church which is his resurrected body.

The Jews, not unnaturally, take these words in another sense (cf. Mt 26:61 and parallels); Jesus did, as a matter of fact, foretell the destruction of the Jerusalem temple (cf. Mk 13:2). *Forty-six years:* the temple was begun, according to Josephus, in the eighteenth year of Herod's reign (that is, in 20 or 19 B.C., according to our reckoning); thus the date indicated for this passage is sometime in A.D. 28. The temple was still in the process of building during the lifetime of

Jesus and was completed only a few years before its destruction by the Romans in A.D. 70

Jn 2:23–25   In the following summary statement that forms the transition to the story of Nicodemus, John shows that he presupposes a knowledge of the Synoptic tradition with its stress on the many miracles of Jesus' ministry. Correspondingly, *the signs* of verse 23 does not appear precisely in its Johannine sense. Jesus, knowing man better than any other man could know, put little reliance on the incipient faith awakened by enthusiasm over his miracles ("signs" in the Synoptic Gospels). It could, it is true, develop into a true knowledge of God in Christ, as would be exemplified in the case of Nicodemus. Too often, however, it would prove to be a hindrance rather than an aid to this knowledge (cf. Jn 6:2, 60).

Jn 3:1–13   Nicodemus was one of those who were attracted by the works which Jesus was performing. As a Pharisee, a member of the Sanhedrin, the high court of seventy-two which formed the supreme governing body of the Jews, and a rabbi, he represents to John the very essence of Judaism, and thus affords the evangelist with another opportunity to show how Jesus has brought in reality what the old dispensation could but promise. Though the circumstances of his visit in the face of official opposition to Jesus explain naturally enough why he would have come secretly *at night,* John probably notes this in an additional meaning: Nicodemus comes from the darkness (cf. Jn 1:5) to Jesus the light, while later Judas will desert him for the darkness (cf. Jn 13:30).

Nicodemus addresses Jesus as *Rabbi,* the title first used by the disciples when he began to reveal himself to them (Jn 1:38). As he had done in their case, Jesus proceeds to offer Nicodemus a challenge to faith far beyond anything he had imagined. *Unless a man be born from above he cannot see the kingdom of God:* the kingdom of God is not to be perceived merely in the marvels that have attracted Nicodemus'

attention; it is to be found only in a spiritual regeneration
(cf. Jn 1:12 f.). The word translated "from above" can also
mean "anew"; the ambiguity permits Nicodemus to take a
literalist surface meaning: *How can a man who is old be
born again?* It is part of the artistic arrangement of the
Johannine dialogues and discourses that double meanings and
initial misunderstandings lead to a deeper exploration of
Christ's teaching.

Jesus proceeds to explain the nature of the rebirth about
which he is speaking. It is spiritual rather than natural. In
speaking of "flesh" and "spirit" he builds on concepts familiar to Judaism from the Old Testament: it is this that
gives point to his words of rebuke in verse 10. Both flesh
and spirit relate to life, but whereas flesh represents all that
is transitory about life, as we have seen (see on Jn 1:14),
spirit is the God-given force by which alone life is possible
(cf. Gen 2:7; Job 10:9–12, 33:4; Ezek 37:8–14). Furthermore, the vital activity of spirit appears under various forms
and in varying degrees: there is a spirit-life which altogether
transcends the normal. Thus the prophet is a "man of the
spirit" par excellence (cf. Hos 9:7); thus, too, the messianic
leader would possess the spirit in a pre-eminent way (cf.
Is 11:1–3), and the messianic times would be characterized
by an extraordinary outpouring of spirit (cf. Ezek 36:27;
Joel 3:1 f., and Acts 2:16–21).

The spirit blows where it will. Jesus employs a play on
words (in Aramaic and Greek the same word "spirit"=
"breath"="wind") to serve as an analogy. Just as the wind
cannot be seen but only perceived in its effects, so it is with
the new spiritual birth of which he has been speaking; it is
imperceptible to fleshly eyes. That Nicodemus, though *a
master in Israel,* cannot understand the relatively *earthly
things* that Jesus has said to him, shows his incapacity at the
present to receive the *heavenly things* which are involved in
the acceptance of Christ in true faith. As yet Nicodemus has
not recognized in Jesus *the Son of Man,* who alone can reveal the heavenly God as he truly is. *We speak of what we
know:* Jesus, representing the true Israel, contrasts his word

with the inadequacy of the knowledge of the Israel for which Nicodemus spoke (vs. 2).

In verse 5 John quotes Jesus as saying that this new birth comes through *water and spirit*. Such words could have been used to Nicodemus, who would have been expected to understand them in terms of a ceremonial baptism like that of John the Baptist, which in fact the evangelist associates with Jesus in the later verses 22–30. However, it is likely that John, who thinks of the Spirit of Jesus' discourse as the divine power animating the Church and evidenced in Christian life, has added the reference to water as a reminder of sacramental baptism. Doubtless, too, the "we" of verse 11 represents the Christian testimony of the evangelist joined to that of Jesus. It is usual in these Johannine discourses for dialogue to merge into monologue, and for the words of Jesus to become those of John. The evangelist's testimony, after all, is to the revelation of Jesus as he himself has come to know it through the continuing enlightenment of the Spirit.

Jn 3:14–21   Nicodemus has now disappeared from the scene entirely, and the Gospel continues to explain in greater detail what is the basis of the spiritual life to be revealed in the Son of Man. It is his redemptive death and resurrection. Alluding to the story of Num 21:4–9 (cf. Wis 16:6 f.), the Gospel states that *the Son of Man must also be raised up* if man is to be brought into the heavenly realm of the life of the Spirit. To be "raised up" for John is for Jesus to be "glorified" (both terms are used of the Servant of the Lord in Is 52:13), and the sense is of both the physical raising of Christ on the cross and his ascent to the Father as Lord and Savior. It is in this character that *everyone who believes in him will have eternal life*.

In turn, the exaltation of Christ, the consummation of his sacrificial life of obedience, is a sign to man of the divine love and will to save. *God so loved the world:* the world, though it is the arena in which evil too often prevails, is itself not evil but the object of God's saving love. This love has been shown to its full extent in God's sending his *only*

Son. The Son has not been sent, in turn, *to judge the world:* not, as one popular idea of the Messiah would have had it, did the Son come crushing God's enemies and scourging mankind, but rather revealing in himself the loving God as the object of the world's faith. Faith brings salvation, but on the contrary willful unbelief is its own condemnation, because it rejects the only source of salvation. If the world as such has, indeed, been judged, it is because *men loved the darkness rather than the light:* here John anticipates his summation of the first part of his Gospel (Jn 12:37 ff., cf. also 1:5, 9 f.). The language of this section has numerous affinities with that of the Qumran literature.

Jn 3:22–30   John continues with a story that is thematically parallel to the story of Nicodemus in verses 1–13, just as the meditation which follows in verses 31–36 corresponds to the one we have just seen in verses 14–21. The parallel serves to confirm the view we have taken of the meaning of the Nicodemus episode for John and also further explains why John omitted any direct mention of Jesus' baptism at the hands of John the Baptist (see above on Lk 3:21 f. and parallels).

After these things, Jesus and his disciples came into the land of Judea. In the present context, this would mean that Jesus left Jerusalem and went into the Judean countryside. However, since this passage is in its present place for thematic rather than chronological reasons, the historical antecedent is unknown and may well have been some phase of the Galilean ministry. *He was baptizing:* John, or the editor of his Gospel, specifies in Jn 4:2 that it was not Jesus himself but his disciples who were doing the baptizing. This baptism was obviously not the sacramental baptism of the Church by which the Spirit is given after the glorification of Christ (cf. Jn 7:39), but a continuation of the baptism of John the Baptist in preparation for the coming of the kingdom; the Synoptic Gospels also represent Jesus' initial preaching of the kingdom as a continuation of the ministry of the Baptist (see below on Mk 1:15). Nevertheless, this event is for John a "sign": a baptism associated with Jesus is here set in opposition to the baptism of John the Baptist and shown to be what has replaced it in the progress of the history of salvation. It would have obscured and interfered with John's thematic treatment had he interrupted it to describe the Baptist's baptism being administered to Jesus.

The location of *Aenon near Salim* where *John was also baptizing* is not certain but is usually thought to have been in northern Samaria. A dispute between the disciples of the Baptist and some unnamed Jew *over purification*, presumably the Jewish purificatory rites (cf. Jn 2:6), furnishes the occasion for the Baptist to complete his testimony to Jesus; the nature of the controversy is not explained and was, of course, irrelevant in view of the greater issues involved. Somehow Jesus' name was brought into the conversation, and the disciples discovered and reported to their master that his renown was now exceeding the Baptist's. The latter's response is to repeat his earlier protestation that he is not the Messiah but only the one who makes a way for him. He stands in the position of *the friend of the bridegroom*, the best man at the wedding who arranged the marriage not for his own but for the bridegroom's sake. His final words sum up his foreordained purpose in relation to Jesus: *he must increase and I must decrease*.

The evangelist notes that *John had not yet been put in prison*. Luke, as we have seen (Lk 3:19 f.), has already described the Baptist's imprisonment. The other two Gospels have completed the story of John the Baptist later on in their chronicle.

Jn 3:31–36   John's commentary which follows both continues and parallels his observations in verses 14–21 above. Again he contrasts with "earthly" knowledge the heavenly truths that have been made known in Christian revelation. Again he marvels over the spectacle of unbelief. *He who receives his witness has set his seal on this, that God is true:* just as Christ is witness to the truth of God, God is witness to the truth of his testimony (cf. Jn

6:27). *Not by measure does he give the Spirit:* prophets
like John the Baptist, the last of a long line, had truly possessed the Spirit of God, but the fullness of prophecy has
come only in the revelation of the Son (cf. Jn 1:17 f.; Heb
1:1 f.). Again the explanation of salvation is found in the
overflowing of divine love.

Jn 4:1–3   Though as usual chronology is not a primary
Mt 4:12   consideration in the development of the Gos-
Mk 1:14   pel, it is likely that John intends to situate
Lk 4:14a   the following story in the period with which
               the Synoptic Gospels begin their history of
the Galilean ministry, after the arrest of John the Baptist
by Herod Antipas. The same Judean leadership which had
looked upon the Baptist's preaching with suspicion, to say
the least (cf. Mt 21:25 ff. and parallels), was now turning
its hostile attention toward the man who was continuing
that preaching and with even greater popular success. For
this reason Jesus left Judea and returned to Galilee.

Jn 4:4–19   *He had to pass through Samaria.* This was
            to follow the most direct route, a three days'
journey, between Jerusalem and Galilee. Jews very often
lengthened the trip in order to bypass Samaria, however, because of the hostility of the Samaritan population (see page
46 and cf. Lk 9:52 f.). The Synoptic Gospels have nothing
about any contacts between Jesus and Samaritans, though
Luke records that he spoke favorably of them on occasion
(cf. Lk 10:29–37); in apostolic times the Samaritans received
the Gospel of Christianity with enthusiasm (cf. Acts 8:1–25).
The *Sychar* of John's text may be the modern village of
Askar, nearby the ancient Shechem, where was *the field
which Jacob gave to his son Joseph* (cf. Gen 33:19, 48:22).
The location of *Jacob's well* where Jesus sat to rest is, in
any case, well known: it still exists midway between Shechem and Askar. John notices these details because they are
to play a part in his story. The disciples left Jesus at the

well and went into the town to buy food, since *it was about the sixth hour,* that is, noon.

This story continues John's thematic pattern and the structure of the Johannine discourses. The woman's misunderstandings permit the deeper sense of Jesus' words to be progressively emphasized, and correspondingly she is offered the opportunity to recognize in him an ever more important figure of faith. Once again a life-giving element associated with Judaism—water, as it happens—is seen to be only a faint reflection of the reality that is to be possessed in Christ.

How is it that you, a Jew, ask a drink of me, a Samaritan woman? expresses surprise twofold. Strict Jews would not associate with the "unclean" Samaritans, much less accept food or drink from them. Neither would they be seen conversing with women: a rabbi would not speak in public even with his own wife. While both John and the Synoptic Gospels show that Jesus was, in general, faithful to the law and customs of his people, they also bring out plainly that there was nothing fanatical or merely legalistic in his observance. Jesus immediately points out that the true *gift of God* with which he is concerned is not the water which he has asked her to give him, but the gift of himself which is being offered to her. *Living water,* like the "rebirth" of which he spoke to Nicodemus, is deliberately ambiguous. The surface meaning, taken by the woman, is the running water of a river or spring. In its figurative sense the expression comes from the Old Testament (for example, Jer 2:13; Zech 14:8) and signifies divine life and grace.

Ironically, the woman asks if Jesus pretends to be *greater than our father Jacob who gave us the well.* The question serves the double purpose of identifying the "water of Judaism" that is being contrasted with Christ and of contributing to the "Johannine irony," that is, to the pattern of John's Gospel in which people so often assert in a superficial way what is true in a much more profound sense. Ironical, too, is the term by which she first addresses him. On her lips the title *kyrie* meant nothing more than *sir,* a respectful but ordinary form of address. It is also, however, the word by

which Christians testified to their faith in their risen Lord
(Phil 2:9–11). It is this word which, still uncomprehending,
she uses after he has explained that the "water" which he
will give not only sustains life but is itself the very source
of everlasting life. This water, of course, is Jesus himself.
John also would expect his Christian reader to think of baptism, which has already been brought in so often in these
early chapters of his Gospel, truly the water which gives life.

As he has done before in the conversation with Nathanael,
Jesus now introduces an apparently irrelevant topic whose
purpose is to show that he is possessed of a mysterious and
superhuman knowledge: *call your husband*. The woman did
not expect to have the literal truth of her reply revealed so
bluntly; doubtless she answered as she did simply to put an
end to a somewhat strange and potentially embarrassing conversation. Now she begins to realize that this is no ordinary
Jew talking to her; she confesses that he must be *a prophet*.

Jn 4:20–38   A prophet indeed Jesus is, but in a way that
far transcends her present understanding.
She puts to him an implied question, in keeping with later
Jewish thinking on the role of prophecy, namely, that it
would intervene to solve disputed questions in the matter of
law and observance (cf. 1 Macc 4:46). According to Samaritan tradition, *our fathers worshiped on this mountain*
of Gerizim at whose foot this conversation was taking place;
the Samaritan temple which had once stood there had been
destroyed more than a century previously, but the site was
still a place of worship as it is to this day for the tiny
Samaritan community that has survived in Palestine. The
Jews, on the contrary, held that only in Jerusalem could
acceptable sacrifice be offered. The resultant controversy between Jew and Samaritan was only one of the issues on
which they were bitterly divided. Jesus answers the question,
at the same time pointing out how irrelevant it already is in
the divine scheme of things. *Salvation is from the Jews*, not
the Samaritans: the one who speaks to her is this salvation
in very fact. And now that salvation has come, neither

Jerusalem nor Gerizim will matter to the God who must be worshiped *in spirit and in truth* (see on Jn 1:17 f.).

In rejoinder, the woman expresses her belief in the coming of *Messiah* who will fulfill the hopes of Jew and Samaritan alike. As we have already seen before, in John's Gospel Jesus accepts this title freely (cf. Jn 1:43–51). However, his words as reported by John contain a further subtlety: *I who am speaking to you, I am* is the self-identification of the God of Israel according to Is 52:6. Furthermore, it is possible that the messianic expectation of the Samaritans—something about which very little is known, though it most likely was developed from the prophetic idea of Deut 18:18 —was such that Jesus could more readily associate himself with it than he could with the nationalistic concepts current in Galilee and Judea.

The rest of the story is acted out in two concurrent scenes. The woman hurries away to her townsfolk to bear to them the message of Philip (cf. Jn 1:45 f.), in her haste *leaving behind her water jug*: John may be insinuating that she had no further use for it, now that she had found the source of living water. Meanwhile the disciples, surprised at finding the Master conversing with a woman but being too well trained to interrogate him about it, now urge him to take the food they had gone to procure. *My food is to do the will of him who sent me and to accomplish his work* sums up the entire life of Jesus. His additional words on the harvest already prepared in Samaria, a harvest they are to reap where they have not sown, doubtless refer to the phenomenal success of the apostolic preaching of Christianity among the Samaritans (Acts 8:4–25).

Jn 4:39–42   The Samaritans fully satisfy the Johannine ideal of the true believer. Having been attracted at first by the woman's report of one who did wonders, they at length come to believe simply because of Jesus' word (cf. Jn 8:30, 10:38), the word of life. *We have heard and we know* (cf. Jn 3:11) *that he is truly the Savior of the world:* doubtless this title, an unusual one signifying

7. ACCLAIM IN GALILEE

Lk 4:31
Mk 1:16–21
Mt 4:18–22
As we saw in the last chapter, Matthew and Luke begin their story of the Galilean ministry at Nazareth, the town where Jesus had spent his childhood and youth and by whose name he became familiarly known as the Nazarene. From Nazareth they take us to Capernaum, and Capernaum is also the first place in Galilee that is mentioned by Mark. We are left to imagine the circumstances that prompted Jesus to make this city the center of his Galilean activity; the attentive reader of Mark's Gospel will note how persistently it features "the house" in Capernaum, the house, that is, of Simon Peter, the eyewitness who traditionally stands behind this Gospel. At Capernaum, too, Jesus taught in the synagogue, as was his custom throughout Galilee.

It is here that Mark, and Matthew following him, places the call of Jesus' first disciples. We have already seen that in John's Gospel a quite different picture is drawn of the same event, in which at least two of the same disciples are involved (see Jn 1:35–42). We do not have the means of harmonizing these separate versions which have been handed down by traditions independent of each other. We can at least maintain, however, that they presuppose historical facts that are not mutually incompatible. It is likely enough, as

John told the story, that Jesus met his first disciples through John the Baptist; as a matter of fact, this present story makes better sense if it is assumed that the disciples were not now meeting Jesus for the first time. The Synoptic account, for its part, reads very much like the factual account of someone who had seen these things happen. We should remember, too, that John is well aware that these disciples were Galileans and not Judeans.

The sea of Galilee is the name used by Mark and Matthew to refer to what Luke calls *the lake of Gennesaret* and John *the sea of Tiberias;* it is a fresh-water lake some thirteen miles north and south and about seven east and west in what is easily the most attractive part of Galilee. *Simon and his brother Andrew* have already been introduced by John's Gospel. The Greek of the Gospel makes it clear that they were fishing with the circular throw-nets still used by the Arab fishermen of the region. *Fishers of men* was an expression already used in the Old Testament (Jer 16:16), there, however, in connection with divine judgment rather than salvation. *James and John, the sons of Zebedee*, who were *mending their nets*, according to Lk 5:7 were Peter's partners in fishing. Mark's mention of *the hired men* left in the boat with Zebedee might suggest that this group had made something of a success of their business.

Mk 1:22–28   Referring   to   Jesus'   synagogue   teaching,
Lk 4:32–37   Mark and Luke note the pleased surprise of the people at *the authority* with which it was presented. This undoubtedly means the authentic voice of prophecy that could be discerned in what Jesus was saying, as contrasted with the traditionalist and repetitive doctrine of *the scribes*. This contrast, and the tensions it aroused, would eventually cost Jesus his forum in the synagogues. Matthew has appropriately transferred these lines to the end of the Sermon on the Mount in which he has preserved a master summation of Jesus' teaching (cf. Mt 7:28 f.).

In this and the following little section Mark has constructed

what might be called "a typical day in the Galilean ministry," featuring a typical exorcism and a typical healing
miracle followed by a summary. This construction has been
followed by Luke but not by Matthew. Matthew, somewhat
surprisingly, omits the story of the exorcism entirely; we
shall have to see if we can discover the reason for this later
on.

The New Testament world accepted demonic possession
as a matter of fact, and the Synoptic Gospels relate numerous exorcisms performed by Jesus and presuppose that
exorcism was practiced successfully by other people as well.
We are not faithful to the Gospel message if we do not take
it as seriously in this respect as we do in all others. While it is
true that in certain instances which we shall have occasion
to note the Gospel may attribute to "a spirit" some affliction
which nowadays we would classify more prosaically as
epilepsy or insanity (and we should remember that well into
the Middle Ages and beyond insane people were commonly
regarded as diabolically possessed), there can be no doubt
that in the generality of cases the Gospel is speaking of the
real exorcism of real devils. This fact causes difficulty for
many present-day readers of the New Testament who are
embarrassed to find a book which otherwise corresponds so
closely to human experience entering in this respect into a
world which sometimes seems to them alien and mythical.
They may even suspect that to some extent it was an embarrassment to the evangelists themselves. It has often been
noted that while John's Gospel is well aware of the many
miracles ascribed to Jesus in the Synoptic tradition, it
actually describes a mere handful of these on its own,
limiting itself to those which it regards pre-eminently as
"signs," and mentions no exorcisms at all.

However, it must not be thought that in any case do the
Gospels deal with miracles for their own sake. Wonder
stories were the order of the day, and in making use of
them the Gospels have been quite sober and restrained by
contemporary standards. Merely to assert that Jesus was a
wonder-worker would have meant little to those who first

heard or read the Gospel, since even more wonderful works were attributed to many others of the past and present and were commonly accepted as true. Even though they are not signs precisely in the Johannine sense, for the Synoptic Gospels the miracles and exorcisms of Jesus are nevertheless signs. They are signs of what Jesus was proclaiming: the breaking in of God's kingdom and saving power, the destruction of the reign of evil. This is why, explicitly or implicitly, these works are always premised on faith in the divine power revealed in Jesus. In an age which thought of evil as personal and experienced it as personal, the exorcisms of the Gospels play a role that is altogether proportionate. The same saving power of God is exercised in our own world in more impersonal ways, but the devils it exorcises are no less real.

The meaning we have just assigned to the exorcisms is clearly brought out in the words of *the unclean spirit* of this story. *What to us and to you* (see on Jn 2:4) points to the essential opposition that exists between the demonic order and *the holy one of God* who has come to put an end to its power. The bystanders understand this. *They were all amazed,* not simply at the sight of an exorcism, but at the power of Jesus' word, which alone sufficed to destroy the reign of Satan. This itself was a *new teaching,* a new *word* as Luke quotes them as saying, a further revelation of whom God had sent among them.

In the imposition of silence which Jesus places upon the unclean spirit in this story we have the beginning of what has been called "the messianic secret," a characteristic of Mark's Gospel which has been partially carried over into Matthew and Luke. Persistently throughout the Gospel story we find Jesus being named by one or another title, usually a messianic title in some sense, usually by the demons but sometimes by others as well, and just as persistently Jesus refuses to allow the title to be heard. Corresponding to this is Jesus' frequent injunction to those who have experienced the works of his saving power that they keep silence about what they have witnessed. Never once in the Synoptic

Gospels does Jesus designate himself Messiah or use the equivalent title Son of David, and never once does he in any clear and unambiguous way accept this designation from others. We have seen that in this respect among so many others the Fourth Gospel is markedly different from the Synoptics.

The term "messianic secret" was first applied to Mark's Gospel by those who felt it was a technique by which the evangelist had explained away an embarrassment of primitive Christianity: by this fictional device the apostolic Church was justified in hailing as Messiah one who was known to have never proclaimed himself Messiah in his own lifetime. Today very few would try to support this thesis. It would, for one thing, leave unexplained the Church's designation of Jesus as Messiah in the first place, to say nothing of the fact that without a messianic claim of some kind on Jesus' part it is impossible to account for his crucifixion. Rather, it would appear that the messianic secret is part of the authentic history of Jesus, though it is easily admissible that Mark has schematized the history in preparing his Gospel. The messianic secret finds its logical explanation in the unique interpretation which Jesus gave to messianism and accepted it as an identification of himself. It was an interpretation so unique as to preclude the possibility of its being expressed simply in terms of Jewish expectation, let alone in terms originated by the powers of this world inimical to the kingdom of God (see above on Lk 4:3–13 and parallel). If we read the Johannine discourses sympathetically with this Synoptic viewpoint in mind, it is not hard to see that in their own way they try to make a point that is rather analogous.

Mk 1:29–31   Mark and Luke now proceed to tell the
Lk 4:38–39   story of a typical healing miracle—typical,
Mt 8:14–15   though the case itself was a special one
which has left its mark on the Gospel transmission, particularly in the vivid form in which Mark has preserved it. Matthew briefly parallels the same story and

so locates it at Capernaum; it occurs, however, at a later stage in his Gospel because of his insertion of the lengthy Sermon on the Mount which we shall begin to consider in our next chapter.

Immediately on leaving the synagogue they entered the house of Simon and Andrew together with James and John. It has been remarked that this somewhat awkward sentence betrays its first-person origin—"we entered our own house in the company of James and John." The mention of *Simon's mother-in-law* is one of the very few in the New Testament which take cognizance of the family affairs of Jesus' immediate disciples (cf. 1 Cor 9:5). The story probably intends to say that her fever (Luke uses a proper medical term to describe the affliction) came as a surprise to the disciples, who had brought their Master home doubtless to take food. Matthew and Mark say that Jesus touched the woman's hand, Luke adds that he "rebuked" the fever. That she was able immediately to rise and *wait on them* dramatizes the effectiveness of the cure. It is to be noted that this is the first time that Simon Peter appears in Luke's Gospel where, however, he is named without explanation as already well known to the reader.

Mk 1:32–34 The "typical day" ends with a reference to
Lk 4:40–41 many cures and exorcisms on this mem-
Mt 8:16–17 orable day in Capernaum. As this was a
Sabbath day, there is a special relevance to the note that these took place *in the evening,* when journeys could be taken and burdens carried without violation of the law of rest. Again Mark's version is the most natural and vivid with its picture of the townsfolk *crowded about the door* of Peter's house. Matthew says that *he cured them all* whereas Mark has "many," but doubtless the meaning is the same (Mark means, in other words, that they were many and that he cured them). Matthew also finds in these events another prophetic fulfillment which is implicit in other descriptions of healing miracles: they are signs of the spiritual healing wrought through the humble sacrifice of the Servant

of the Lord (Is 53:4). To Mark's reiteration that Jesus *forbade the demons to speak because they knew him,* that is, they would have identified him as the Jewish Messiah, Luke adds a more explicit designation by the demons which Mark has reserved for his summary description in 3:11.

Mk 1:35–39   The following episode is also intimately con-
Lk 4:42–44   nected with the preceding by Mark and
              Luke; it is omitted by Matthew. *In the morning at an early hour while it was still night* again strikingly evokes the memory of an eyewitness, suggesting Peter's surprise and dismay at finding Jesus gone; Luke's paraphrase is in better Greek, but his account is pallid by comparison. Jesus *had gone away to a secluded spot where he was at prayer;* but Peter and his companions (Luke again says simply "the crowds") *tracked him down,* in Mark's graphic phrase, certain that they are bringing him welcome news that will persuade him to return quickly: *Everyone is looking for you.* Thus ingenuously presented we see in fine relief the contrast between the good-willed but naïve enthusiasm of those for whom the kingdom of God has already come in power and the meditative Christ who knows how far from realization is the work he has come to do. There is an apparent variation in the conclusion of the story as told by Luke: the best reading of the text is that *he was preaching in the synagogues of Judea* rather than of Galilee. However, the difference is probably only apparent, since Luke sometimes uses "Judea" to mean "Jewish land" in general, that is, Palestine (cf. Lk 23:5; Acts 10:37, etc.).

Lk 5:1–11   It is at this point that Luke has inserted his
             own version of the call of the first disciples, a version that differs in certain obvious respects from that of Matthew and Mark. In it Peter is featured almost to the exclusion of the others, and a wonder is related of which we did not hear before. There would seem to be no doubt, however, that the stories go back to the same event. Luke has

preserved this independent variant of the tradition and placed it here seemingly because he intends it to be the beginning of a unit developing the theme of the calling of the Twelve concluded in Lk 6:16.

In this story the fishermen are *washing their nets* rather than drying them. Jesus' expedient of avoiding the press of the crowds by teaching from the boat is also related in Mk 4:1 f. and was probably a practice that he adopted often. The Sea of Galilee abounds in fish, so that it is not the size of the catch, though this was remarkable, but the extraordinary knowledge of Jesus that is seen as a wonder. Peter has begun by calling Jesus *Master* (*epistatēs*, a word found only in Luke): here not "teacher," as in the parallels, but rather "leader," one whose business it is to command. At the sign of the Lord's power he realizes that even this was an inadequate designation and is struck with chagrin at the contrast with his own human frailty. Luke concludes the story by saying that *they left everything and followed him.* These disciples were only fishermen, it is true, whose way of life was at best precarious. However, they gave up everything they had, and no man can give up more than this.

Mk 1:40–45   Luke now rejoins Mark to tell the story of
Lk 5:12–16   the cleansing of a leper; both of the evan-
Mt 8:1–4   gelists locate the story in the context of
              Jesus' circuit of the Galilean cities after his departure from Capernaum. Matthew has his own brief parallel to the story which, however, he has attached immediately to the Sermon on the Mount as its sequel, doubtless in order to bring out how Jesus' authority in word (cf. Mt 7:29) was also an authority of action.

"Leprosy" is used in the Bible to refer to a variety of skin diseases, none of which may have been precisely what we understand as leprosy; this does not lessen the fact, however, that the diseases were loathsome and painful, and often incurable. In those days of primitive hygiene and lack of resources against contagion, the law perforce adopted a harsh attitude toward lepers. They were forced to live apart, not to enter cities, and to warn away any who would come near them. The leper in this story had violated the law by entering a town, a sign of the faith that drove him on and which is implicit in his dignified statement: *If you will, you can cleanse me.* Equally remarkable is the gesture of Jesus: *stretching forth his hand, he touched him.* It was the simple word of the Lord which healed the man; the touch was a sign of sheer compassion. Jesus' injunction to the man to *show yourself to the priest* and perform the ritual sacrifices (cf. Lev 14:2–32), while consistent with his own obedience to the Law of Moses, was also a necessity if the cure was to be officially certified and the restored leper once more admitted into society.

Mark's version of the story contains some important notes that have disappeared in the parallels. The best reading of the text has it that Jesus *was angry* as he stretched forth his hand. (Most of the manuscripts have instead that he "was filled with compassion"; but this reading seems to be an obvious change made by early copyists who were unable to find a cause for the Lord's anger.) At what was Jesus angry? Possibly at the violation of the Mosaic law, which he revered as the revealed will of God. More likely, however, is it that it is the same emotion that is implied in verse 43, a verse extremely difficult to translate which suggests that Jesus' command to the former leper was accompanied by an inarticulate indignation (the same verb is used to express his reaction to Lazarus' death in Jn 11:33, 38). It is the presence of evil itself which angers Jesus, evil manifest in its works of human suffering and death. He was no clockwork faith-healer unconcernedly scattering miracles in his wake, but a man committed to a life-and-death struggle in which he was deeply and emotionally involved. Mark's Gospel is testimony to an aspect of the personality of Jesus the God-Man which we ignore or gloss over only to our loss.

The messianic secret is continued in Jesus' command that the man he had healed was to *say nothing to anyone.* As was so often the case, the command went unheeded. The

Gospels speak again of the enthusiasm over Jesus that spread throughout Galilee, and it is this background that provides the setting for the following episodes.

Mk 2:1–12   Having described somewhat the popular suc-
Lk 5:17–26   cess that had followed Jesus' progress through
Mt 9:1–8   Galilee, Mark now begins to indicate where
               the opposition to Jesus lay. The scene is again
Capernaum. The evangelist has joined together five conflict narratives, most of them also pronouncement stories featuring the Lord's teaching on one or another point, which bring out the hostility which Jesus had aroused on the part of some of the elements in official Judaism. In this tropical arrangement Mark has been closely followed by Luke. Matthew, who as we have seen pursues a distinct outline of his own, has divided the series into two sections and inserted them elsewhere in his Gospel.

In Chapter 1 we commented briefly on the role that the conflict story served in the development of the Gospel material. These narratives—we will easily note that they are somewhat standardized, reduced to bare essentials, and consequently lacking in some of the freshness of the eyewitness recollections that Mark has recorded thus far—are reflections of the preoccupations of a Church that preserved them primarily for their catechetical values, the solutions they offered to problems that beset nascent Christianity during the formative period of the Church. We should try to discern those preoccupations as we study them, in addition to recognizing the role the stories play in the life of Jesus and in the written Gospel.

The introduction to the story in Mark's Gospel may have been taken from the evangelist's eyewitness source rather than from the ecclesiastical tradition on which the stories mainly depend. It depicts a realistic picture taken from Palestinian life which has been refracted by Luke and omitted by Matthew. After his tour of Galilean cities Jesus is again *at home* in Capernaum, presumably in Peter's house, with the crowds pressing about the door as before while *he preached the word to them.* It is this situation that explains what occurred with the paralytic man. He was being *carried by four,* one at each corner of the light mattress or mat that was *the bed* of the poor man: Matthew and Luke substitute a more elegant Greek word for "bed" than the common term used by Mark. Finding the doorway impossibly blocked, the paralytic's friends hoisted him to the low roof of the house, *made an opening,* then handed him down to Jesus still on his pallet. This was not quite as spectacular a thing as it might seem to us: the roof of a Palestinian house would ordinarily have been of beaten earth and twigs or loose flat stones easily displaced. Luke, paraphrasing the account for readers familiar with the more formal architecture of the Mediterranean world, speaks of them going *through the tiles*—rather a different kind of project! At any rate, their action was dictated by a single-minded faith that could not but please Jesus.

Instead of a word of healing, however, Jesus tells the man that his sins are forgiven. This does not mean, certainly, that Jesus shared the naïve conception of physical suffering as a personal retribution meted out for specific sins (cf. Jn 9:2 f.); he did, however, see a radical connection between physical and moral evil, and it is this connection that constitutes the healing miracles as signs of the saving presence of God. Thus he goes to the root of the matter in saying, *Your sins are forgiven.*

Matthew and Mark speak of *the scribes* as the opponents of Jesus on this occasion; Luke refers to *the scribes and the Pharisees.* In context the same persons are meant: it was the scribes or rabbis, the "professional" Pharisees, whose sense of orthodoxy was offended by Jesus' teaching. In view of the role of the conflict stories in the catechesis of the apostolic Church, specific names for the various elements of official Judaism sometimes tend to be used indiscriminately. The scribes accuse Jesus of *blaspheming* by arrogating to himself a power which belongs to God alone, the power to forgive sins. Jesus' sign, therefore, must be understood as a demonstration that he truly possesses this power, not that he is merely declaring that God has already forgiven the man. On the other hand, it is not precisely correct to see in it a proof of his divinity: this would be to accede to the scribes' position rather than to refute it. The function of the sign is to show that he, the man whom they all knew, rightly exercised a divine prerogative. This is the meaning the story had in the Church's tradition, as is brought out in the conclusion which Matthew has substituted for the rather conventional ending in the parallels: *the crowds gave glory to God who had given such power to men.* In Matthew's Gospel this episode is part of a section in which the powers and prerogatives of the Church are shown to be extensions of the powers and prerogatives of Christ. *Which is easier to say:* paradoxically, the more difficult thing, the pardon, is proved by something that is relatively easy, simply because the latter is palpable and evident to all in its effects.

In this passage, and habitually in all of the Gospels, Jesus refers to himself as *the Son of Man.* The meaning of no other New Testament title has been more hotly debated, and it is probable enough that it sometimes means more than one thing in various contexts. In the present episodes, for example, it is likely that the etymological sense is often being stressed (Aramaic *bar nasha*=Man, with an emphasis on the human estate). As a title, it certainly cannot be separated from the description in Dan 7:13 f. in which the eschatological Israel is represented as "one like a son of man" who has "received dominion, glory, and kingship . . . his dominion is an everlasting dominion that shall not be taken away, his kingship shall not be destroyed." In many passages of the Synoptic Gospels Jesus speaks of the Son of Man as the eschatological judge and savior, and it is reasonable to conclude that he has concretized in himself this figure of the redeemed and redeeming Israel, especially, as we shall see, when this figure had been uniquely combined by himself with the even more significant one of the Servant of the Lord. In John's Gospel, where eschatology is more often than not presented as "realized" here and now, the Son of Man has this especial significance. It is also possible, though this is uncertain, that Son of Man had a messianic meaning for at least some Jews. It is equally possible that behind the Son of Man figure in the Book of Daniel and other Jewish apocalyptic thinking there may lie a concept shared with other Near Eastern peoples of a primordial Man, first-created of God and principle of all life. At all events, the Son of Man seems to be integral to the kingdom of God as it was preached by Jesus. In Mark's Gospel especially, the title is seen to be part of the Messianic secret: it was distinctive and calculated to excite interest, bound up with Israelite soteriology yet not associated with a particularist messianism, and above all capable of being filled with a new content by Jesus who made it his own.

Mk 2:13–17   The second conflict story is introduced by
Lk 5:27–32   Jesus' call of another disciple, named *Levi*
Mt 9:9–13   by Luke, *Levi* [the son] *of Alphaeus* by
Mark, and *Matthew* by Matthew. All three evangelists later on list a Matthew, but no Levi, as one of the Twelve, the apostle which tradition has associated with the authorship of the First Gospel. Double names were not uncommon; however, the fact that Luke and Mark know this man only as Levi may well indicate that they were unaware of his identification with the Matthew of the Twelve. He was *sitting in his toll booth*, evidently a collector of taxes and tolls in the employ of Herod Antipas at the border city of Capernaum. As such, he was not one of the "publicans," the taxgatherers for the Romans, but in Jewish eyes he undoubtedly belonged to the same social class. His occupation was probably quite lucrative, and thus his decision to follow Jesus involved a greater sacrifice in some respects than that of the earlier disciples who, after all, could go back to fishing at any time. It is Luke who notes that *he left everything*.

Levi gave a banquet to which he invited his friends, and the friends of such a man in such a line of business were inevitably "not the best kind of people." Those who are called *sinners* were not primarily loose-livers or notorious scofflaws, however, though to be sure some of these may also have been present. To the scribes—Matthew and Luke again have *Pharisees,* while Mark with closer accuracy writes *the scribes of the Pharisees*—they were "sinners" who could or would not keep the Law according to the scribal interpretation: it is little exaggeration to say that in this category were included most of the people who were not scribes (cf. Jn 7:49). Those, for example, who had to deal with Gentiles in their business of making a living were habitually unclean according to the scribal idea of legal purity. Hardly anyone but a professional student of the Law could master the casuistry and traditional lore that were involved in the strict practice of scribal Judaism. The uninstructed and non-practicing masses of a formally Catholic country today, or the unchurched majority of any major city, would correspond almost exactly to the "sinners" of the Gospel.

The text does not say that the scribes were present at Levi's banquet, though they easily could have been, given the informality of Oriental meals. Their objection was made to a known and habitual practice of the Lord. His answer was, of course, a norm of action for the Church of all time. *It is not the healthy who need a physician, but the sick:* it is the business of Christ, and of Christ's Church, to seek out those whom a complacent society might regard as its offscourings. There is no sentimentality or false mystique about the basic goodness of the common man in Jesus' words: he recognizes that they are indeed sick, whatever they may think of themselves, just as by the same token "the healthy" may not actually be in such good health as they imagine. In precisely the same vein he says, *I have not come to call the just, but sinners.* For good measure, Matthew quotes the Lord as employing a rabbinic formula to explain to the rabbis of the Law how his conduct exemplifies the spirit of Hos 6:6 and is therefore a prophetic condemnation of their own attitudes: *Go and learn what this means, "I desire mercy, and not sacrifice."* The scribes used external conformity to the Law as the criterion and checklist to determine who was the just man and who the sinner. Jesus did not deny for a moment that externals are a powerful index to a man's soul; this is a consistent biblical teaching (cf. Mt 7:15 f.; Jas 2:14–17, etc.). But externals, especially carefully selected externals, have a way of becoming religion itself instead of remaining its flower and fruit. Formalism is the temptation of the righteous, and the means by which they become self-righteous.

Mk 2:18–22   It is fairly easy to see the meaning that the
Lk 5:33–39   following episode had in the catechesis of
Mt 9:14–17   the apostolic Church. By means of it the Church both justified its practice of fasting by a saying of the Lord and also defined the spirit which differentiated Christian fasting from every other kind. The event that is presupposed could have occurred virtually any-time during Jesus' public life, though it seems to be from a time after the Baptist's removal from the scene. Luke simply connects it with the preceding passage, though Mark does not. Matthew has the Baptist's disciples themselves pose the question, while in Mark it is simply "they" who ask Jesus.

The situation seems to have been this. The Baptist and his followers imitated the Pharisees in the practice of periodic fasts over and above the one fast that was prescribed by the Law for the solemn Day of Atonement. Mark's expression *the disciples of the Pharisees* is somewhat puzzling, but he appears to mean nothing more or less than those who sub-scribed to the Pharisaical interpretation of Judaism. In this respect at least Jesus deviated from Pharisaical practice, and his disciples naturally with him. Moreover, he justified his contrary practice not on the score that such fasting was at best optional but on the radical significance that fasting must have if it is to be more than an empty observance. *The sons of the bridegroom* is a Semitic expression meaning the friends and companions of a bridegroom at his wedding feast. A wedding feast is no place for fasting, obviously. But it is precisely a wedding feast that they are celebrating who rec-ognize in Jesus, however imperfectly as yet (cf. Jn 3:25–30), the bridegroom of the messianic kingdom. Therefore they should take no part in the fasts of those who do not recognize this kingdom, whose fasting is a penitential preparation for a kingdom to which they still look in the future. *The days will come when the bridegroom is taken away from them:* this is a veiled reference to his death. There is a fasting proper to Christians which, however, finds its motivation in the Christian event itself and not in its Jewish heritage. Christian fasting has its explanation in the new revelation of the mystery of the Cross.

Concluding this episode Mark (or the catechesis on which he drew) has quoted two little parables of the Lord, both of which illustrate the impossibility of effectively combining incompatibles. In context, of course, the incompatibles are Judaism and Christianity: now recognized as such by a Church that had gone through the painful experience of the Judaizing crisis. *Raw cloth* is no good to patch *an old garment* because the inevitable shrinkage that it will undergo will result in a greater rent than before. *New wine* still undergoing fermentation cannot be contained in *old wineskins* weakened with age and transport. It is interesting to note Luke's paraphrase of the first parable, which underlines the folly by having the patch torn from a new garment. Luke also adds a third parable which, from another standpoint, teaches the same lesson. A man used to good *old wine* can hardly be persuaded to drink raw new wine along with it: the two do not mix. These examples, incidentally, effectively show the difference between a parable and an allegory, a distinction whose importance we shall see later.

Mk 2:23–28
Lk 6:1–5
Mt 12:1–8

The final two conflict stories revolve about the question of the Sabbath. While Mark and Luke keep them within the context of the first part of the Galilean ministry, Matthew has reserved them for a later period in his Gospel where he treats of the opposition to Jesus in a way proper to himself. These stories point up the almost superstitious reverence in which the Sabbath was held by the Jews. It would, indeed, be difficult to exaggerate the importance

of this observance in the Jewish mind; we must remember
that it was by the Sabbath above all that the Jew distinguished himself externally from the sea of paganism that
surrounded him, and therefore quite apart from its religious
value as honoring the Creator God it had an emotional
claim on him that some other laws and customs did not.
By the same token, it was over the Sabbath that early
Jewish Christianity came into easy conflict with non-Christian
Judaism, and this explains the popularity of this kind of
story in the Gospels.

His disciples began to pluck ears of grain; Luke adds
that *they were rubbing them in their hands.* It was to this
that the Pharisees objected. The Law did not forbid eating
from a neighbor's field (Deut 23:26), but it did forbid
harvesting on the Sabbath (Ex 34:21). In the strict Pharisaical view, what the disciples were doing constituted harvesting; it was one of the thirty-nine works which the rabbis
counted as violations of the Sabbath. Even to discuss business or to plan one's work for the morrow was forbidden. It
is only just to add, however, that while rabbinical opinions
ould be cited that were even narrower than the one ascribed
the Pharisees in this story, there were always other rabbis
  o followed a more liberal view.

Dealing with rabbis, Jesus uses rabbinical argumentation,
which is argument from precedent. *Have you never read
what David did* refers to the story in 1 Sam 21:1–6. When
David was in danger of his life from King Saul he begged
food of the priest Ahimelech (Mark has "when Abiathar was
high priest," associating the story with Ahimelech's far more
famous son whose priesthood was identified with David's
reign); Ahimelech, having nothing else to offer him, gave
him the showbread of the sanctuary (cf. Lev 24:5–9), which
ordinarily was reserved for sacred purposes alone. The lesson
is obvious: human need takes precedence over ritual law.
The other precedent given by Matthew is to the same effect:
*on the Sabbath the priests in the temple profane the Sab-
bath.* What would normally be considered work violating
the Sabbath is considered lawful for the priests because it

is necessary to fulfill duties more pressing than the Sabbath law. *A greater than the temple is here:* this statement probably is in tune with the final sentence cited by all the evangelists, that the Son of Man is lord of the Sabbath in virtue of his character as fulfillment of what the temple had only imperfectly represented (so also Jn 2:19–21). It is also possible, however, that it echoes in other language the principle cited by Mark: *the Sabbath was made for man and not man for the Sabbath.* The rabbis themselves cited such a principle as this in justifying work on the Sabbath that was necessary to save a man's life. Jesus takes it much farther, however, in insisting that the human condition as such, not just its preservation under extraordinary circumstances, takes precedence over every ritual law however holy. Matthew again cites Hos 6:6 in much the same sense as before: if the Pharisees would be truly religious, they would judge the disciples not by the letter of a law but by their adherence to its spirit.

Thus the Son of Man is Lord even of the Sabbath! Lu? puts these words in the mouth of Christ, but this is evident from Matthew and even less so from Mark. It is ? that the statement was originally a Christian comm? the foregoing episode (which, after all, is not about ab? of the Sabbath but about its proper observance), a comment recognizing in the risen Lord of the Church the one who had replaced the Sabbath of the Jews. It is still possible, however, that this is a saying of Jesus playing on the ambiguity of the Aramaic *bar nasha*="son of man"="man": man himself is superior to the Sabbath.

Mk 3:1–5   The second story involving the Sabbath also
Lk 6:6–10   describes a healing miracle and leads to
Mt 12:9–13 a further pronouncement of Jesus. Luke says
            that it took place *on another Sabbath,* which
has led to a curious reading that appears in most of the manuscripts of Lk 6:1: "on the second first Sabbath." Probably an ancient copyist inserted "first" in this verse in view of Lk 6:6, while another corrected it to "second" because of Lk 4:31; eventually both words got into the text

which then made very little sense but was able to inspire some interesting commentary at times.

In this story only Luke specifies from the outset that a conflict is joined with *the scribes and Pharisees;* only at the conclusion of the story do Matthew and Mark agree that it was indeed these who were watching Jesus *that they might accuse him* of Sabbath violation. The man *who had a withered hand,* possibly a victim of infantile paralysis, afforded Jesus with the occasion of testifying to the word of God in the face of the hostility that surrounded him. The rabbis would concede that what was necessary to save a human life could be done on the Sabbath, but that any healing or medication that could be put off was forbidden. Again Jesus establishes a principle on a quite different plane of thought. *Is it lawful on the Sabbath to do good or to do evil, to save a life or to kill it?* Once more he asks that a judgment be made not out of the casuistry involved in considering a law as an absolute in itself, but rather from an enquiry into the meaning of law as the communication of the will of a merciful and beneficent God. Within such a context, does every act of man blur into the one concept of "forbidden work"? Or is it not relevant to ask whether such and such an act furthers the same purpose for which the law was given, while another does not? Does the God who established the Sabbath to help rather than to harm man intend that it should be the occasion of suffering and pain?

Jesus' plea for mercy rather than sacrifice is greeted with a sullen silence. Mark says that *he looked round at them with anger,* and understandably so. Grieving as well as angry, he quickly brings the episode to a close. *Stretch forth your hand!* This was his answer to his own question and his witness to their small-minded vision of God.

Matthew has drawn on a source also known to Luke (see on Lk 14:1–6) to add to this story another precedent used by the Lord, this time taken from rabbinical casuistry concerning the Sabbath law. If a man's *one sheep,* his only property, were to be in danger of loss by falling into a pit, he could save its life without violating the Sabbath. But *of*

how much more value is a man than a sheep! Yes, the
rabbis might answer, but rescuing the sheep constituted an
emergency, whereas the healing of a man could be deferred.
Yet they do not answer, and with cause. Such an answer
would imply that their concern for a man's property—for the
concession was obviously not made out of consideration for
the sheep—outweighed their concern for the man himself.
It is interesting to note that Jesus' argument could not have
been used against some of the Jews of his time, who were
more consistent, and also more rigorous, than the rabbis
with whom he was speaking. The so-called "Zadokite Document," the sectarian rule of a group pertaining to if not
actually identified with the Jewish sect of Qumran, contains
this specific regulation: "No one is to foal a beast on the
Sabbath day. Even if she drop her young into a cistern or a
pit he is not to lift it out on the Sabbath."

Mk 3:6   And so, the Gospels now tell us, Jesus' enemies
Lk 6:11   found a common cause in their opposition to
Mt 12:14   the new Teacher of Galilee. Mark says that
these Pharisees *took counsel with the Hero-
dians*. The Herodians were the Jewish supporters of the house
of the Herods, in this case those who were influential with
the tetrarch Herod Antipas. Since they undoubtedly shared
in the pagan atmosphere that pervaded Herod's court, for
the Pharisees to seek their advice was tantamount to consort-
ing with publicans and sinners. Stranger alliances than this,
however, have been made against a common peril. We are
not told that the Herodians themselves had anything against
Jesus. Their influence might be used, nevertheless, to induce
Antipas to deal with Jesus as he had already dealt with
John the Baptist.

Mk 3:7–12   To counterbalance this picture of implacable
Mt 12:15–21 hostility, Mark now presents a summary
Mt 4:23–25 statement on the phenomenal success of
Jesus' preaching, a description with which
he introduces his main treatment of the Galilean ministry.
Luke reproduces this Marcan material: he has already used

part of it earlier in his Gospel (see Lk 4:40 f. paralleling
Mk 1:32–34 above), and he will use the remainder to introduce his equivalent of the Sermon on the Mount which
we shall see in our next chapter. Matthew's parallels, which
we consider here, are somewhat similar. Partly he has imitated
Mark's summary statement in the three verses he has placed
immediately before the Sermon on the Mount, the great
discourse in which he has epitomized the height of the
Galilean ministry. He has made use of a like summary to
conclude his version of the two Sabbath controversies we
have just seen, which as we know he has located in a different part of his Gospel in pursuit of his own theological
outline.

What all these summaries conspire to produce is a single
effect: the fame of Jesus, largely premised on the signs of
his healing miracles and exorcisms, was now becoming widespread not only among the Jews of Galilee and Judea but
also among those of the immediate Diaspora of the neigh-
boring territories of the north and south and east. The cries
of the demons, *You are the Son of God,* whose testimony
Jesus continually refuses to accept, have probably been re-
phrased in the Gospel in the light of Christian faith (so also
Mk 5:7; compare Mk 15:39 and Mt 27:54 with Lk 23:47).

Matthew's contribution to these passages is, as usual, a
citation of Old Testament prophecy (Is 42:1–4) which he
finds fulfilled in these events. The true Servant of God who
by the evangelist's time has fulfilled the earnest of these
former days in order to *proclaim justice to the nations,*
pursues his spiritual destiny in the quiet assurance of the
power of God, without the stridency of any compelling prop-
aganda or the triumphalism of a King Messiah: this is
Matthew's explanation of the "messianic secret." It is the
lengthiest quotation of the Old Testament in the First Gospel.

Mk 3:13–19   One final detail completes this picture of
Lk 6:12–16   Galilean success and enthusiasm: the choice
Mt 10:1–4   by Jesus of the twelve special disciples
              called by the evangelists apostles (but
rarely, except by Luke), and whom we tend to think of

as *the* apostles on whom the Church was founded (Eph 2:20). Certainly the Gospels, all of which in varying degrees have in mind the interests of the existing Church for which they were written, treat the selection of the Twelve as an event of special importance, over and above the call of the disciples already described. Both Mark and Luke say that the designation of the Twelve took place on *the mountain,* evoking a theme which repeatedly occurs in the Gospels and which is doubtless intended to recall the decisive events in Old Testament history when the word of God came to Moses (Ex 24:12–18) or Elijah (1 Kgs 19:8 ff.) on "the mountain of God." Luke adds that *he continued in prayer to God all night:* a note which he often prefaces to acts that are of special significance in the life of Jesus. Mark and Matthew say that Jesus *gave authority* to the Twelve such as he himself possessed, and in the Acts of the Apostles Luke habitually shows various ones of the Twelve, and especially Peter, standing in relation to the early Christian community precisely as Jesus had stood in relation to his contemporaries. There can be little doubt, therefore, that the Church which produced the New Testament looked on the apostolic Twelve as its link with Jesus, just as there can be little doubt that Jesus chose the symbolic number twelve in relation to a new era in the salvation history of Israel (cf. Mt 19:28; Lk 22:30).

However, if the New Testament manifests great interest in the Twelve as an apostolic college, the same can hardly be said for its concern with them as individuals save in a few instances. This becomes evident, first of all, when we compare the lists of the Twelve as they appear in the Synoptic tradition, including the second list given by Luke in Acts 1:13.

The lists, we see, are fairly stylized. They follow a tradition which had divided the names into three series of four, in which Peter always appeared first, Judas Iscariot always last, the second and third quartets were always headed by Philip and James of Alphaeus respectively, and the rest of the names had no particular place of order.

Mark	Luke	Acts	Matthew
Simon Peter	Simon Peter	Peter	Simon Peter
James and John of Zebedee	Andrew his brother	John	Andrew his brother
	James	James	James and John of Zebedee
Andrew	John	Andrew	Philip
Philip	Philip	Philip	Bartholomew
Bartholomew	Bartholomew	Thomas	Thomas
Matthew	Matthew	Bartholomew	Matthew the publican
Thomas	Thomas	Matthew	James of Alphaeus
James of Alphaeus	James of Alphaeus	James of Alphaeus	Thaddaeus
Thaddaeus	Simon the Zealot	Simon the Zealot	Simon the Cananaean
Simon the Cananaean	Judas of James	Judas of James	Judas Iscariot
Judas Iscariot	Judas Iscariot		

Furthermore, while the lists do, by and large, refer to the same persons, there are also some discrepancies. We have already seen (above on Mk 2:13–17 and parallels) that it is probable that Mark and Luke did not identify "Levi the tax-gatherer" with Matthew the apostle, as Matthew definitely does; Mark spoke of him as "Levi of Alphaeus," but the only "of Alphaeus" in the lists of the Twelve is the second James. Simon the Cananaean and Simon the Zealot are the same person: "zealot" is simply Luke's correct translation of a Semitic term (Aramaic *qan'ānā*) used to characterize members of a politico-religious party which in later times spear-headed a fanatical resistance to Roman rule in Palestine. But it is by no means certain that the Thaddaeus of Mark and Matthew was known to be the same as the Judas (whom we usually call Jude) of James listed by Luke. (To complicate the matter further, some of the Greek manuscripts of Mark and Matthew have the name Lebbaeus instead of Thaddaeus.) John, though he also speaks of the Twelve (Jn 6:70), never gives us a list of them. As we have seen, he mentions by name Peter, Andrew, Philip, and Nathanael; he also includes in his Gospel the names of Thomas and Judas Iscariot, and at various times he presupposes the presence of one or more unnamed members of the Twelve. His Nathanael appears nowhere in the Synoptic lists; if he is to be identified with anyone there, the most likely candidate is Bartholomew (Aramaic *bar tolmai*=son of Tolmai, a "family" name).

All of this suggests that while the institution of the Twelve was of the utmost importance to the New Testament Church, it was with the insitution rather than with the personalities of the apostolic college that the tradition was concerned. Aside from Peter and the sons of Zebedee and, of course, Judas Iscariot, the members of the Twelve rarely appear as distinct personalities in the Gospels. This is not as surprising as it might at first appear. The Church of the New Testament, after all, was interested in those aspects of the tradition which vitally affected it, and it was the apostleship itself rather than its original components that was of the most concern to a Gentile Church remote from Palestine. We have no authentic information about the activity of most of the Twelve after the first days of the Church in Jerusalem, but it is likely enough that they remained identified with Jewish Christianity, particularly, perhaps, with the Galilean Christianity about which we know practically nothing. By the time the Gospels were written this Christianity had all but disappeared. Meanwhile the apostleship had broadened, and other apostles like Paul and Barnabas had opened up a new age for the Church of which the Gospels are a product.

Apostle means "one who is sent," even as Jesus is shown in these passages to commission the Twelve to go forth and speak in his name. The title, as well as the office, therefore, doubtless derives from the Lord. Two other terms here may need explanation. Mark says that Jesus nicknamed the sons of Zebedee *Boanerges, that is, "sons of thunder."* Behind the word which Mark transliterates as "Boanerges," scholars have suggested there may lie a Hebrew *bnê rogez* or *bnê regesh,* either of which roughly (but only roughly) can mean "sons of thunder." But what does "thunder" mean in this connection? Perhaps Lk 9:54 gives some kind of indication. Or perhaps Mark, not knowing the origin of the nickname, found a popular etymology in the Greek word for "thunder" (*brontēs*). *Iscariot,* applied to Judas the betrayer by all the evangelists without explanation, remains a puzzler. It is usually understood as representing the Hebrew *ish qerioth,* that is, "the man from Kerioth" (a Judahite city mentioned in Jos 15:25). This is not very satisfactory, but it is equiprobable with any other alternative that has been proposed. Obscurities of this kind testify to the antiquity of the tradition on which the Gospels drew.

8. THE KEYS OF THE KINGDOM

Mt 5:1–2   In the foregoing chapters we have some-
Lk 6:17–20a   what tended to slight Matthew, bringing
in his parallels to the Marcan or Lucan material to the disregard of his own way of arranging things.
This has been done out of practical necessity in view of
the limits that we have set on ourselves in reading the Gospels
in harmony, for the reversal of the process would have
made the more or less common order of Mark and Luke
incomprehensible. Now, however, Matthew comes into his
own as we begin to study one of the chief contributions he
has made to the Gospel story, which is, as a matter of fact,
probably the most famous passage in all Christian literature,
the Sermon on the Mount.

We speak of it as the Sermon on the Mount because that
is what Matthew called it, utilizing the symbol of *the mountain* which we have already noted above in Mark and Luke
(see on Mk 3:13–19; Lk 6:12–16). Matthew makes a point
of the mountain because for him Jesus is a new and greater
Moses proclaiming a new and greater law from the source
of divine revelation. The Sermon is the first of the five lengthy
discourses in which Matthew has mainly summarized the
teaching of Jesus; he has placed it appropriately in the
midst of the Galilean enthusiasm over Jesus' initial preaching
of the kingdom because it epitomizes the spirit of the

kingdom as Matthew knew it to have been realized in the
Church. Luke, who has a much shorter version of what was
undoubtedly the same sermon, states more matter-of-factly
(and more realistically) that Jesus addressed the crowds on
a level place. Luke's purpose in reproducing the discourse is
not so programmatic as Matthew's. Having described Jesus'
choice of the Twelve, he used his own account of the
Galilean acceptance of Jesus (see on Mk 3:7–12 and Mt
4:23–25 above) as a preface to the sermon as Jesus' proclamation of the kingdom to the Twelve and to the multitudes. In these latter he sees "the poor of the Lord" who
now have the Gospel preached to them (cf. Lk 4:18).

That Matthew and Luke found the record of this sermon
in the common source they have used independently of
Mark seems to be evident enough, despite the difference in
length (one hundred and nine verses in Matthew against
thirty in Luke) and purpose with which it appears in the
two Gospels. Neither version pretends, of course, to be a
stenographic account of any single sermon preached by our
Lord: in both cases the sermon has been adapted to the
Gospel. It is equally certain that Matthew, who has done the
most with the sermon, has also introduced far more changes
than Luke. He has imposed on it a rigid outline more appropriate to a literary composition than to oral delivery, and
into this outline he has fitted various sayings of the Lord
which often appear elsewhere in the other Gospels (and, for
that matter, which sometimes appear elsewhere in his own
Gospel as well). The original moment of the sermon is
usually more perceptible in Luke than in Matthew, in view
of the sense in which it figures in these two Gospels;
however, all Christian history is testimony to the success of
Matthew in synthesizing its perennial significance for all
Christians of all time. That the Sermon on the Mount is only
one of the five discourses of Christ in Matthew's Gospel
should warn us that in the intention of the evangelist it is
not all of Christian teaching. It has, for all that, captured the
heart and spirit of Christianity in a way that nothing else
ever has.

Mt 5:3–12   The differences between Matthew's and
Lk 6:20b–23 Luke's versions of the Sermon appear im-
             mediately from the first words, in the Be-
atitudes with which it begins. In Matthew's Gospel there are
eight Beatitudes (originally, perhaps only seven), and in
Luke's four; in the first instance they have been put in the
third person and have a wider application, in the other
they have the form of direct address. In both Gospels,
however, it is important to observe, the Beatitudes and the
rest of the Sermon are addressed to Jesus' *disciples* (Mt
5:1b–2; Lk 6:20a): the Sermon on the Mount is not a collection of idealistic poetry but a proclamation of Christian
values and (especially in Matthew) a realistic exhortation
to a standard of virtue that is possible only through the
power given by the Spirit of God.

A beatitude, translated *blessed . . .* or *happy . . .* , is a
fairly common literary form in both the Old and the New
Testaments (cf. Pss 2:12, 33:12, 40:5; Mt 11:6; Lk 1:45,
etc.). Almost invariably it involves the possession of a present
good, which in turn, explicitly or implicitly, is the earnest of
an even greater good to come. The Gospel Beatitudes are
eschatological: they look forward to a blessedness that is to
come, a consummation of the divine plan of salvation. However, they find the beginning of this same blessedness in the
here-and-now situation that is the result of Jesus' coming and
his saving word. They are, therefore, a combination of
"final" and "realized" eschatology.

Blessed are the poor in spirit is Matthew's equivalent of
Luke's *Blessed are* [you] *poor.* The two do, in fact, mean
much the same thing, though Luke has preserved the form
of proclamation to a distinct audience which was, in point
of fact, poor; the entire first generation of Christianity drew
its membership basically from the economically and socially
underprivileged, like the Galilean peasantry. Nevertheless,
Luke is not saying that there is anything blessed or happy
about belonging to the social class of the poor—the idealization of the sturdy virtues of the poor, a romantic notion de-
vised by comfortable philosophers who have never experi-

enced the degrading effects of an unwanted, grinding poverty, is not an error propagated by the Bible. Poverty of itself is not blessed, though one may be blessed for voluntarily embracing it: in which case it is his motive that makes him blessed. Neither, of course, is Luke speaking of this voluntary poverty that was later to be made the object of one of the three vows of Christian perfection, taken as a means of imitating more literally the penitential life of Jesus. He is not speaking of it directly, that is, though he does include the idea: some of those to whom Jesus was proclaiming his kingdom had, in fact, literally made themselves poor for his sake (Levi, for example, Lk 5:28). What he is saying is: Blessed are you, my disciples, who are poor. The blessedness comes from discipleship, but in their poverty they fulfill an eschatological promise. From Old Testament times, because of a long history of social oppression and injustice, the poor, the *anawim,* represented above all those who, having no worldly means of their own to fight the battle of life, placed their whole reliance on God and his vindication. When a person wished to give himself a special title to God's saving help, he called himself a poor man (cf. Ps 40:18). At long last, says Luke, the cry of the poor through the ages has been heard: *yours is the kingdom of God.*

Hence the meaning of Matthew's paraphrase. To be poor in spirit is not precisely or simply to have the spirit of poverty, but to have the spirit—that is, the mind, the attitude of being—of the *anawim,* to be conscious of standing before God always naked and defenseless, trusting in him and him alone. It is no less than this that Matthew lays down as the indispensable quality of a Christian. It is a quality far more easily asserted than lived, and far more embracing than to be, or to think that we are, "detached" from worldly goods.

The next two verses of Matthew's Gospel appear in reverse order in many of the Greek manuscripts. In fact, since *Blessed are the meek, for they shall inherit the land* is a citation of Ps 37:11, it is believed by many that this verse is an ancient interpolation into Matthew's text, introduced as a commentary on the first Beatitude. If this view is correct, the primitive number of Matthew's Beatitudes would be reduced to a symbolic seven, corresponding to patterns found elsewhere in his Gospel. Whether or not this is the case, it is true at all events that there is little if any difference in meaning between the two Beatitudes. "Meek," though traditional, has never been too accurate a rendering of what is meant by the operative word here. The "meek" are also the *anawim,* patiently enduring what must be endured in their confident expectation of God's justice. The "land" is a reference to Palestine as the land of God's promise; already in Old Testament times (the psalmist of Ps 37:11; cf. also Ps 25:13; Is 57:13, 60:21, 65:9) the original inheritance of the promised land by Israel was seen as a type of the eschatological kingdom of God, as it is also in the New Testament (see Heb 4:1–13).

The next two Beatitudes, found both in Matthew and in Luke though in a different order, likewise constitute a commentary on the first. *Blessed are you that hunger now,* Luke quotes the Lord who was speaking to people who were physically hungry. Matthew translates this as *those who hunger and thirst for* God's vindicating *justice:* not in any selfish spirit, but that God's sovereign will be done (cf. Pss 36:11, 40:11, 85:11). These *shall be satisfied* in the kingdom of God wherein every desire for what is right and just will be fulfilled. Similarly, Luke's *you who weep now* but who *shall laugh* is rendered by Matthew as *they who mourn . . . shall be consoled.* The causes of the *anawim's* mourning were many. The end of this mourning, as had long ago been prophesied, was in the consolation that Israel would find in the establishment of God's kingdom through the ministry of his Servant (cf. Is 40:1 ff., 61:1–3, etc.).

From the more or less passive qualities of the *anawim* Matthew passes to quite active attributes in the three following Beatitudes which he alone reproduces. *Blessed are the merciful* enshrines a cherished Old Testament idea: that the principle by which God has joined man to himself and by which in turn man preserves his union with God and with his fellows is the single one of loving-kindness, covenant fidelity. It is this concept (*ḥesed*), especially beloved of the prophets, that defines the meaning of the "mercy" which God prefers to sacrifice (Hos 6:6; see on Mt 9:13 and 12:7 above). The corporal and spiritual "works of mercy" of traditional piety fit precisely within this concept, faithfully echoing the biblical doctrine that man's service to man is the measure of his loyalty to God. *They shall obtain mercy:* the *ḥasîd*, the man of *ḥesed*, is already blessed in the possession of God's gift which he shares with others, and this blessedness is the token of the final mercy that he will obtain from God.

Pure of heart is another expression that we habitually somewhat mistranslate, which at least can give an erroneous impression owing to differences of idiom. "Pure" is used here in the same sense in which we might speak of "a lie, pure and simple," that is, whole, integral, entire; and "heart" for the Semite is not pre-eminently a metaphor for man's emotional life but rather a surrogate for his entire self: a man *thinks* in his heart (Gen 8:21; Eccl 8:5, etc.). What we should understand by the pure of heart, therefore, is the "simple," in the best sense of this often misused word (see also Mt 6:22–24, 10:16). These *shall see God:* see above on Jn 1:15–18. The vision of God which they have through faith in this life is in all substance the eschatological vision of God (cf. Jn 14:9; 1 Cor 13:12).

Somewhat surprisingly, the word *peacemakers* appears nowhere else in biblical literature, though the idea is an ancient one. "Peace" (*shalom*) was a sacred word for the Semite, denoting a positive state of wholeness and productivity rather than the merely negative absence of hostilities that we sometimes tend to associate with it; "peace" was the greeting by which he announced his benign intentions toward man. It is no wonder, then, that unending peace and the kingdom of God become identified (Is 9:6). In Eph 2:14 Paul speaks of Christ concretely as "our peace." Those who in their lives and works further this peace of

God, in the last day *shall be called God's children,* for this they have been all along (cf. 1 Jn 3:1).

Matthew and Luke come together again for the final Beatitude. It is, in a way, a summation of all that have gone before, and seemingly Matthew signals this fact by ending it with an "inclusion," a repetition of the promise of the first Beatitude: *theirs is the kingdom of heaven. Those who are persecuted for the sake of justice,* Matthew further explains, are those persecuted *on account of me,* and Luke, *on account of the Son of Man.* The "justice" in question, therefore, means here what it ordinarily means in Matthew's Gospel: the way of salvation as it has been revealed by God in Jesus Christ. This use of the word justice, to signify the true way of life made known by God, is peculiarly associated with the prophetic vocabulary of the Old Testament. Fittingly, therefore, the Christian who undergoes persecutions and indignities for the cause of his religion is likened to the prophets and promised a "prophet's reward" (cf. Mt 10:41). The Church of the New Testament was fully persuaded that the patient and joyful endurance of persecution was a sign of its prophetic character willed by God (cf. 1 Thes 1:4 ff.; 2 Thes 1:4 ff.).

Lk 6:24–26 In his commentary on the final Beatitude, Matthew adopts the direct address of the original sermon form. Luke, who has preserved this form all along, now has a proper contribution to make in the "woes" that accompany and complement the four Beatitudes of his version of the Sermon. The woes need not have been addressed to any specific persons in the crowds which had flocked to hear Jesus; they are apostrophes directed in traditional fashion against those who represent the exact opposite of the *anawim* (cf. Is 65:11–16). As is evident, they simply reverse the blessings of the Beatitudes, and they should be understood in this sense. While primitive Christianity counted in its membership few persons of influence or wealth and, like the *anawim* of the Old Testament, could almost without qualification identify the rich as its enemies (cf. Jas 5:1–6), the Gospels never make the mistake of finding evil in things rather than in people. They are agreed, however, and Luke above all makes a point of it (cf. Lk 12:16–21, 16:19–30), that the wealthy man far too easily misses the purpose of his existence simply through his pursuit of "the good life," just as the good esteem of men far too often can be a sign that one has never risen above the aspirations of this world (cf. Jn 15:19; Jas 4:4). *The false prophets* are those who confused their own hopes and dreams with the word of God. They told complacent or evil men what they wanted to hear (cf. 1 Kgs 22:1–28; Jer 27–28, etc.), and thus won their praise.

Mt 5:13–16   Matthew himself continues the Beatitudes by appending to them two little parables of the Lord which further define the character of the true disciple of Jesus. The same sayings of Christ we shall meet in other contexts in the Gospels of Luke and Mark; there are also some echoes in the Gospel of John. Because the specific context can mean a different application of the saying and therefore a different interpretation in the concrete, it is necessary to see each passage as it occurs in the Gospels. It is the proper function of authorship, of course, that each evangelist should have made the words of the Lord his own and have integrated them into the form and design of the Gospel that is peculiarly his; in the strictest possible sense, too, it is in this dimension that we read the teaching of Christ as inspired Scripture. In some instances we have good reason to believe that the evangelists drew on collections of the Lord's sayings which had preserved his words without reference to their original historical contexts; they consequently fitted these into their narratives in various applications.

The reason for the association of *salt* and *light* is obvious: both are necessities for life. The Christian character has profound significance not only for God and the Christian himself, but also for the entire world. As of old God chose Israel to be a light to the nations, so it is with the Church:

a city set on a hill which cannot be hid. By mirroring in their lives the Christian virtues and testifying to the salvation wrought in Christ, the followers of Jesus "salt" the world, functioning for its life as salt functions in flavoring and preserving food. They give light to the world by their *good works,* compelling men to *give glory to the Father* whose grace has made such things possible. This is Matthew's expression of the idea of "witness" which is so prominent in the Gospels of Luke and John. It explains the warnings and injunctions here attached to the parables which themselves take the form of parables, borrowing their analogies from everyday Palestinian life. The salt that was in common use was often imperfectly refined and chemically impure; it could lose its saltiness and therefore its value. The Palestinian house would ordinarily be illuminated by a single lamp, often enough a mere saucer of oil in which floated a lighted wick; if such a lamp was to do its job properly it had to be set in the clear, on a stand from which it could cast its light unimpeded. What is involved in Christian witness, in other words, is simply that the Christian be truly himself, that he always act precisely as his Master has intended him to act. This is far removed, of course, both from an ostentatious parading of good works that gives witness to the worker rather than to God, and from the self-conscious compulsion to "give good example" that often distorts Christian witness into playacting.

Mt 5:17–20 Having set forth the Christian's duty to testify to God through his good works, Matthew now explains in the Lord's words what is the distinctive nature of the Christian righteousness that offers this testimony. It is characteristic of this Gospel that such a definition would be made in terms of its relation to Jewish law and practice; however, it would also have been inevitable that Jesus himself would have chosen these terms. The introductory principle is stated in a passage that is entirely proper to Matthew, with the exception of one verse that is found in a different context in Lk 16:17.

Do not think I have come to abolish the Law and the prophets. Probably no other verse of Matthew's Gospel has caused more controversy than this. "The Law and the prophets" is contemporary Jewish language for "the Bible," or in Christian language, "the Old Testament." In context, there can be no doubt that what is meant is the revealed will of God as set forth in the Old Testament, specifically in the Law of Moses: in Jewish thinking the prophets of the Old Testament functioned pre-eminently as interpreters of the Law. Jesus seems to be saying, then, that the Old Testament law remains forever in effect: *till heaven and earth pass away* is doubtless popular idiom for "never." The rest of the text appears to bear this impression out. Jesus insists that *not one iota, not one "horn" will disappear from the Law,* that is, not one *yod,* the smallest letter of the Hebrew alphabet, which was sometimes written as a simple dot, and not one *qots:* the little protuberance that distinguishes, for example, the letter ב (*b*) from the letter כ (*k*). *Till all things come about:* again, the meaning is probably "till the end of time," ascribing a practical perpetuity to the Law. He goes on to say that whoever disregards *one of the least of these commandments* (the rabbis distinguished between the "light" and the "heavy" precepts of the Law) will be excluded from the kingdom of God. And so on. Yet the New Testament—with Matthew's Gospel very much included!—is at one in the conviction that the Mosaic law has been superseded by the law of Christ, that Christians are entirely free of its precepts.

That Jesus himself said these words, or words very much like them, there can be no doubt. They constitute the kind of defense that he would have inevitably been called upon to make in his controversies with the rabbis. They are consistent with his own practice as we see it reflected in the Gospel stories, which portray him as keeping the Law faithfully, though without fanaticism or literalism. It is not surprising, therefore, that some interpreters imagine the original context of these lines to have been other than that of Matthew's Sermon, on some occasion, for example, when in hyperbolic Oriental language Jesus was expressing his here-and-now teaching on fidelity to the Law which had been called into question. Or, if Matthew's context is to be preserved, they understand the passing away of heaven and earth, etc., to refer to the old era which Christ was bringing to an end and which ceased to be with his death, resurrection, and the emergence of the Church: Jesus taught the permanence of the Mosaic law, in other words, but only for his own lifetime.

Neither of these explanations is particularly convincing, and certainly neither of them gets at what Matthew means by these sayings in his context, the only context in which we possess them. Neither is the solution to be found in applying Jesus' words only to a part of the Mosaic law, as though he were speaking of the permanence of its moral prescriptions and keeping silence about the rest. Neither Jesus nor Matthew, neither the New Testament nor the Old Testament, would have made any distinction between the commandments of the Law, moral, ritual, or otherwise: all of them were equally the expressed will of God.

Rather, we must first see carefully what "the Law and the prophets" signifies in Matthew's Gospel, then understand in this light what it is for Jesus *to fulfill* this law. "The Law and the prophets" is the Old Testament revelation expressed in law, to be sure, but by no means the letter of any law. It is, instead, the divine word itself as revealed by the Law and the prophets but transcending their imperfect utterance. The Golden Rule, the law of universal love: these are "the Law and the prophets" (Mt 7:12, 22:40). They convey the spirit of the Law of God, in other words. But taken at the letter only, obviously they are not simply convertible with God's revealed will; neither is any letter of the legal or prophetical books of the Old Testament, nor all of them put together. The God who once revealed himself in law and prophecy has now made himself known by a Son who is the stamp of his very being (Heb 1:1–3). Christ fulfills the Law not by transmitting another law to replace it but by revealing a vision of God at which the letter of the ancient law could only hint. Christ himself is the new law, and it is the life of Christ that the Christian must lead. Thus we see the meaning of the *righteousness exceeding that of the scribes and Pharisees:* not only quantitatively but also qualitatively the Christian must lead a life of obedience to God's will which surpasses the legal piety of the Old Testament.

Faithful to the Law, Jesus nevertheless taught that true fidelity to the Law as will of God sometimes entailed the disregard of the Law's letter; we have seen this borne out in the conflict stories of our preceding chapter. The lesson of his life is the exact opposite of legalism. The apostolic Church learnt this lesson well and found true precedents in Jesus' life and teaching when, with the guidance of the Spirit of God, it recognized that the Mosaic prescriptions were only a vanished shadow of a substance now possessed in Christ (cf. Col 2:16f.).

Mt 5:21–26   Matthew proceeds to illustrate what is meant by a righteousness that exceeds that of the scribes and Pharisees by a series of six contrasts which have as their point of departure an enunciation of the Mosaic law. These will be correctly understood only when it is recognized that they do not attempt to pit one law against another; rather, they show how a sovereign and divine good once expressed in the Law—and expressed well, for that matter—must now be pursued in a personal dimension that escapes the confines of law. For the most part these contrasts are proper to Matthew, but one of them is paralleled by Luke and occasional verses are found elsewhere in the other Gospels.

You have heard. In the situation of Jesus' Sermon, those addressed would not be such as had read the Law themselves, but who had heard it read and taught in the synagogues. *It was said to the ancients:* thus it was revealed to the original recipients of the Law. *You shall not kill:* the contrast begins with a citation of one of the Ten Commandments (Ex 20:13; Deut 5:17), but equally important is the reference to *the judgment* that is to be exercised against those guilty of bloodshed (Ex 21:12; Deut 17:8). In banishing uncontrolled blood vengeance as the sanction against murder and substituting for it the judicial processes of civilized society, the Law of Moses was eminently the word of God for Israel. *But I say to you:* Jesus consciously sets forth his word as revelation, on the plane of what was "said" before. Not, however, to oppose revelation to revelation or to contradict the spirit of the Law: the rabbis, too, understood that hatred and contempt of one's fellow man were implicitly forbidden by this commandment. It is precisely the spirit of the Law—"the Law and the prophets" as we have defined it—that constitutes the way of life in the kingdom of God, rather than the letter of any law. Hence Jesus' teaching, though phrased in the juridic terms of the parallel which illustrates it, obviously has nothing to do with law in the accepted sense of the word: *judgment, the council* (the Sanhedrin), *gehenna* do not determine actual legal penalties for specific violations of law, but simply emphasize the malice of hatred which is every bit as bad as murder. Similarly, no "degrees" of malice are here being expressed in exclusive terms: *raca* (which means something like "blockhead") and *you fool* are random examples of the unwholesome kind of anger which is alien to the Christian spirit.

Two little parables have been joined to this pronouncement to underscore its positive implications. Both parables bring out the primacy of fraternal charity in the Christian life, though with somewhat different emphases. In the first place, reconciliation with one's neighbor is seen as the touchstone of one's good relations with God, which are signified by external worship but not replaced by it. Secondly, the time for reconciliation is now; there is an eschatological urgency to Christian charity, which on no account can be deferred. *You will not be released until you have paid:* this clause has nothing to do with regard to eschatological punishment but is a parabolic detail. The comparison is being drawn between the urgency of fraternal harmony and the prac-

ticality of settling a debt out of court rather than by awaiting the process of law, which according to the customs of
the times included the possibility of a debtor's prison till the
debt was paid. The Christian is being reminded of God's
coming judgment, it is true, but nothing is implied concerning the nature of the judgment itself or its penalties.

Mt 5:27–30   The second contrast also begins with one
of the commandments of the Decalogue,
the prohibition of adultery (Ex 20:14; Deut 5:18). Though
the letter of this law was originally concerned exclusively
with the rights of possession and the stability of the family
and of society which are jeopardized through adultery, the
Jews knew that in keeping with its spirit lustful desires and
intentions were also contrary to the will of God. Again it is
in this spirit that Jesus roots his "new law." *He has already
committed adultery with her in his heart:* in Semitic thought,
the "heart" of man is man himself in his inmost being. Here,
then, is wherein sin really consists. If sin is an act of alienation, it has already taken place when man has willed the
alienation of himself from God or his fellows. "Am I my
brother's keeper?" (Gen 4:9) gave verbal expression to a
sin whose outward expression was the first murder.

Matthew quotes the Lord as employing two hyperbolic
examples which dwell on the power of sin to destroy man
and what man must do to avoid such a destruction at all
costs. *If your right eye . . . your right hand,* if any part
of man however noble and necessary, if any thing however
precious, would lead him to sin, it must be ruthlessly cast
aside rather than that the whole man should perish. Spiritual
writers customarily cite this passage in warning against the
"occasions" of sin, that is, objects that are not sinful in themselves but owing to circumstances can lead to sin.

In these and the preceding verses we find our first
Gospel references to *gehenna*. Gehenna was originally the
Hebrew *gê hinnom,* "the valley of (the sons of) Hinnom"
to the south of Jerusalem, which doubless derived its name
from the tribe or clan which had inhabited it. It acquired an
unsavory reputation owing to its use as a place of human

sacrifice during the time of the kings (2 Kgs 23:10), and later it became a charnel and a refuse dump (Jer 7:32), a scene of fire and corruption. In Jewish literature and in the New Testament the name has been applied to the place of eternal perdition, the abode of the evil dead, thus "hell" as we now customarily use this English word.

Mt 5:31–32 Another prescription of the Mosaic law which marked its enlightened legislation as a blessing given to the Old Testament people of God was its regulation of divorce (Deut 24:1–4). Divorce itself was an institution taken for granted by the people of Israel in company with all others of their time, members of societies whose primary concern was for the survival of the race and the prerogatives of the males who perpetuated it and gave it their names. The same considerations justified polygamy and weighted the scales against a recognition of women's rights over against those of men. What the Law did was to insist that when a man decided to divorce his wife—there was, of course, no thought that a woman could divorce her husband!—he must *give her a certificate of divorce*. This was for her protection, lest she be later accused of adultery when she was married to another man. The dominant male, in other words, though his right to divorce went unquestioned, was not allowed to have it all his way. In some fashion the rights of woman and her dignity were being recognized. This was the spirit of the Law.

And it is this spirit that continues as the law of Christians. As we shall see elsewhere (on Mt 19:3–9 and parallels), in his teaching on marriage Jesus goes behind the letter of the Mosaic law and insists that it is the Creator's will that it be a monogamous and indissoluble union. The Old Testament had recognized this view of marriage as an ideal, but had never implemented it legally. Now a new voice of revelation makes the ideal a reality. Henceforth not merely an irregular divorce, but any divorce, will constitute a remarried woman an adulteress, for marriage is once and for all.

Matthew tempers the proclamation of the abolition of divorce with the well-known clause: *except in the case of immorality.* An equivalent clause appears in Matthew's version of the Lord's later *ex professo* pronouncement on marriage and divorce, and we shall see its meaning there.

Mt 5:33–37   The fourth contrast Jesus draws not merely with the letter of the Law requiring fidelity to oaths sworn in the letter of God (cf. Ex 20:7; Lev 19:12; Num 30:3; Deut 5:11) but also with certain casuistic practices by which the spirit of the Law was violated. The Jews, out of reverence and to avoid taking the name of God "in vain," would customarily substitute various equivalent expressions for it: thus, habitually, "kingdom of heaven" rather than "kingdom of God" in Matthew's Gospel. A man would swear, then, *by heaven,* meaning by God, or *by Jerusalem,* the holy city, or even avoid sacred connotations altogether, swearing *by the earth* or by his own honor. Hence arose many fine legal distinctions concerning the relative value and obligation of oaths sworn in this or that way. Jesus rejects this casuistry. An oath is an oath; by whatever formula, the purpose of an oath is to call into witness the God of all truth who cannot be distinguished in any way.

The spirit of the Law was to honor the sacred character of the plighted word. This spirit should prevail in the kingdom of God, Jesus goes on to say, in a Christian speech that is its own guarantee. *Swear not at all:* this is not a divine law prohibiting legitimate authority from requiring oaths or forbidding Christians to satisfy its requirements; it is a call to a higher recognition of what the Old Testament had already sensed (cf. Sir 23:9–11), that oaths are at best a compromise with a sinful and disordered world, that in the society of man as willed by God they have no part to play. That is why Jesus says that beyond the Christian's simple "yes" or "no" (cf. Jas 5:12) *anything more than these comes from evil* (or, *from the evil one*): it acquiesces in a condition of human intercourse that has been made necessary by sin and evil.

Mt 5:38–42   *An eye for an eye and a tooth for a tooth*
Lk 6:29–30   expresses the so-called law of talion or exact
                compensation repeatedly stated in the Law
of Moses (cf. Ex 21:24; Lev 24:20; Deut 19:21). Apparently harsh in its positive formulation, it was in reality a law of mercy shared by all civilized peoples of antiquity. Its sense was *only* an eye for an eye, *only* a tooth for a tooth, thus insisting on the principle of strict justice in human affairs and excluding what would otherwise have been unrestricted private vengeance. It is by the law of talion, of course, that society is governed today, and indeed it would be difficult to imagine how it could be otherwise. Justice must be at the basis of every genuine law, and without law society cannot survive. Neither the Jews nor the modern state which governs by law, nor the Old Testament itself, for that matter, have interpreted talion as a perpetuation of literal eye-gouging or the knocking out of teeth. Talion merely insists on proportionate indemnification, proportionate and not disproportionate reciprocity under law.

And with this there can be no quarrel: it is doubtless as enlightened a legal principle as we shall ever have. Yet here precisely can it be seen perhaps best of all why the letter of even the very best of laws is a letter that kills. It kills because man cannot live by law alone, not even by the very best of laws. Man is well advised to obey the law, which is a lamp to his feet (Ps 119:105). But this does not give him life. What gives him life, and what makes meaningful his submission to law, cannot itself be formulated as law, even though, paradoxically, Paul can call it "the law of the Spirit of life in Christ Jesus" which has set him free from law (Rom 8:2), even though, as we have seen, Matthew can think of it as "the Law and the prophets" or simply "the Law."

Not to the judge or jury whose duty it is to vindicate the rights of the injured, but to the injured person himself, Jesus says, *do not resist the evil man.* The "evil man," in context, is the man who inflicts an evil upon another: whether he does so from evil or good intentions is immaterial to

the situation. Jesus gives four examples to illustrate his meaning—a blow on the face, a lawsuit, guidance or carterage
levied by the military police, even robbery or extortion—all
of which add up to the same injunction: do not insist upon
redress, upon your rights, but yield even beyond what may
be demanded by circumstances. Luke parallels Matthew in
recalling three of these examples from his version of the
same Sermon; in his Gospel, however, which omits Matthew's
lengthy development of the nature of Christian righteousness
in relation to the Mosaic law, they appear as illustrations of
the radical law of Christian love with which Matthew deals
in his final contrast.

As the Lord's words are not laws in the accepted sense
of the word, it is obvious that they lay down no absolute
rules to govern Christian conduct in every conceivable case.
The Christian must submit himself to the guidance of the
Spirit and a rightly formed conscience, that he may be
prepared to do the right thing at the right time. Love does
not conflict with justice; it always satisfies justice even if it
goes beyond its demands. But it should be insisted upon
that Jesus' teaching is in no way the assertion of an un-
realizable ideal, as though the ideal itself were its sole justification for being uttered. It is altogether practical, from the
standpoint of human society itself. There are numerous
contemporary evidences of this. If everyone were to insist
at all times on an exact retribution for every injury, if violence
were continually to be opposed to violence, the fruit would
be endless enmity and hostility which would render the
society of man impossible and choke off the growth of the
human spirit. Love, however, is as contagious as hate. There
must be, if an order of justice is ever to be established, the
prophetic figure who takes the first step by foregoing his
own rights to redress, who witnesses to the power of love
over hatred and fear, who wins for society as a whole what
he does not demand for himself. And if this is true for the
human estate as such, it must be true above all for the
Church whose mission it is to stand before the world as the
prophetic figure of what God wills the world to be.

Mt 5:43–45 Matthew draws his final contrast be-
Lk 6:27–28, 31 tween Law and law leading from the
concept of love, which as we have al-
ready noted is basic to what has been enuciated in the foregoing. *You shall love your neighbor* are the words of Lev
19:18. Nowhere in the Mosaic law, it is true, do we ever
find anything like *you shall hate your enemy*. It might be
thought, however, that by omission the Law had at least
left itself open to such an interpretation through its silence
on the question: who is my neighbor? (cf. Lk 10:25–37).
Semitic thought expresses itself in black and white, not in
greys, and it makes an easy semantic transition from "not
love" or "less love" to "hate" (cf. Lk 14:26). Moreover,
in context the "enemy" does not refer so much to personal
as to official hostility, to the enemies of the state and of
religion, therefore, to the persecutors of the Church. Senti-
ments that a man might feel ashamed to acknowledge concerning another individual human being personally hostile to
him, he often expresses even proudly when they can be
directed against "the enemy" of his race, his nation, his
religion—we do not have to go back to the Jews of the first
Christian century to verify the truth of this. But as far as
the contemporary scene of the Gospel is concerned, we may
have an idea of what Jesus was talking about in certain of
the Psalms whose language we find somewhat embarrassing in
this respect (cf. Pss 58:7–12, 137:7–9, etc.). The Qumran
sectaries acknowledged as an obligation correlative to the
love of God and his friends, "to hate all the children of
darkness, each according to the measure of his guilt, which
God will ultimately requite."

The spirit of the law of love was to reverence the human
dignity that is the creation of God, to recognize in every man
the divine image (Gen 1:26 f.) and to find joy and peace
in the one human family. The letter of the Mosaic law had
expressed this spirit not only by enjoining love of one's fellow
Israelite, but also, under certain conditions at least, love of
the foreigner: this in an age when "foreigner" and "enemy"
were often synonymous (in some languages the two words

are the same). Now Jesus expresses this spirit in Christian
terms. Love must be universal because God has now shown
the family of his fatherhood, radically or potentially already
present in the creation of mankind itself, restricted no longer
to a particular people or nation but extended to its full potential in the Church. The Christian must love his fellow
Christian for what he is, and he must love every other man
for what he should be: for what, in God's intention, he already is as well.

That which is new about the Christian dimension of love
is that it does not judge men by its concept of neighbor but
rather adjusts its concept of neighbor to fit man. In this it is
urged to find its example in God himself, *who makes his sun
rise on the evil and the good* indifferently, *and rains on the
righteous and the unrighteous.* It is not, obviously, that there
is no difference between good and evil, or that the Christian
is supposed to pretend to like evil things that are done to
him. It is simply that such considerations are irrelevant to
love, which must disregard them. That these considerations
have a habit of getting in the way of love is to put the
situation mildly. The Gospels have intentionally set the duty
of Christian love within the context of its severest test and
proof. In doing so they have left us in no doubt that it is a
hard and demanding way of life having nothing to do with
sentimentality or an ingenuous romanticism. One can easily
persuade himself that he loves "mankind," which he has
never encountered except as an abstraction of his mind.
It is a different matter entirely to love a person who has
made himself known in ways that are altogether unlovable.

Because the measure of love is man himself and not man's
often unlovable ways, Luke has appropriately inserted here
his version of the Golden Rule that Matthew has put later in
the Sermon (Mt 7:12). The man we know best of all is the
one who is our self. If in this sense we make ourselves the
norm of our conduct toward others, we shall be following
the way of love. Love shows itself above all in seeking the
good of the loved one. The good that we would have others
to do for our self that is known to us but perhaps hidden

from them is the norm of what we must do for these other
selves which are often hidden from us by intent or by circum-
stance.

Mt 5:46–48   The final words of the evangelists on the
Lk 6:32–36   subject of Christian love insist once again
                  on its disinterestedness and universality. In
love itself there is nothing extraordinary. Everyone finds it
easy to love his own, to reciprocate love: everyone, says
Matthew, in words originally intended for Jews, *taxgatherers*
and *Gentiles* not excepted; Luke translates *sinners* as a
"Gentile" equivalent. To love in this fashion is only natural,
certainly, but it does not transcend the capabilities of a sinful, imperfect world. It has no dynamic power to advance
the human spirit. To be *merciful* as God is merciful, on the
other hand, to be *kind to the ungrateful and the selfish,* is to
rise above the static condition of sinful man and to enter
into the perfection of God and his kingdom. It is to offer to
man a vision of himself and his worth as they are known
and loved by God, who knows man as even man cannot
know himself.

9. TREASURE IN HEAVEN

Mt 6:1–4   As we begin the second part of the Sermon on the Mount we are still under Matthew's guidance. Just as Luke did not attempt anything like Matthew's detailed analysis of Christian righteousness in terms of its contrasts with the Law of Moses, neither has he any parallel to this next section in which Christian piety is outlined against the backdrop of certain contemporary Palestinian practices. As is immediately seen, whereas Matthew's previous chapter dealt with the spirit of Christianity as expressed in some of its guiding principles for life, this chapter begins by considering some of the specifically religious observances that also manifest its peculiar spirit. A general principle is first asserted, which is then illustrated by three examples.

The general principle is to *beware of practicing your religion before men in order to be seen by them*. What is understood here as "religion" is denoted by the same word ("justice" or "righteousness") which Matthew used above in relation to the total moral and social life of the Christian; here its application is to works done in the explicit name of religion. Obviously this principle does not contradict what was said in Mt 5:16. A truly Christian life is by its nature a public affair which men can and will see. The point made here, however, is that it must be a life lived for God, and for God in man, seeking the approval of God and not of man.

The first example that illustrates this principle has an easy application to religion as we know it today. To *give alms* is, literally, to "do mercy": as we have seen above (on Mt 5:3–12), "mercy" is one of those qualities in which man best achieves the end of religion, which is to become God-like. In this concrete and practical sense we take it for granted that "mercy" (*eleēmosynē*) and "charity" are pre-eminently works of religion; this is part of our Jewish heritage and does it honor. If, on the other hand, "eleemosynary" sometimes evokes an image of something less than disinterested and reciprocated kindness, if we tend to call Christian love by some word other than "charity" in order to avoid misunder-standings, it is partly because of what is being described in these Gospel verses. Man, who is incurably nominalist, sin-cerely believes that beautiful words ennoble his deeds. This we should carefully bear in mind. The *hypocrites* of these passages were not persons who consciously led double lives; they were, as they thought, devoutly religious people.

Having a trumpet blown in synagogues and streets prob-ably is to be taken at the letter. Collections for the poor, which were efficiently organized in Jewish Palestine, were announced by the sounding of a trumpet. The temptations that this offered for conspicuous giving may be imagined when we consider that it was the equivalent of all that our modern organized charities can do to set forth the solid advantages of good-doing. *Let not your left hand know what your right hand is doing* is a graphic way of saying that almsgiving should be *in secret*. It is not, quite evidently, that a point should be made of secrecy, which is often, like the celebrity *incognito*, the surest way of attracting atten-tion. Rather, it is one's motive that should be secret, hidden both from man and from oneself. Almsgiving should be for God and the sake of his poor, and neither to excite the admiration of others nor to induce a feeling of euphoria and self-satisfaction.

Mt 6:5–8 The second example of pure religion has to do with prayer. If the conspicuous doing of good deeds is a perennial temptation offered to religion, conspicuous praying—and it is about conspicuous praying that these verses are concerned first of all—holds an even more obvious peril, where religion's interest is quite vested. The peril increases in proportion to the public rather than the personal character of the prayer, it seems. A man who would quite rightly be ashamed to pray openly merely to impress another human being with his godliness, nevertheless often feels compelled to make a public display of the prayer of the godly community with which he identifies himself. This is one aspect of what we have recently learnt to call triumphalism, which appears to be the manifestation of a basic insecurity in regard to spiritual realities, seeking reassurance about these by appeal to what the world recognizes as evidences of success. Jesus' contemporaries found occasion for their triumphalism in prayer where they found it for obvious almsgiving, *in synagogues and on street corners.* By the same token, Jesus was not condemning prayer in common any more than he was condemning alms or synagogues (cf. Mt 18:20). The *room* in which one prays to God *in secret* does not necessarily shut out others to pray to God in secret; it shuts out those whom we would have admire our piety.

Jesus also says that in prayer we must *not babble like the Gentiles.* The Greek verb found in this verse appears to have been coined by Matthew from an Aramaic expression meaning, roughly, "speak nothing at great length." Probably the Gentiles acquired a reputation for windy prayers with the Jews owing to the multiple names and attributions under which they invoked Deity. Jesus is also doubtless thinking of the lengthy pagan formulas to whose mechanical repetition a quasi-magical efficacy was often attached. However, his emphasis is on the quality of prayer rather than its quantity: *your Father knows what you need before you ask him.* The Christian who knows through Christ that God is his loving Father stands already in that serene relation to him that is prayer itself and that renders superfluous the elaborate honorifics which the pagans felt it necessary to bring to the objects of their worship.

At this appropriate place Matthew has introduced that ideal example of Christian prayer which is ascribed to the Lord himself and which has always been a feature of the Christian liturgy (Mt 6:9–15; Lk 11:1–4). This prayer, the Our Father, exists in a shorter form in Luke's Gospel, but in a different context, where it will be more convenient for us to examine it (see page 33, Vol. II). Appropriate though its insertion may be at this point, it also interrupts the structural pattern into which Matthew has cast the Sermon on the Mount, which now sets forth the third and last of the Lord's examples of sincerity in religious practice.

Mt 6:16–18   Fasting, as we have seen (above on Mk 2:18–22 and parallels), was a religious observance taken for granted both by the Jews who first heard the Sermon on the Mount and by the Christian Church for which Matthew wrote his Gospel. Whereas in the earlier catechetical passage (placed later on, as it happens, by Matthew) the Gospel was concerned with the difference in meaning between specifically Jewish and specifically Christian fasting, here the purpose is, as above, to warn of the dangers to religious simplicity that lurk in any work for God that is performed under the eyes of men.

The fasting with which the first-century Church was acquainted was, externally at least, a complete and thorough-going act of penance. The oil which the Oriental considered so necessary to keep his head clean and fresh was laid aside. The hair was left uncombed and the face went unwashed. The feet were left bare against the cruelty of makeshift roads and paths. The whole man, in other words, was engaged in the fast—or so it would seem outwardly—and not just the control of his appetite. This, of course, was as it should be, provided that the whole man was so engaged inwardly as well. The occasions were all present, however, for the same conscious or unconscious hypocrisy which could vitiate alms-giving or prayer. Jesus does not reject the externals of fasting so much as he inculcates the motive with which they must be used, visible only to *your Father who sees in secret*. The Christian must not *go about looking dismal* for the edification of man, himself included. Though many religious people cannot be persuaded of this, such practices, which try to employ religion as a lever and a tool foreign to its avowed purpose, ultimately repel rather than attract; men can ordinarily discern very well what has been staged for their benefit and what they have merely been allowed to see.

Mt 6:19–21 From this point down to nearly the end of the Sermon on the Mount, Matthew's arranging hand becomes particularly evident. Almost every verse is paralleled elsewhere in the Gospels, usually by Luke, but usually also not in the context of this Sermon. We shall have to see most of the parallels in their own proper context and content ourselves for the present with seeing to what ends Matthew has disposed the material. Opinions differ as to how he intended the remaining outline of the Sermon to be read. The simple and seemingly satisfactory solution that is followed here is that in Mt 6:19–7:12 the evangelist has gathered together various sayings of the Lord to make up seven pronouncements on the spirit with which the Christian should approach this or that aspect of life. Needless to say, some of these concerns overlap and no attempt should be made to draw a hard and fast distinction between them.

The first pronouncement, on true riches, follows easily from the preceding section on right motives. The man who has it as his single-minded rule to please God rather than men will readily understand that it is *treasures in heaven* that he must seek, that is, the good will and rewards of God, rather than earthly riches. We are reminded, first of all, that while the latter are fleeting, the former remain forever. *Moth and rust* are not mere figures of speech as applied to worldly wealth: in the world of the Gospel money was not counted in stock shares or banknotes but in rich stuffs, metals, and the like. The important thing is, however,

that *where your treasure is, there your heart is also.* The
principle is as applicable to a pauper as to a millionaire.
Even if a man dies poor, he may have spent his life coveting
what the world has to offer. There his heart has been, and
there it will remain for what it is worth to him.

Mt 6:22–23   The following two verses, which Luke inter-
                   prets in quite a different way (Lk 11:34 f.),
are somewhat perplexing in their Matthaean context. Doubtless they were, or were built upon, a popular parable of the
time that was useful in various applications. It is, at any rate,
entirely Semitic in its inspiration.

The preceding verses spoke of the heart of man. Now we
hear that *the eye is the lamp of the body.* This seems to
offer us a clue to the connection of thought intended by
Matthew. Through the eye light is brought into a man: thus
the Semites thought of the process of seeing. *If the eye
is evil,* that is, if it is unsound, blind, or failing, then the
light cannot penetrate and the *whole body will be full of
darkness.* A man's eye, then, has much the same relevance
here to his body—his person—as does his heart. If it is fixed
on God, the source of all light, then all will be as it should
be. If it is not, then what would normally be *light in you,*
as coming through the eye, will in actuality be *great darkness.*

Mt 6:24   The theme of divided allegiance in man, or
                potentially divided allegiance, with heavenly
and earthly riches suggested as the source of division, leads
to the third pronouncement: *You cannot serve God and
mammon.* The principle is illustrated by a parable, *no man
can serve two masters,* whose truth, and its consequences,
are immediately evident to anyone who has had to try to do
so. (On the Semitic dichotomy "love" and "hate," see on
Mt 5:43 above.) It is possible that Matthew presupposes
the etymological meaning of mammon. This word, which in
popular speech meant simply money or capital, appears to
have been derived from the same root from which Hebrew
took its words for "faith" and "trust" (compare the analogous

development of "trust" in a financial sense in English). At any rate, as summing up all that can inspire confidence in this world, "mammon" admirably contradicts the God in whom the poor of the Gospel must place their trust.

Mt 6:25–34 The fourth pronouncement, an extended dis-
Lk 12:22–31 course on trust in God, also follows quite naturally in this context. That Luke has reproduced elsewhere the same discourse differing in no point of substance shows that the two evangelists have made use of a common traditional catechesis. Though the Lucan context differs from Matthew's, the teaching of the discourse is so similar in the two Gospels that we can take the passages together.

As they appear in Matthew's Gospel these words are among the best known of the Sermon on the Mount; they are also among the most frequently misunderstood. On occasion they have been invoked to justify a quietistic waiting on divine providence, or, in more profane and prosaic terminology, shiftlessness. They have been praised, chiefly on account of the parables of the birds and the flowers of the field, as a kind of poetic idealization of a life that has never been and cannot be on this world, but which is beautiful to contemplate—from a distance. Above all, they have been most often quoted in indictment of a social or economic class by members of a conflicting and corresponding class which apparently believed they were written for its vindication. The discourse has nothing to do with any of this.

The first point to note about it is that it is addressed to everyman. *Food* and *clothing:* are there any goods of man more basic than these? Everyone sitting before Jesus as he taught, everyone who has subsequently read his words or heard them preached, has had these two concerns constantly in his mind throughout life. And it is of these that Jesus says *do not be anxious.* Not to be anxious is not to have no care. Not to be anxious is to care very much, but to care in measure and in faith. Has not God given the greatest gift, which is life itself? And if so, then may he not be trusted to provide what is necessary for life? The Gospel does not oppose prudent planning and discretion. What it rejects utterly is the kind of planning that dispenses with providence, the quest for a security that would make faith superfluous.

It is this principle that is illustrated by the parable of *the birds of the air* (Luke has *the ravens,* possibly in allusion to Ps 147:9). The point is not that the birds do no work but that they go about their daily rounds without anxiety for the morrow. What the birds do instinctively man should do of set purpose, if he truly believes that the God who cares for these least of his creatures cares even more for him whom he made in his image and likeness. Decent care is one thing, anxiety another. *Who by being anxious can add one measure to his lifespan?* Contrary to an impression carefully cultivated by propagandists of various kinds, no one can assure himself of even an additional moment of existence by eating and drinking the right things at the right time or by taking any amount of therapeutic precautions. These may all be helpful in their way, but their way does not afford a mastery over the life which is in the hands of God. The Christian life from beginning to end is, or ought to be, an act of faith in the Author of life. It is this faith that gives, or should give, a distinct dynamism to the life of the Christian, who begins works whose end he can never see, who often finds his Christian duty to lie precisely in the direction of what the world knows as folly.

The lilies of the field of which the second parable speaks are not the tall, stately flowers of classic beauty with which we are familiar. They are the tiny wild flowers and scarlet anemones that dot the hills and fields of Palestine in the spring, contributing to the land a gaudiness that explains the comparison to the robes of an Oriental monarch like Solomon. They have but a brief life in the thin soil, after which along with the other grasses they are *thrown into the oven* as fuel in lieu of wood, which is ordinarily scarce and precious. Their very transitoriness adds to the force of the example. If God is so solicitous for such things, how much more will he be for his children? The conclusion, then: live not as *Gentiles* ("the nations"; Luke, deferring to the Gentile origin of his readers, has *the nations of the world*), that is, in Jewish thought, those who have no belief in a personal God of providence, who think, or who act as though they think, that man has been put into the world simply to exist and survive, to feed, to sleep, to propagate, and to die. Live rather for God's kingdom, and trust him for what else is necessary. The Christian's day-by-day task, Matthew adds (vs. 34), is responsibility enough without worry over the future.

Mt 7:1–5   If the first four pronouncements of this series
Lk 6:37–42   were fairly logically connected, the final three appear to be rather disparate. They are bound together, however, and also tied to the preceding by their common concern over certain definite Christian attitudes. The first of them is paralleled by Luke in his version of the great Sermon, and here, interestingly enough and quite by exception, it is Luke rather than Matthew who has expanded the text by borrowing from other parts of the Gospel.

Judge not that you be not judged, says Matthew. Luke has it, *and you will not be judged.* The variance seems to be slight, but when the two are read in separate context it is seen to be more significant. There is a finality, a once-for-all note in Matthew's text that is lacking in Luke's. Judgment, says Matthew—and in his Gospel "judgment" almost invariably means the judgment of condemnation—is the prerogative of God. Take from God this prerogative, and you call down upon yourself God's judgment. It is as simple as that. Instructions of this kind were especially relevant in the eschatologically minded community of primitive Christianity.

Luke sees these words rather as part of the Lord's teaching on Christian love, with positive as well as negative implications. The *measure* of the forgiving disposition one manifests toward others is the measure by which one asks to be forgiven by God—except that God, who gives without measure (cf. Jn 3:34), will recompense such a man far beyond his deserts. Luke compares God, or those whom God uses as the instruments of his beneficence, to a generous, honest merchant who pours out without stint the grains he sells in the market place.

Luke also introduces two parables (used otherwise by Matthew, the second by John as well) to lead into the second lesson of this passage, which deals with the judgment of others that often masquerades as fraternal correction. *Can a blind man lead a blind man?* He can, of course, but with obviously disastrous results. Anyone who has been witness to the casual ways of the Palestinian in respect to unfenced cisterns, wells, quarries, and, nowadays, excavations in the middle of concrete footpaths, will know what the Gospel is talking about. *No disciple is above his teacher:* no one can teach more than he knows, and thus his student *when fully taught will be like his teacher* at best. All this is to say what the Lord's proverb quoted by both Matthew and Luke puts so graphically: before setting oneself up as an example to others, judging and correcting them, one must set his own house in order. Otherwise such correction is only presumption and hypocrisy. With typical Oriental hyperbole the proverb pictures the hypocrite of this kind offering to remove a splinter from his neighbor's eye while his view is blocked by a whole log of wood lodged in his own eye.

In Matthew's purview of wholly negative judgment, the injunction to *cast the log from your own eye* is doubtless ironical. No man will ever be in a position to judge his fellow as Matthew understands judgment without condemning himself once and for all. Luke, in his context of fraternal charity, does envision a judgment that works to the benefit of the neighbor. He does not mean, of course, that correction can be given only by the perfect. For Luke the log that must be cast from the eye is the evil to which a man is blind, or which he excuses in himself while condemning it in others. It is this that constitutes his judgment hypocrisy.

Mt 7:6   The connection which Matthew intended this present verse to have with the preceding or the following context is not too clear. Was he thinking of judgment here as Luke does, that is, in terms of fraternal correction, and applying the Lord's saying to the situation in the sense of Prov 9:7: "He who corrects an arrogant man earns insult"? Verbally, the saying means that holy things should not be exposed to the contempt or the disinterest of those who will not or cannot properly appreciate them. It is probably a proverb reflecting Jewish usage, in which *dogs* and *pigs* signified Gentiles. (Not necessarily intended as an evaluative judgment; it was simply that, like the Gentiles, dogs and pigs were ritually "unclean" according to the Law of Moses.) The first- or second-century Christian writing known as the Didache cited these words of Jesus as requiring the withholding of the Eucharist from the unbaptized. We understand them rightly, too, when we recognize that unbelievers have a right not to be annoyed by the public display of what may be quite sacred to us and equally meaningless to them.

Mt 7:7–11   Appropriately enough, Matthew concludes
Lk 11:9–13   his series of seven pronouncements with these
words on the power of Christian prayer. Luke has the same passage almost verbatim with this, but in an entirely different context where it is attached to a parable which he alone relates. Since the context hardly affects interpretation in this case, we can take the two Gospel pericopes together.

The theme of the efficacy of prayer is common in the Gospels. Prayer will be answered, says the Lord, not simply because it is persistent, though his exhortation is to perseverance in prayer, but because God is our *heavenly Father*. He is this, of course, because we have been constituted his children through Christ. By the same token, we have no right to expect an answer to our prayer if we are not living as his children, for in such a condition we are refusing to acknowledge his fatherhood. There is, therefore, no automatic or guaranteed prayer on which we can depend apart from the grace of Christ. Our Christian life must be our prayer.

The passage uses several parables to illustrate a fortiori the confidence that may be reposed in God's willingness to answer prayer. Who, if his son calls to him for something to eat, will give the child instead a useless or harmful thing— a stone in place of bread, a viper instead of a fish? No true father would do such a thing. If human beings, then, sinful as they are, act thus toward those whom they love, how much more will the good God *give what is good to those who keep asking him.*

Luke also asks, what father would give his child a scorpion in place of an egg? The parallel is somewhat curious: while there is some superficial resemblance between a stone and the flat, round loaves of the Near East, and between some snakes and some fishes, there seems to be none between an egg and a scorpion. Probably all these examples were taken from contemporary proverbs. Luke's other variant is rather more important: *the heavenly Father will give Holy Spirit to those who keep asking him.* He has taken occasion to emphasize the most precious of God's gifts to his children, the motive and end of all the rest.

Mt 7:12 It is at this point, less appropriate perhaps than that chosen by Luke (above Lk 6:31), that Matthew has quoted the teaching of the Lord that we know familiarly as the Golden Rule. He has placed it here, it seems, because he sees in it a summation of all that has gone before—thus he calls it *the Law and the prophets* (see above on Mt 5:17-20)—and in Matthew's mind the instructional part of the Sermon on the Mount is now being brought to a conclusion. What will follow this, to end the Sermon, is a series of four combined exhortations-warnings which invite the Christian to recognize the seriousness of his commitment to Christ's message.

The Golden Rule has precedents in the Old Testament (cf. Tob 4:15) and in Jewish teaching before Christ. The formulation of the great Rabbi Hillel (about 20 B.C.) is most famous: "Do to no one else what is displeasing to you; this is the whole Law, and everything else is commentary." The Jewish examples are negative in expression whereas Jesus' pronouncement is positive. It has sometimes been objected that the very positive character of the Golden Rule turns it into an idealism that is unworkable in practice. Others, quite to the contrary, have protested at its lack of idealism since it invites a man to use himself as a norm of moral conduct. To deal with the second objection first, we should observe that the Golden Rule requires that we do to others as we would *want* them to do to us, not as we necessarily expect it to be done or as it has been or is being done. The self, therefore, is the norm of no one's conduct except one's own, and that only to the extent that it is the norm of the human condition—the only norm, as it happens, that is valid for every man. It is in this sense that charity begins at home (see above on Mt 5:43–45 and parallel). As for the rest of it, it is true enough that the Golden Rule can easily come into conflict with the enlightened self-interest that is the dictate of the natural law. The law of Jesus frankly demands a standard of conduct that transcends what may be normally expected of man because it is addressed to man as possessing the more than normal fullness of life which is the gift of the Spirit of God. That man can and does possess this life and live in accordance with it has been proved by the example of countless Christians. That not all Christians live to its fullness the life that has been given to them, that even the majority does not, is a statistical fact that cannot be denied.

Mt 7:13–14 Terminating the Sermon on the Mount, Matthew lists four exhortations of the Lord which offer some kind of commentary on what we have just been discussing. If Christians are not invariably what their calling professes them to be, this may be laid to their not having heeded Jesus' warnings implicit in these final statements on the kingdom of God.

The doctrine of "the two ways" is ancient in religious

thought; it is found in the Old Testament (e.g., in Ps 1), at Qumran, frequently in the New Testament and with other early Christian writers, and in various pagan religions as well. As expressed here in Jesus' words Matthew has applied it to the teaching of the Sermon on the Mount; later on we shall see Luke employing it in a quite different context (see on Lk 13:22–25). Here its purpose is to insist on the great difficulty of the Christian way in contrast to the way which man is more naturally disposed to take. It is a way that one must *seek in order to enter:* to find it he will do well to rely on no help of man but follow Jesus only.

The passage is a parable and must be interpreted as such. The narrow gates of a city were little used, while the larger ones would naturally attract the greater traffic. In the same way, a narrow lane is not as well traveled as are the main highways. This is the basis of the comparison which Jesus intends: one way is enticing, the other is not. There is no judgment passed on how many do, in fact, find *the gate that leads to life* and how many do not. Neither are we told how many continue on *the rough road* once they have found it.

Mt 7:15–20   The second exhortation is a warning against *false prophets.* There would seem to be no doubt that by *wolves in sheep's clothing* Matthew understands false teachers within the Church itself. As the New Testament makes very plain, heresy has plagued the Church from the very beginning. The malice of heresy is not that it manifests an independence of mind—independence of mind may or may not be admirable depending on a variety of circumstances—but that it peddles falsely as the word of God precisely that from which the word of God has come to save us: the hopelessness and inadequacy of the unregenerate human condition. Like the false prophets of the Old Testament who prophesied the thoughts of their own hearts rather than God's (cf. Ezek 13:2), the false teacher may have honestly confused his own imaginings with the will of God. His sincerity, however, does not make his doctrine the less pernicious.

By their fruits you will know them. Matthew applies the
parable of the fruit trees (see above on Mt 3:7–10 and
parallel) as a test of prophecy. Some of the worst heresies—
Gnosticism, Jansenism, Quietism, for example—have been
proposed as superior kinds of Christianity. They were rightly
judged not by their claims but by their effects, which were
to distort the image of God in human lives, to substitute
pride for piety, and to make Christian charity the bond of
a sect. Other heresies would distort Christianity in other
directions, converting the Gospel into a pious Stoicism, equat-
ing it with bourgeois respectability, with tribalism, with the
good life, or any number of alien philosophies. Jesus' words
are addressed to every Christian, who must have a sound
eye and ear for the Gospel and be able to detect false
notes and discern bad fruits from good. These he acquires in
a true and prayerful life of the Spirit in which he knows
God. Relatively few false prophets will ever be formally
condemned by the Church as heretics. The purity of the
Gospel is every Christian's responsibility.

Lk 6:43–45 Luke has used this same parable, also as
part of the conclusion of his version of the
Sermon, but his application of it is quite different. In his
Gospel the parable is a continuation of the teaching on true
fraternal correction (see on Lk 6:37–42 above), and therefore offers the would-be judge of others a criterion by which
he may gauge his worthiness to act as reformer. In the
same spirit he adds (vs. 45) a saying on the necessity of
making *the mouth* (what a man says) agree with *the heart*
(what a man is). Matthew has this same combination of
sayings in a later and different context (see below on Mt
12:33–37).

Mt 7:21–23 It is easy to see how the following verses
Lk 6:46   in Matthew's Gospel relate to what has
just gone before. If the Christian must be on
his guard against false prophets, there is an even more in-
sidious enemy that may be lurking within his own person.

It is so easy to deceive oneself with good intentions and brave words. The Lord whose name may come so readily to our lips will never be deceived, however. Matthew puts this saying in the context of eschatological judgment, and there is a chilling finality to the words *I never knew you*. It is not merely that faith must be proved by good works; what gives the appearance of being such works can also be illusory. Paul speaks of a faith such as can remove mountains, yet leave its possessor as nothing in the sight of God (1 Cor 13:2). The only works that count for a man are the works that come from his heart, that show what he truly is as a Christian: this is what it is to do *the will of my Father*. A man may have worked miracles in Christ's name and have been the instrument of grace for many others. But he may have been only a channel for a divine power that has never touched him personally. Only through the opening of his own heart will God's grace have flowed into his own life to bring forth the good fruits that mark him as a true Christian.

Luke begins his peroration on the Sermon with a verse that is substantially in the words and spirit of Mt 7:21. He has a parallel to the remainder of Matthew's text in a later, also eschatological, context (cf. Lk 13:26 f.).

Mt 7:24–27   Both Matthew and Luke conclude the Ser-
Lk 6:47–49   mon on the Mount with the Lord's parable
                       of "the two houses." It is interesting to see how each has made use of it. Matthew contrasts the *house built on rock* with that constructed *on sandy ground*. This version presupposes the simple conditions of Palestinian living. It was and is vital to the Palestinian peasant that he set up his dwelling near the precious water supplies, such as are the wadies, the water courses which for most of the year are only trickling streams or dry sandy soil. The temptation is to build on the level wady bed rather than to seek the higher rocky ground. In the rainy season, however, the wadies can become torrents within a moment; even seasoned travelers in the Near East have been overtaken by disaster

in these flash floods. Luke has cast the parable in a less regional setting, drawing the contrast between houses provided and unprovided with deep, firm foundations.

The meaning of the parable, in any case, is not too difficult to see. It is easy enough to hear the Lord's words and to admire them: even unbelievers frequently do this. It is another thing to take them into our hearts and make them part of our lives. But if we do not do so, we deserve to be compared with the foolish builder of the parable. Unlike the unbelievers, we have committed ourselves to these words and we shall be judged by them. What should have been for us the source of life, therefore, can easily become the occasion of our destruction. As one commentator on Luke has put it: "The audience are left with the crash of the unreal disciple's house sounding in their ears."

Mt 7:28–29   Matthew concludes the Sermon on the Mount with a formulaic statement which he repeats almost identically when ending each of the five major discourses which determine the outline of his Gospel (cf. Mt 11:1, 13:53, 19:1, 26:1). In turn, this formula is reminiscent of that used to terminate the discourses of Moses in the Book of Deuteronomy (cf. 31:1). In this instance the evangelist has fittingly incorporated into his summary statement the words used earlier by Mark in connection with Jesus' teaching in the synagogues, concerning the contrast remarked by the people in comparing it with the ordinary teaching of their rabbis (see above on Mk 1:22 and Lk 4:32).

10. PARABLES OF THE KINGDOM

Lk 7:1–10
Mt 8:5–13
Both Luke and Matthew follow the Sermon on the Mount with the story of a healing in Capernaum (Matthew, however, having prefaced to it another healing story which we have already seen on page 150 when dealing with Mk 1:40–45 and its parallels). From now on, as will soon be made evident, Matthew and Luke tend to draw wider and wider apart in the separate use they have made of the Gospel material they share supplementary to Mark. For a variety of reasons we have chosen usually to follow Luke's order rather than Matthew's, but we shall also try to remind ourselves as we go along of what distinct purposes Matthew had in mind in his ordering of events. Just as the Sermon on the Mount, the first of the great discourses, was in some measure prepared for by the narrative of Mt 1–4, the text of Mt 8–9 leads into the missionary discourse of Mt 10: in these chapters Matthew thinks of Jesus as exemplifying in his words and deeds the spirit of the instruction he will give to his disciples in the second discourse. In like manner, Mt 11–12, some of which we have already seen paralleling the conflict stories of Mark and Luke, are the introduction to the parables of Mt 13, which Matthew has constituted the third of the Lord's discourses by which he seeks to explore the mystery of faith

and unbelief. Luke's order does not, in this respect, have these complications. Basically he has followed and will continue to follow Mark's story of the Galilean ministry, though for the moment he is drawing on a source that was not used by the Second Gospel.

As we have noted above (on Jn 4:46–54), the story that we find before us in all likelihood goes back to the same event that gave rise to the somewhat different story found in the Fourth Gospel. It is not at all difficult to understand why the story in its present form should have had great appeal for Matthew and Luke. The man who figures most prominently in the episode is a Gentile; not only that, but of him the Lord said *I have found no Israelite with faith like this!* It was to precedents like this that the Gentile churches of Matthew and Luke could appeal when they set the events of Jesus' life in relation to the existing Christian condition. Though in his earthly ministry Christ had confined his preaching to the people of Israel, there was inherent in his proclamation a concept of universal salvation that made the postresurrection mission of the Church to the Gentiles a logical development divinely willed. Matthew would go even further than this (cf. vss. 11 f.); in his view the Church signifies not only that the privileges of Israel have been extended to the Gentiles, but that a new elect people has replaced the old (cf. Mt 21:43).

There remain some differences in the story as it appears in Matthew and in Luke. Both Gospels speak of the man as *a centurion,* not, presumably, as the commander of a hundred men within a Roman legion, but as an officer in the service of Herod Antipas, who doubtless organized his civil and military forces on the Roman pattern. In Luke's account the centurion never speaks to Jesus directly but only through emissaries, first a group of the Jewish city-fathers, then some of his own friends. This doubtless tells us something of the man's character and also his status. The Jews say that *he loves our nation and he built our synagogue for us.* Probably, therefore, he was not a proselyte, a convert to Judaism, but like many of his contemporaries a good pagan who felt drawn to the Jews through similar convictions about the nature of God and the moral law. Luke takes for granted that the centurion's solicitude was over one of his slaves (*doulos*), which in itself was somewhat extraordinary. From Matthew we might gather that it was the centurion's son who was ill (*pais*=boy but also servant; Luke has *pais* in vs. 7).

According to the usual interpretation of the Law, a Jew would become legally unclean from association with a Gentile in his home. The Jewish elders were apparently disturbed by no scruples in this regard, nor was Jesus, but the centurion shows extreme delicacy, professing himself *not worthy* that Jesus should come to his house. Such delicacy, in turn, accompanies a faith in Jesus' serene *authority* which requires no bodily presence to work its will. It is this quality of faith that earns Jesus' accolade.

Lk 7:11–17   Matthew continues the preceding story with two passages concerning Jesus' works of healing which we have already seen above in other contexts. Luke's sequel is this story of the raising to life of a widow's son, another wonder which Jesus performs merely by his word. This is the first Gospel passage we have encountered which actually describes the restoration of life to a dead person, and it is given to us by Luke only; however, all four Gospels contain similar stories and the fact itself was taken for granted by the New Testament and the rest of early Christianity. It is not by chance that in this account Luke for the first time calls Jesus *the Lord*, the name by which the apostolic Church acknowledged Christ as divine Savior, the conqueror of death and giver of life (cf. Phil 2:9 f.).

Nain (Hebrew *na'im*, fair; modern Arabic *nēn*) is today a rather squalid Muslim village of some two hundred souls, in the plains near Nazareth. It is possible that it may have been a larger town in New Testament times: the site has never been excavated archaeologically. By established custom burials took place outside the town walls; thus Jesus, *his disciples*, and the *great crowd with him* met this funeral cortege just as it was passing out through the town gate on the way to the burial ground. Luke's story contains a large number of incidental details that point to the human interest he found in this event. Most important to him, however, is its prophetic significance: *God has visited his people* (cf. Lk 1:68). *He gave him to his mother* evokes the memory of the great prophets Elijah and Elisha (cf. 1 Kgs 17:23; 2 Kgs 4:36) to whom similar wonders were ascribed in this Galilean region. Hence the acclaim of the people: *A great prophet has risen among us!*

Lk 7:18–23 Luke takes occasion from the widespread
Mt 11:2–6   attention which Jesus had attracted through
                works like the one just described (vs. 17) to introduce the story of the Baptist's query which he shares with Matthew. Though Matthew has placed his briefer version of the story elsewhere in his Gospel, the context is really much the same: *John in prison heard about Jesus' works.* Luke has already mentioned the Baptist's imprisonment (Lk 3:20); Matthew, who will explain the circumstances later (Mt 14:3 ff.), previously said only that John had been arrested (Mt 4:12). That the Baptist, though in prison, could maintain contact with the outside world and send messages through his disciples is in keeping with what we are otherwise told in the New Testament about the normal conditions of imprisonment.

There can hardly be any doubt that both Matthew and Luke believed that the Baptist had already designated Jesus as the awaited Messiah (see above on Lk 3:21–22 and parallels). Nevertheless, it seems to be evident enough that the Baptist here was asking a real question, and on his own behalf: *Are you he who comes—the Messiah—or shall we look for someone else?* If the question is somewhat puzzling, Jesus' answer appears to be more so. It was the works of Jesus which occasioned the question in the first place, yet it is only to the works that Jesus points (with the implied reference to messianic texts like Is 26:19, 29:18 f., 35:5 f., and especially 61:1: the Servant of the Lord) by the way of reply, telling the disciples to *tell John what you hear and see*. What are we to make of all this?

Seemingly we are confronted again by the disparity of Jewish and Christian thought concerning messianism. The Baptist believed Jesus to be the Messiah: his works proved that he was. But this being the case, why was he, John, languishing in prison while tyrants like Antipas still lived in security? When would the messianic kingdom be inaugurated as it should, in a burst of power and with the terrible might of the wrath of God, crushing all opposition and establishing right for ever? The Baptist's question, then, came to this: Since you are the Messiah, why are you not acting like the Messiah?

To such a question Jesus could reply only as he did. The signs of the messianic era which the Baptist has recognized are not a prelude to something else that is to come: they are a proclamation of the kingdom as it is, a kingdom which triumphs not by crushing its opposition but by submitting to it, a kingdom whose principal figure is one who is Servant of all. Though John the Baptist does not yet realize this, he himself has already begun the final course of a life which, like Jesus' own, will be a testimony to the kingdom as it really is. Faith in Jesus' word alone can extract meaning from such a life. Therefore, *blessed is he who is not scandalized in me*.

Lk 7:24–35   Both Luke and Matthew continue the pre-
Mt 11:7–19   ceding episode with the testimony of Jesus
to the Baptist. It is quite evident that for this testimony they have depended upon a traditional source elaborated in the apostolic Church; however, there is every reason to suppose that it goes back to an authentic setting in the life of Jesus, who must have been called upon more than once to declare himself in relation to the Baptist.

Jesus offers his testimony by asking the crowds to offer their own: it is their testimony which he accepts. Why had they sought John out? Because he was just like any other weak and fickle human being, *a reed shaken by the wind?*

Obviously not. Because he was *someone luxuriously clad*: pre-eminent among men according to the standards by which the world recognizes pre-eminence? Hardly; such people were rather those who were now persecuting the Baptist. *A prophet*, then? *Yes, and more than a prophet!* Here in Matthew and Luke are cited the words of Ex 23:20 and Mal 3:1 which in Mk 1:2 were joined to the Isaian passage which all the evangelists use to identify the Baptist in his relation to Jesus and his kingdom (see above on Lk 3:3–6 and parallels). It is this, in fact, that finally determines the greatness of the Baptist: he is the greatest of the prophets, and no man is greater than he, because of his immediate proximity to the kingdom which he announced. By the same token, *the least in the kingdom is greater than he.* This is stated not to disparage the person of the Baptist but to further define his position in the history of salvation. *All the prophets and the Law delivered their message until John*: the Baptist is the last of a most distinguished prophetic line, but he remains within that line. As a child of grace, John of course shares in the New Testament just as did all the other holy people of the Old Testament; but he has not been destined to take an active part in the kingdom which he prophesied. His glory, says Matthew, is to have been *Elijah* the precursor (again see on Lk 3:3–6 and parallels). Luke omits this reference, since immediately before he has represented Elijah as a type not of the Baptist but of Jesus himself (see above on Lk 7:11–17).

It is probably best to take verse 12 in Matthew's text as a parenthetical remark suggested to the evangelist because of its topical connection with John and the kingdom. Much the same words appear elsewhere in Lk 16:16, but probably in a quite different sense. Matthew seems to be alluding here to real violence directed against the kingdom since the time of the Baptist: either persecutions directed against the Church, or Jewish attempts to establish a political kingdom by military force in Roman Palestine, or something similar. The meaning is far from clear.

Luke also encloses a parenthetical remark in verses 29 f. All the Gospels make the point from time to time that while the religious and political leadership of the people tended to be lukewarm or actively hostile toward both Jesus and the Baptist, the people as such were disposed to receive them.

Yet in the long run the leadership won out, as it has a way of doing, just as popular enthusiasm has a way of waning. Jesus came unto his own and his own did not receive him, as he knew they would not. The parable with which the two evangelists conclude this passage does not deal with the rejection of Jesus by the Jews as an issue of polemics— it is really incidental that *this generation* happened to be Jews. The parable is the story of everyman to the extent that he remains a part of this generation, a child of this world which blinds itself to the light of the word when the word will not conform to its tastes. This generation, says the Lord, is like wayward children who demand that everyone adjust to their mood of the moment. John the Baptist came among them leading an austere life and preaching repentance: they would have none of this. *He has a demon:* he is a fanatic! Jesus, on the contrary, though closely associated with the Baptist, exercised perforce a quite different kind of ministry, living not in solitude but in normal fashion among normal people, seeking out those who needed him the most. What laxity! Living in pleasure and with low company!

Wisdom is vindicated by her works, says Matthew. The wisdom of God's word (cf. 1 Cor 1:21) as manifested in the Baptist and in Jesus, cannot be, as this generation would have it, at one and the same time too narrow and too free. It is the world that is wrong, not wisdom. Had the world been able to read the signs of the times (cf. Lk 12:54–56), it would have seen the meaning both of the Baptist's penitential preaching and the joyous proclamation of Jesus. *Wisdom is vindicated by all who are her children,* says Luke. The faithful few who know how to discern wisdom in what is foolishness to men are wisdom's children (cf. 1 Cor 1:22–25).

Lk 7:36–50   Matthew continues in his Gospel with Jesus'
lament over the cities of Galilee, a passage
which fits in very well in this context of faith and unbelief,
which however we shall see later on (see below on Lk
10:13–16). Luke gives us in this place a story reported
only by him, doubtless intended to illustrate the way in
which God's wisdom can find its children in quite unlikely
places.

The scene which Luke describes is very similar to a later
one set in relation to the narrative of Jesus' passion and
death by both John and the Synoptic Gospels (Mt 26:6–13;
Mk 14:3–9; Jn 12:1–8); so similar is it, in fact, that Luke,
who as we know avoids even apparent repetitions, has omitted the second episode in telling his Gospel. The two stories
are quite distinct, however, with different principals and
different purposes in different locales. Because of their fundamental resemblance—the action of a woman concerning our
Lord at a banquet—it appears that in oral transmission details from the two stories have become intermingled, with
the result that they are now even more similar than they
originally were. The name "Simon," for example, which appears quite unheralded in verse 40, has doubtless been borrowed from the second event, which according to Matthew
and Mark took place in the house of "Simon the leper." The
anointing of Jesus, too, which in the present story is something of an anomaly, may be an intrusion from the later
setting in which an anointing is the whole point of the
account. As will be seen, the influence has been reciprocal,
and some of the particulars of the other story as it now
appears in the Gospels undoubtedly owe their origin to this
tradition preserved by Luke.

It is not entirely clear why *one of the Pharisees asked*
Jesus *to eat with him.* Possibly he had been included in a
general invitation to a banquet, for curiosity's sake; while
the Pharisee does not appear to have been particularly hostile
toward Jesus, neither did he treat him as an honored guest.
There was a certain woman in the city, a sinner: the meaning
is that she was a notorious sinner, doubtless a prostitute.

She had recently repented, as the story will show, but either this was as yet unknown or, as so often happens, her life had already acquired for her a permanent reputation as far as respectable society was concerned. Undoubtedly she was an intruder in the house, but as we have already seen Palestinian gatherings were semi-private at best. Learning that Jesus was present at the meal, *she stood behind him at his feet.* The Jews of Palestine often adopted the Roman custom in taking food: reclining on mats surrounding a low table (one side of which was kept free for the waiters), leaning on the left arm and eating with the right hand. Thus a person's feet would be behind him; the sandals were also removed at meals.

It is likely enough that the woman came with nothing more definite in mind than to see Jesus, to be close to him. Overcome with emotion, however, she kneels at his feet, weeping. Her tears fall upon his feet and, in the most natural way possible, she looses her hair and uses it to blot away her tears. As we suggested above, the detail of the ointment and her anointing of Jesus' feet are best explained as intrusions from another story. Anointing the head was customary (see vs. 46), but there was no purpose or precedent for anointing the feet. The Pharisee, in any case, was scandalized at this public display and contemptuous of Jesus for permitting himself to be made the object of it by such a person.

The lesson of the Lord's parable, quite plainly, is: he who is forgiven much, loves much, while *he who is forgiven little, loves little.* He contrasts the mean spirit shown by the Pharisee in his minimal hospitality with the exuberant manifestation of the woman's love. The Pharisee had little love in his make-up because he was not conscious of having been loved; he had not experienced the incredible mercy of God's forgiveness because he did not know that he had done much to need forgiveness. The woman knew all that the Pharisee did not. She had repented of her evil life, doubtless as the result of Jesus' preaching. Her faith had saved her (vs. 50). Aware of the divine love that had been shown her, she loved much in return. It was *because of this,* Jesus said, *because she has loved much,* that he can confirm with all authority that *her sins, many as they are, have been forgiven her.* The parable has a great deal to tell us about the nature of love as Jesus understood it.

Lk 8:1–3 Having related one woman's story which obviously meant much to him, Luke now mentions several other women who, like this woman, had been the beneficiaries of Jesus' healing ministry. It is one of Luke's engaging qualities that he has striven to give women their proper place of prominence in his Gospel set in the man's world of Palestinian Judaism. This apparently summary statement that Luke has given us is actually of some importance in explaining how Jesus and his little band of disciples were maintained in their preaching activity through the support of several well-to-do women. *Mary* was *called Magdalene* presumably because she was a native of Magdala on the west shore of the Sea of Galilee; this city is today only a ruin. Luke introduces her here apparently for the first time, and there is no reason to suppose that she was the unnamed woman of the preceding episode, though popular tradition has made this association. There is no reason, as a matter of fact, to think that the Magdalene had ever been a notorious sinner: *from whom seven demons had gone out* need be nothing more than the Gospel's way of saying that she had suffered from some extraordinary mental or physical illness. We know nothing further about *Joanna, the wife of Chuza, Herod's steward.* Chuza could have been in either the civil service or the private employ of Antipas. Neither do we have any further information about the *Susanna* whom Luke mentions, though he speaks of her as someone with whom his readers would be presumed to be familiar.

Mk 3:20–21 After our lengthy excursion into the Gospel story that is proper to Matthew and Luke we now return to the story of the Galilean ministry as it was disposed by Mark. This present little section has the distinction of being one of the very few Marcan passages that have been utilized neither by Matthew nor by Luke. The reason that they have omitted it seems to be quite evident: despite its brevity, it raises more questions than it offers explanations, and the two later evangelists did not want to bother with its problems.

Mark says, not in connection with any specific context (having just given his list of the Twelve), that Jesus *came home:* Capernaum is doubtless meant. As before, the news is quickly spread abroad and almost immediately an enthusiastic crowd has gathered about the door of the house, jostling, questioning, and merely getting in the way of Jesus and his disciples, *so that they were not even able to get a bite to eat. Hearing of this,* we are told, *his own people went out.* Who are "his own people" (literally *hoi par' autou=* those on his side)? It is generally taken for granted that they were the close relatives of Jesus who appear in the next passage that we shall consider (Mk 3:31–35 and parallels). This assumption is probably quite correct; it should be observed, however, that it is not entirely certain, for the expression can mean other things. They went out, the text says, *to take charge of him.* Or should it be read, to take charge of *it,* that is, of the crowd? Either reading is possible from the Greek. Assuming, again, that Jesus is meant, the sense seems to be that of his relatives, disturbed by the notoriety which he was attracting to himself and doubtless out of sympathy with it (cf. Jn 7:5), were resolved to draw him back into the family seclusion: he was becoming an embarrassment to them. *For they said* [or, "it was being said"?], *"He is out of his mind"* [preferable to "it"=the crowd again, which could have been out of "its" mind]. The allegation is not of insanity, precisely, but of fanaticism, lack of balance.

The function that Mark intended this somewhat obscure passage to serve in his Gospel is itself not too clear. Presumably he intended it to parallel what he has immediately following: the incredulity of Jesus' own family more than matched by the malicious charges of the scribes. At any rate, there is no sequel, and we hear no more about what Jesus' "own people" did or intended to do. The encounter with the scribes we shall see later on in a better context.

Mk 3:31–35   It is probable that Mark associated *the*
Mt 12:46–50   *brothers* of Jesus who appear in this next
Lk 8:19–21   passage with "his own people" of the pre-
               ceding. Both he and Matthew have put the
story immediately before the "day of parables" in which the Lord speaks at length on the mystery of the kingdom of God; Luke has put it immediately after. The situation is not incidental: Jesus' doctrine of a kingdom that takes precedence over every earthly tie (cf. Mt 8:21f., 10:37) is being illustrated in his own life.

Jesus' teaching is perfectly straightforward and clear. He has come to establish a family of faith (cf. Rom 8:29), and they make up this family who *do the will of God* as he does it. This is a common New Testament teaching (cf. Jn 15:14); from the Pauline epistles and the Acts of the Apostles we know that "brother" was the customary title by which the early Christians recognized one another, a usage which continued an Old Testament precedent. Neither Jesus nor the early Christians thereby minimized natural relationships (even though Luke has considerably toned down Jesus' "rejection" of his family in this passage for fear that it might be misunderstood); it was merely a question of establishing priorities.

Who were those whom this Gospel story names the brothers and sisters of Jesus? For insisting that they were cousins or at any rate something other than uterine brothers and sisters Catholic interpreters have sometimes been charged with departing from the plain sense of Scripture merely to uphold the Church's belief in the permanent virginity of Mary. It is true that Catholic interpretation has been colored by this belief, but it is equally true that the ancient tradition on which the belief rests cannot simply be disregarded in the interpretation of the New Testament. It would be hard to see how the tradition could ever have developed had it been thought that any scriptural passage opposed it.

As a matter of fact, the early Church appears to have been fairly of one mind on this subject, with Tertullian in the third century forming a singular exception following his lapse into heresy. The Gospel and other New Testament references to Jesus' brothers presuppose Semitic usage, which makes "brother" do for half brothers (Gen 37:16), nephews (Gen 13:8), cousins-german (1 Chron 23:22), more remote cousins (Lev 10:4), and relatives in general (2 Kgs 10:13). Later we shall see that at least some of those whom it calls Jesus' brothers the Gospel itself explicitly states were sons of another woman than Mary the mother of Jesus.

Mk 4:1–9 A matter of much more absorbing interest
Mt 13:1–9 to the Gospels is now introduced to us by
Lk 8:4–8 the common Synoptic account of the parable of the sower. We have already seen a considerable number of parables in what the Gospels have given us of Jesus' teaching, so much so that we hardly need to be told now that parables were a predominant feature of his preaching in Galilee. It is now, however, that the Synoptic Gospels choose to take up Jesus' parabolic teaching *ex professo*. This is particularly the case in Matthew's Gospel, which has taken up Mark's "day of parables" and expanded it to the symbolic number of seven parables, converting it into the third of the major discourses of Jesus which constitute the outline of the First Gospel.

There was, of course, nothing particularly original about Jesus' teaching in parables. Parables have been in use among almost all peoples from time immemorial. They have been particularly popular with Orientals, who like to use their imaginations as well as their minds in learning and in teaching. The Old Testament is filled with parables of various kinds, which is one reason for the fact that it is such enduring literature. Parables were a common teaching form for the rabbis of Jesus' day, and in his lavish use of parables therefore our Lord was simply adopting, as a good teacher should, an instructional method with which his hearers were quite familiar.

It may be helpful to distinguish the different kinds of parable which we encounter in the Gospels. The simplest form is the *parabolic saying*, which may be what we would ordinarily call in English a proverb, a simile, or a metaphor. Essentially this is to talk in pictures: "You are the light of the world"; "You cannot put a new patch on an old garment." What may be termed the *parable* proper is the immediate development of this, a figure of speech that makes its point through the short description of some action or fact. The parable of the sower is a parable in this sense. Finally, we have the *parabolic story*, a further enlargement in which the parable becomes a complete short story with a cast of characters and a finished action: we think immediately of the good Samaritan or the prodigal son. To all of these we give the name parable in a general way, for they have in common what is essential to a parable: to teach something by comparing it with something else. The "something else" is invariably a familiar reality, in the light of which the hearer of the parable is invited to take a closer look at the something new that he is being taught.

Ordinarily the parable is content with performing its essential function of making a simple comparison: it has one point to make, and one only. Especially in its developed forms, however, the parable easily verges upon *allegory*, from which nevertheless it should be firmly distinguished. An allegory is a sustained metaphor, in which a whole series of details is systematically related to the details of another reality. The Johannine figure of the true vine and its branches has the character of an allegory: Christ corresponds to the vinestock, his disciples to the branches of the vine, God to the vinedresser, and so forth. Like the parable, the allegory can be either quite simple or very involved, depending on the degree to which it is developed. A modern work like *Lord of the Flies* is a good example of the artistic use of complicated allegory.

The parable sometimes verges on allegory, we have said. In other words, we do not exclude the possibility that some of the Gospel parables may occasionally go beyond the one point proper to the parabolic comparison and make other points as well. That is to say, the parable may at times contain allegorical elements. This is definitely not the rule, however. In the well-known parable of the good Samaritan, for example, it is pointless to ask for the "meaning" of details like the road to Jericho, the inn, the innkeeper, the oil and wine, and the rest. Such details are present merely to make up a vivid and interesting story, merely to constitute the parable in the first place. They have no allegorical significance beyond the single message of the parable, which is that everyman, however separated by race or nation or religion, is everyman's neighbor. It is essential to recognize this difference between parable and allegory, for otherwise it is very easy to misread the parables and understand them in ways quite foreign to their original intention. When the Lord says that the way to destruction is wide and well traveled, he is speaking a parable, not an allegory (see above on Mt 7:13 f.). He is saying that the road to hell is as easy to find as a busy public highway; he makes no pronouncement concerning the number of those who actually travel this road. If the Lord's sayings in Mk 2:21 f. and parallels were allegories rather than parables, we would have to conclude that they were unhappily stated, since each of them concerns a good thing that is old being spoilt by something new—and *ex hypothesi* the latter would be his own new teaching. As parables, however, the sayings do not intend to establish any such relationship. They merely illustrate the principle that the new and the old cannot be mixed.

The allegorical potential within the parables, it should be added, has sometimes been exploited by the Church or by the evangelist in adapting their teaching to situations other than the original ones in which they were uttered. We shall see an instance of this in a moment. We have already observed how certain of the parables appear in different contexts in the several Gospels, where they invariably take on different shades of meaning. The evangelists also have a tendency to connect in topical or logical grounds parables that originally had a separate existence. In practice we must first of all interpret the parables as we find them in the Gospels, whatever may have been their historical context in Jesus' preaching. This is, after all, to get at the inspired meaning of the Scripture. In some instances, however, by comparison of one Gospel with another, by taking into consideration the known tendencies of this or that evangelist, or simply by scrutinizing the parable itself independently of its present context, we may with greater or less probability reconstruct the process by which the parables have passed from their existential situation in Jesus' proclamation of the kingdom into the existential situation of the Gospel teaching.

Let us test this assertion by considering the parable of the sower apart from the explanation that is later given to it. *The sower went out to sow:* Jesus takes a familiar picture from Palestinian life. Farming methods in the Near East were and are crude and prodigal. Having broken the soil by perfunctory plowing, the sower simply walked through the field scattering seed on either side by the handful. He did not expect all of it to take root. Some would inevitably fall on the beaten path instead of the plowed area and thus remain on the surface to be trampled on or eaten by birds. Some would be scattered in areas where there is only a thin layer of soil over bedrock: this is the geological description of much of the land of Palestine. In such ground the rain does not seep away so quickly and the excess moisture would cause the seed to germinate immediately and begin to grow. But it would be a premature growth that could not last; the sun and the plant's lack of roots would soon finish it off. Still other seed would fall among thorns, which rob the soil of its nourishment and choke off the growth of the grain. Finally the rest of the seed—the bulk of it, let us hope—would fall where the sower wanted it to fall, in his good ground where it would prosper in varying degrees.

He who has ears, let him hear! Thus the Lord issues his challenge to understanding. But what was his meaning? In the circumstances of the Galilean preaching, seemingly he intends the parable to illustrate how the kingdom was being proclaimed. It would—it already had—encountered much opposition and much indifference. Nevertheless, now was the one and only time of sowing in view of the anticipated harvest. Now, therefore, was the one and only time for decision: a second chance would not be offered. The parable is an eschatological summons to heed the all-powerful word of God which can, if men will but permit it, produce fruit *thirty, or sixty, or a hundred for one.*

Mk 4:10–12   Following Mark, all the Synoptic Gospels
Mt 13:10–17   here insert an explanation of Jesus' use of
Lk 8:9–10   parables in answer to a question of the
                disciples. It may well be, as many scholars
suspect, that this explanation had originally to do with all
Jesus' teaching, not his parables exclusively; even if this is so,
however, it has been most aptly applied to the parabolic
teaching because of the inherent obscurity of the parable as
a literary form. What is unfortunate, nevertheless, is that
these verses have sometimes been interpreted as meaning that
Jesus used parables as a deliberate means of hiding his teaching from the multitudes. This certainly cannot be the sense
of the Gospels. Parables were not intended to conceal meaning but to clarify it. Their obscurities, which were only relative, were not designed to make them pointless riddles but
to challenge the hearer to penetrate more deeply into the
realities which they signified, just as the apparent absurdity
of a paradox challenges us to examine more closely the truth
it expresses in an unusual way.

Still, as the evangelists knew full well, Jesus' teaching,
however much he had intended it for all, had been widely
disbelieved and unheeded. What was the providential explanation of this fact? *To you,* says Jesus, that is, to his
disciples who have believed him, *has been given the mystery
of the kingdom of God; but to those outside* the community
of faith, *everything appears in parables.* This statement evidently depends on the material meaning of the word "parable"—that is, roundabout speech, enigma, riddle. He says,

then, first of all, that the same word which was light and truth for those who would believe could merely increase the darkness for those who would not see. This, as we know, is a common affirmation of the New Testament (cf. Jn 9:39). Matthew, who says the same thing more simply, adds (in vs. 12) a saying which Mark and Luke reproduce further on. His meaning is doubtless eschatological: the present loss or gain represented by unbelief or faith points to the eternal loss or gain that will follow in the final judgment.

But Mark and Luke go on to record the Lord as saying that he teaches in parables precisely *in order that* those destined not to believe *may look but not see, hear but not understand,* and so on. It is these words that cause most of the difficulty with this passage. Matthew may have been sensitive to the difficulty when he changed Mark's "in order that" to "because": the Lord conceals his teaching in parables *because* the people look but do not see, etc. It is doubtful, however, whether this alteration really changes Mark's meaning, particularly since Matthew, as is his custom, takes the opportunity to cite in full the "offending" passage from Is 6:9 f. that is implicit in the texts of Mark and Luke. Is Jesus saying then, after all, that his teaching is a deliberate source of confusion to those who lack faith?

Rather, we must understand the evangelists as finding a prophetic precedent for the present events in Israel's past and as citing the Old Testament in this spirit. God had commanded Isaiah: "Go and say to this people: 'Listen carefully, but you shall not understand! Look intently, but you shall know nothing!' You are to make the heart of this people sluggish, to dull their ears and close their eyes. Else their eyes will see, their ears hear, their heart understand, and they will turn and be healed." It was not that he willed Isaiah's preaching to have these results, but that he knew that it would. He willed the repentance that Isaiah's words would never effect, yet his mercy compelled him to offer grace in the full knowledge that it would be rejected. Even so, the Gospels tell us, what happened in Isaiah's time was now being repeated when one greater than all the prophets preached the fulfillment of all prophecy. Again the intention was otherwise, and again the result was the same.

Matthew concludes this section by appending a saying of Jesus for which Luke has found an even better context in another part of his Gospel (cf. Lk 10:23 f.). Here the blessedness of the believing disciples is contrasted with the sad state of those who look but do not see, listen but do not understand.

Mk 4:13–20
Mt 13:18–23
Lk 8:11–15
Faithful to his principle that the Lord explained all things to his disciples (Mk 4:34), Mark, and the other Synoptists with him, has inserted at this point an explanation of the parable of the sower. When it is read attentively, however, it speedily becomes evident that it is not so much an explanation of the parable as it is an adaptation of it to somewhat different purposes. Though the explanation begins with the assertion that *the seed is the word,* almost immediately it becomes instead the different kinds of men who receive the word. Various of the details of the parable have now been allegorized: the birds of the air, for example, appear as Satan, the tempter. No longer is it a question of the triumph of the kingdom over every opposition, of faith versus unbelief, but rather of various depths of faith and of the vicissitudes to which faith is subject.

The conclusion appears to be irresistible that this is an explanation given to the parable by the apostolic Church at a time when the conditions that it presupposes—persecutions, for example, and the lure of wealth—had become sources of danger to the fervor of Christian faith. The language and style of the passage confirm this conclusion. By no means, however, is its value thereby lessened at all. Quite to the contrary, it is a precious testimony to the way in which the word of the Lord remained living in his Church and was recognized as relevant to the present and future as well as the past.

Mk 4:21–25   Mark continues his treatment of the par-
Lk 8:16–18   ables, and Luke concludes his, with a series
                 of the Lord's sayings that had evidently
been composed into a unit by one of the oral or written
sources of tradition upon which the written Gospels depend. In Mark the schematic memory device by which the
sayings were linked together has also been preserved:

> verse 21: And he said to them . . .
>   (a) saying about the lamp and lampstand
>
> verse 22: For . . .
>   (b) saying about the hidden thing
>
> verse 24: And he said to them . . .
>   (c) saying about measure for measure
>
> verse 25: For . . .
>   (d) saying about haves and have-nots

Luke's version of this collection seems to be a summary of
Mark's; among other things, (c) has been truncated. Luke
also has (a), (b), (c), and (d) as individual units distributed throughout his Gospel (Lk 6:38, 11:33, 12:2,
19:26). Matthew, too, who does not reproduce the present
series (though we just saw him use [d] in Mt 13:12 above),
likewise has his own, and different, distribution of (a), (b),
(c), and (d) a second time (Mt 5:15, 7:2, 10:26, 25:29).
Both Matthew and Luke brought (c) into the context of the
Sermon on the Mount, but each gave it a different application.

What is the meaning of the series in this context? Because
of the artificial connection of ideas, the evangelists' intention
is not too clear. Possibly it is this: If there is at present any
obscurity about Jesus' teaching, it is not for the purpose of
keeping mankind forever in the dark. It will be the function of
his disciples to explain his teaching. Therefore they must
understand it in all its depth. Continual application will
deepen their understanding, but neglect of it will cause them
to lose what they thought they possessed. Even they can

prove to be the rocky ground where the seed of faith has been unable to grow.

Mk 4:26–29 The common theme of sowing has induced Mark to continue his "day of parables" with this one concerning the seed which grows of itself. Luke has finished with parables for the moment, but it is somewhat curious that Matthew, the great collector of parables, should have passed this one by. Perhaps it was because his concern throughout is with the part played by the believer in the furthering of the kingdom, and this parable was not easily adaptable to such a viewpoint.

The parable, in fact, is wholly taken up with the idea that the kingdom is the work of God and not of man. Just as the seed contains within itself an inner power that governs its life and growth, so the kingdom possesses its own dynamics beyond the sufferance or control of man. Of course, what is not said in the parable should not be pressed for implications that it does not intend. Man's part in the kingdom is not merely passive. The point is, however, that the kingdom is proof against both its enemies and friends alike, who cannot divert it from the "harvest" intended by God (Mark quotes Joel 4:13) either by malice or by well-intentioned bungling. The message is not insignificant for Christian faith and hope.

Mt 13:24–30 A message of equal significance is conveyed by this next parable related by Matthew only, again connected with the preceding by the figure of sowing. Here we see a wealthy farmer *sowing good seed in his field* and then entrusting it to the care of his servants. *While they were asleep*, however, *his enemy came* and oversowed the same field, this time with weeds, called *zizania* in the Gospel, a particular kind of grass that looks very much like wheat until it has fully developed. Such stories of revenge were well known in the East, where the desire to get even might lie hidden for long years awaiting a suitable opportunity to repay with interest.

In this story the master restrains the impatient zeal of his slaves, who are all for rooting out the weeds immediately even at the expense of losing the wheat. Rather, the time of harvest must be awaited. The lesson seems to be clear. The coming of the kingdom has not meant an automatic triumph of good over evil. The same field in which the seed of the word has been planted has also been sown with weeds. The time of God's eschatological judgment must be awaited with patience. And with faith. Good men are always subject to the temptation to despair over the apparent permanence of evil.

Mt 13:31–32 Though Matthew has put the preceding
Mk 4:30–32 parable in the context of Jesus' instruc-
Lk 13:18–19 tion of his disciples, it is very likely that it
was originally a response to his adversaries. It answers the objection: If the kingdom has really come, why has nothing happened? why do the evil yet prosper? The same judgment may be made concerning the following two parables, both of which Luke has placed, doubtless quite rightly, in relation to one of the Lord's controversies with the Jewish leadership in the synagogues.

What could be less like the kingdom of God as men had fondly anticipated it than the tiny band of Jesus' followers, disreputable, most of them, in the eyes of the world? It is precisely for this reason, Jesus replies, that the kingdom of God is *like a mustard seed*, the smallest seed known to a Palestinian farmer, which quite marvelously in a short period of growth is transformed into a veritable tree. The evangelists would have especial cause to recall this parable, they who had seen the Church develop in a short lifetime from a peculiarly Jewish institution into a movement in which men of all nations were finding a home. To call the mustard plant *a tree* (Matthew and Luke; Mark, more realistically, *the largest of the bushes*) is not too great an exaggeration, since it sometimes grows to a height of ten or twelve feet; however, there is an allusion here to an Old Testament figure of worldwide empire (cf. Dan 4:9, 18; Ezek 17:22 f., 31:6).

Mt 13:33   Much the same lesson is taught in the
Lk 13:20–21   parable of *the leaven,* omitted by Mark.
                 The mysterious action of yeast, quietly and
inexorably transforming the dough in which it has been
hidden, was another familiar analogy to illustrate how the
kingdom, tiny though it was, could eventually entirely
overcome its hostile environment. The unrealistically large
amount of flour that appears in the parable—*three measures*
are well over a bushel, or something like three dozen gallons
—serves to emphasize the point uncompromisingly.

Mk 4:33–34   Mark concludes his "day of parables" with
Mt 13:34–35   a summary statement. Because, as we have
                 seen, Mark relates Jesus' parabolic teach-
ing to the "messianic secret" by which he revealed himself
only by degrees, he makes a point that this method taught
the people *in a way they could understand,* while *privately
he explained everything to his disciples.* Matthew follows
Mark in the summary statement, and characteristically he
finds an Old Testament (that is, "prophetic") precedent for
the parabolic teaching in the words of Ps 78:2.

Mt 13:36–43   Matthew, however, unlike Mark, has not
                 yet done with Jesus' parables of the king-
dom. What follows is entirely proper to his Gospel, and he
has further separated it from what has gone before by noting
that it was a private instruction to the disciples, *in the house*
away from the crowds.

Matthew begins with an explanation of the parable of the
weeds (vss. 24–30 above), the only other passage in the
Gospels like the explanation that was given to the parable of
the sower. This second explanation has the character of the
first: it is a later application of the parable made by the
Church. The parable, first of all, has been allegorized,
though without any appreciable change in meaning thereby.
The perspective of the final judgment remains paramount.
What seems to have been changed, however, is the precise
effect of God's judgment on the kingdom: it is now a purifi-

cation *gathering from his kingdom all stumbling blocks and evildoers*. The evil over which the kingdom triumphs, in other words, is internal to it as well as external. In keeping with this, a distinction seems to be made between the kingdom of the Son of Man in verse 41 (the Church on earth?) and the kingdom of the Father in verse 43 (the eschatological kingdom?): compare 1 Cor 15:24. The lesson of this extension of the parable is quite as important as that of the parable itself. If good men are tempted to despair over the perdurance of evil, the temptation is the greater when evil is found in the very temple of God. However, the point previously made remains valid: a premature weeding would destroy the kingdom and nullify its redeeming power.

Mt 13:44–46   Matthew has just been speaking of the kingdom under the figure of seed sown in a field. It may be the tenuous connection formed by the word "field" that caused him to introduce here the double parable that begins with the kingdom as *a treasure hidden in a field*. Be that as it may, the point that is made by these two little parables is quite a different one: that no sacrifice is too great in order to acquire a place in God's kingdom. The relevance of this teaching both to our Lord's preaching and to the catechesis of the Church is obvious.

The idea of a treasure trove is exciting under any circumstances, but it could especially quicken the imagination in Palestine, where the civilizations of thousands of years lie below the surface of the ground, and a man with a plow may easily turn up a treasure in a field. Treasure found in this way belonged by law to the owner of the field: the parable presupposes that the man who found it was a sharecropper. In this instance the kingdom is figured as presented as it were by chance; in the parable of the *merchant's search for fine pearls* it is represented as the object of a lifelong quest. Both kinds of men find their way into the kingdom, and both have a common duty once they have found it.

Mt 13:47–50   Matthew's final parable continues the thought expressed by the parable of the weeds and especially by the explanation given to that parable. It is aptly situated in a context of instruction of Jesus' disciples, for it gives an answer to a question that would most naturally have been asked by those whom he had destined to be fishers of men. To whom must the kingdom be offered? Jesus' reply is that they must fish as with *a dragnet,* which is indifferent to its catch, dredging up in its path *things of every kind* (and not fish only). The sorting out will be left to God and his angels of judgment. Meanwhile, the Church can no more dissociate herself from sinners than could Jesus depart from the company of tax-gatherers and prostitutes that gained him a bad reputation in certain quarters. It is to make sinners into saints that the kingdom is preached.

Mt 13:51–53   Matthew concludes the parabolic discourse with a saying of the Lord that is a little parable in itself. To Jesus' question whether his disciples have understood the mystery of the kingdom of God their answer was a perhaps overconfident yes. On this assumption, then, he continues, *every scribe who has become a student of the kingdom of heaven is like the head of a house who can bring out of his storeroom both new things and old.* Just as a prudent householder knows what he has on hand and has seen to it that he has on hand the necessary provisions that must be acquired from time to time if he is to be a generous and capable host, so has the new "scribe" that has risen in Israel learnt to perform his task with equal efficiency. He has become a student of the kingdom as the scribes of Judaism were students of the Law. As there is a Christian interpretation of the Law that illuminates the old figures with new light (see Chapter 8, and especially on Mt 5:17–20), so is it with the Christian understanding of the kingdom of God. There is no doubt that the evangelist considers himself to be such a Christian scribe, and his Gospel to be this new kind of scribal instruction.

The "day of parables" ends with the conventional formula with which Matthew has concluded each of Jesus' major discourses (see above on Mt 7:28 f.).

11. REJECTION IN GALILEE

Mk 4:35–41
Lk 8:22–25
Mt 8:18, 23–27

After the parables, Mark and Luke now resume their story of the Galilean ministry. We rejoin Matthew, too, at the stage in his Gospel in which he is developing the picture of Jesus the model of missionaries, preparatory to the missionary discourse which the Lord gives to his disciples in chapter 10. Matthew, as we have seen and shall continue to see, is by far the most independent of the Synoptic Gospels in his ordering of the traditional material.

For an undisclosed reason, Jesus decides to cross to the other side of the Sea of Galilee, apparently using Peter's boat. Other boats also accompanied him, but presumably they turned back in the storm that ensued. As usual, Mark has the most vivid and lifelike account of what happens, giving evidence of dependence on an eyewitness. The sudden *squall* (so Mark and Luke; Matthew uses a word that properly means a much greater cataclysm) is not extraordinary. The Sea of Galilee, about 685 feet below sea level, is surrounded by mountains almost on all sides. Particularly at night (*as evening drew on*) a storm can quickly develop: as warm air from around the sea rises, cool air rushes down from the mountains to take its place, often causing a violent wind. At the northern end of the sea there are valleys to the east and west which help to funnel the wind over the water. Within the matter of a half hour the normally glassy surface can be transformed into chopping waves of seven or eight feet, more than enough to be a danger to light fishing craft.

The scene in the boat as it begins to ship water is one of the Gospel's best efforts at portraying both the essential humanity of Jesus and those qualities that caused other men to recognize in him that which transcended their human estate (Matthew brings this out in verse 27, saying that *the men marveled*). Jesus was asleep in all confidence, and doubtless honest bone-weariness from his labors, on *a cushion*, probably a wooden or leathern seat in the boat that doubled for this purpose. Mark's record of the disciples' appeal for help includes the tone of exasperation uttered by men in straits for which they hold Jesus responsible: *Master, do you not even care that we are perishing?* Matthew's, on the other hand, echoes the cry of liturgical prayer: *Save, Lord!*

There is no doubt that the Gospels recognize in Jesus' quieting of the storm an exercise of the same kind of power by which he cast out Satan and worked miracles of healing (Mk 4:39 quotes him as using the same command to the sea that is addressed to the demon in Mk 1:25). "Nature" miracles of this kind no less than the healing miracles pointed to the inbreaking of God's kingdom, a restoration of order which is the essence of the biblical idea of creation, and a subjection of all things to the rule of God and his Messiah. Such was the interpretation of the primitive Church, based on the evidence of competent witnesses. The witnesses themselves, in this passage under discussion, had not yet reached this interpretation, but their wonderment at what they had seen led them in its direction.

Mk 5:1–20   After the storm on the lake, according to
Lk 8:26–39 all the Synoptic Gospels, Jesus and his
Mt 8:28–34 disciples *came to the other shore;* Luke
            adds *opposite Galilee,* for technically they
were now in the territory of the Decapolis. Mark and Luke

(according to the evidence of the best manuscripts) call this *the land of the Gerasenes,* which is the first of the difficulties presented by this story. The story presupposes a site by the shore, but Gerasa, the modern Jerash, is some thirty miles away to the southeast. Matthew (in the best manuscripts) revises Mark's geography to read *the land of the Gadarenes,* but this is no real help: Gadara is still a good six miles from the shore. A variant in the manuscript of all three Gospels, but especially of Luke, reads *the land of the Gergesenes;* it is now generally agreed that this is the result of a "correction" supplied to the text by Origen in the third century, who was thinking of the Girgashites (in Greek, Gergesites) of the Old Testament (cf. Gen 10:16, 15:21; Deut 7:1; Jos 3:10, 24:12). There are other variants as well, all of which show that the geographical difficulty was recognized almost from the very beginning, by apparently everyone except Mark. It is likely enough that Mark, whose knowledge of and interest in northern Palestinian geography is rather casual, intended merely a generic reference to the Decapolis, of which Gerasa was a prominent town best known to him. However, there is a site on the eastern shore of the Sea of Galilee almost directly across from Magdala which seems to fit most of the requirements of the story. Here the bank is narrow and there is a precipice, while the mountainside contains natural caves, the customary location of *the tombs* presupposed by the Gospels. There is also a ruined village nearby which existed in Jesus' time; today it is called Kursi, but in Aramaic this would have been Kersa or Gersa. The similarity in names is at least suggestive.

An obvious discrepancy between the Gospel accounts that immediately springs to the eye is the number of demoniacs that are featured: one by Mark and Luke, two by Matthew. It might be easy to think of Mark and Luke passing over a second man without mention, since the person about whom they do speak became well known to the infant Church as a kind of pre-Christian evangelist of Christ to the Decapolis. Mark's story especially leaves us in no doubt that this is no routine recital but a documented history of a well-known

event involving a well-known person. On the other hand,
however, Matthew, or the tradition on which he depended,
shows a strong favoritism for two's. The two of this present
story may represent his way of catching up on or summariz-
ing the Gospel narrative. As we saw, he omitted the story of
the possessed man given in Mk 1:23–28; perhaps for this
reason, therefore, he now adds another demoniac to the one
which he found in Mark's Gerasene account. In a quite similar
way, as we shall see later on, Matthew (in 20:30) speaks
of two blind men to Mark's one, having omitted an earlier
story about a blind man described in Mk 8:22–26. In Mt
26:60 it is only Matthew who makes a point of there being
two witnesses at Jesus' trial. And there are other instances.
It may be that the fondness for two's has something to do
with the requirement of the Mosaic law for valid testimony
(Num 35:30; Deut 19:15; cf. Jn 8:17 and Mt 18:16), or it
may be due simply to the vagaries of the oral tradition on
which the evangelists depend.

This story at one and the same time is unique in the
Gospels and also partakes of characteristics common to other
descriptions of exorcisms. As before, the demons call Jesus
by name, simultaneously recognizing his authority with God
and fearing it; one present-day commentator has observed
that "these conceptions are perhaps less contrary to today's
psychiatry than they would have been fifty or sixty years
ago." Through the mouth of the insane man whose frenzies
are so graphically depicted by Mark, an appeal is made by
the forces of evil that Jesus *torment them not*. Matthew
speaks of a torment *before the time* and *here*, in the
Decapolis, introducing an eschatological note and taking
cognizance of Jesus' activity in a pagan land. On Jesus' en-
quiring the man's name (to know another's name, according
to universal ancient belief, is to possess some power over
that person), according to Mark and Luke he identifies himself as *Legion*, a term borrowed from the Roman military
unit composed of something over six thousand men. This can
be taken either as demoniacal arrogance and boasting or as
a cry of anguish wrung from the demoniac himself, recogniz-

ing the turmoil within his person. At all events, the exorcism follows in any case.

It is the circumstance of the exorcism involving the *herd of swine*—another indication that this event took place among Gentiles—that has always occasioned the greatest difficulty in this story. What was the purpose of this gesture? As far as the fact itself is concerned, it would not be contrary to the reality of the Gospel account to imagine the swine's headlong flight as caused by the paroxysms that usually accompanied exorcism. It was, certainly, an effective way of dramatizing the deliverance that had taken place. In the conversation between Legion and Jesus, however, the Gospels doubtless indicate their interpretation of what happened. Mark says that the demons asked not to be sent *out of the country*: another ancient belief put territorial limits on demoniacal activity; Luke has it that they asked not to be cast *into the abyss*. Probably Mark and Luke agree with Matthew, then, in understanding the episode of the Gerasene/Gadarene swine as exemplifying the preliminary character of Jesus' onslaught against Satan in the exorcisms of his public life. The exorcisms were evidence that the kingdom had indeed come, but the final banishment of the forces of evil would take place only in the eschatological age brought in by the redemptive death and resurrection of Christ.

Luke and Mark conclude the story by adding various details about the man who had been exorcised, who was instructed to make known what the power of God had effected for him. Matthew omits these details but joins the other Gospels in remarking how the inhabitants besought Jesus *to depart from them*. This doubtless speaks volumes about the hierarchy of values cherished in rural Gentile society. Understandably awe-struck by what had occurred, they nevertheless could not bother to discover whether this man's mysterious power was destined for their good or their ill. They could only see in Jesus a threat to their settled way of life. Their pigs were more important to them than the life of the spirit.

Mk 5:21–43   Mark and Luke continue the story with two
Lk 8:40–56   connected miracle events that are set in
Mt 9:18–26   Capernaum; Matthew has the same nar-
              rative, before which, however, he inserts
three passages that we have already seen above in parallel.
As usual, Mark's is the lengthy, detailed account which in this
instance is abbreviated by Luke and condensed even more
by Matthew.

Jairus, unnamed by Matthew, was doubtless quite a distinguished person, and thus his humble mien in Jesus'
presence testifies to his sincerity and the urgency of his
appeal. He is called *a ruler* by Matthew and identified
by Mark and Luke as *one of the leaders of the synagogue.*
The leaders of the synagogue were the lay officials who not
only determined the order of its services (see above on Lk
4:16–22a) but exercised other functions of prestige in Jewish
society. Jairus' prominence undoubtedly accounted for the
great crowd which accompanied Jesus and his disciples
responding to his request. In Matthew's Gospel, Jairus' request is from the beginning for a restoration of life: this is the
only such miracle recorded by Matthew. Also Matthew notes
that Jesus *rose* to accompany Jairus: the First Gospel has
Jesus at table in the house of Levi at this juncture (cf.
9:10) rather than just having recrossed the Sea of Galilee.

The story of the healing of the *woman afflicted with a
flow of blood for twelve years* is drastically reduced to a few
lines by Matthew, but Luke's and especially Mark's accounts
contain various items of interest that should by no means
be overlooked. For one thing, whereas Mark offers a fairly
testy commentary on Near Eastern medicine to which his
own experience might have contributed—*having suffered
much from many doctors and spent all she had, and having
got no better but rather become worse*—Luke says instead
that *she had not been able to be healed by anyone* (the
having spent all her means on doctors of some Lucan
manuscripts is probably a harmonizing addition to the text).
A touch of this kind leads us to suspect that Col 4:14
should be taken at the letter and that Luke was using a

euphemism dictated by the code of medical ethics. Far more important, however, are the reactions of Jesus to the woman's approach, particularly as related by Mark.

The woman believed that she would be healed *merely by touching his garment;* Luke and Matthew speak of *the tassel of his garment,* referring to the Jewish practice prescribed by Num 15:38 f. and Deut 22:12. This was not necessarily superstitious in intent. Jesus said that it was the woman's faith that saved her, and the desire to achieve physical contact with the object of one's faith is not unsound. Her touch was covert because legally she was unclean (cf. Lev 15:25–27; Num 19:11). Jesus' question and Mark's notation that *he was looking about in the crowd* indicate a genuine search for information, not playacting. Similarly, Peter's and the other disciples' somewhat exasperated reactions, pointing to the jostling and milling crowd surrounding Jesus, suggest accurate historical recollection rather than dramatic invention. Mark's explanation is that *he perceived that the power which proceeded from him had gone forth.* All of this adds up to a primitive and perhaps ingenuous appreciation of Jesus' consciousness of his role as the instrument of God's healing power, toned down or omitted in the parallels, but all the more valuable for these reasons. This is a passage that must be taken into firm consideration whenever it is a question of determining the extent to which the expression "emptying" in Phil 2:7 means precisely what it says. Jesus partook of our human condition wholly and exactly. The Gospel insists, at the same time, that he was an active cause and not merely a passive occasion of the divine power operating in and through him.

Faith had cured the woman and would save Jairus' daughter. Jesus told the distraught father to disregard the message of death and to *believe* (in Mark, *continue to believe*). Disregarding also the professional mourners (cf. 2 Chron 35:25; Jer 9:16 f.) and others present who greeted with mocking skepticism his assertion that the girl was *not dead but asleep* (cf. Jn 11:11), he entered her chamber, taking with him her parents and three of his disciples, Peter and the two brothers James and John. These three form a select group within the Twelve, which on more than one occasion is accorded an extraordinary witness to his works. Mark recalls the Aramaic words of Jesus' command to the girl, paraphrased by Luke and omitted by Matthew. Literally, *talitha kum* means "little girl, get up." The noun is the feminine form of *talya,* a word which in Aramaic signifies "lamb," "child," or "servant" (cf. Jn 1:28–34; cf. also the ambiguity of *pais* in Mt 8:5–13). A great number of manuscripts of Mark have *talitha kumi,* which is "better" Aramaic, and for that reason evidently an elegant scribal correction of the original text. Mark and Luke conclude the story with Jesus' usual injunction to keep the matter quiet for the preservation of the "messianic secret" (a motive that did not obtain in pagan Gerasa/Gadara).

Mk 6:1–6a   Pursuing Mark's chronicle, we now come to
Mt 13:54–58 a passage which intentionally achieves a
Lk 4:22b–30 climax in the Second Gospel: the rejection
of Jesus by the people of Nazareth and the beginning of the end of the Galilean ministry. Though Matthew's order of events is different, he too has placed his parallel version in somewhat the same position in his Gospel. It follows there the "day of parables" and begins the narrative section leading into the fourth of Jesus' major discourses (ch. 18), a section in which we see the Lord concentrating more and more on the instruction of his disciples and more or less resigned to continued rejection by people and leaders alike. Luke, as we remember, has an entirely different sequence for this episode, having set it at the beginning of the Galilean ministry (see above in Chapter 6).

Luke (in 4:16–22a) has described for us the synagogue procedure presupposed by Mark and Matthew as they open their accounts. Jesus' teaching on this day was the culmination of many words and works which his compatriots had witnessed or about which they had been told. *Where did he get all this?* Such questions as Mark and Matthew quote could have been asked in honest admiration, as is certainly the reaction depicted in Lk 4:22a. Do the Marcan and Matthaean versions of this story come, like the Lucan, from a fusion of experiences at Nazareth, friendly as well as hostile? This may be. Whatever the original import of the questions, however, as they now stand the evangelists intend to show them as hostile, the accent resting on the repeated deprecatory *where*. For the Nazarethites are about to illustrate the principle of human nature expressed in a thousand proverbs and by Jesus in the saying earlier ascribed to him by Jn 4:44 and now by the Synoptics: *a prophet does not go unhonored except in his native country*. Familiarity, which breeds contempt, is also an obstacle to faith. The people of Nazareth already knew too much about Jesus, or thought they knew, even to believe their own eyes and ears which told them that he was more than they could ever know.

Luke has the Nazarethites identify Jesus as *the son of Joseph*, Matthew as *the carpenter's son whose mother's name is Mary*. Both these versions employ routine language. Much more unusual is Mark's (according to the best manuscripts) *the carpenter, Mary's son*. The supposition, here and elsewhere in the Gospels, seems to be that Joseph is dead, and it is only to be imagined that in Nazareth Jesus would have been associated with his father's craft both in fact and in the mind of the people. What is completely extraordinary is that a man should be called by his mother's name: in Jewish mouths this would imply a reflection on his legitimacy, which does not appear to be the intention of the text. It is probable, therefore, that this is Mark's title for Jesus and, if so, perhaps an indication of his acceptance of the tradition of Jesus' virgin birth explicitly affirmed elsewhere by Matthew and Luke.

Matthew and Mark quote the Nazarethites as citing in evidence against Jesus apparently all the closest of his relatives they can name: his father and mother, *his brothers*, four of whom are named, *and his sisters, all of whom are here with us*—the last, seemingly a larger group, would represent Jesus' women relatives who had married into various

families of Nazareth. Of the four brothers mentioned, *James,
Joseph* (in Mark, *Joses*), *Judas, and Simon,* at least the first
two are elsewhere identified as sons of another woman than
the mother of Jesus (Mk 15:40, 47; Mt 27:56). If the James
of this list was the "other" James among the Twelve, he was
the son of a man named Alphaeus (Mt 10:3 and parallels).
If the Judas of the list is the person to whom tradition
ascribes the Epistle of Jude, the Scripture makes him a
brother of this same James (Jude 1).

Because of their lack of faith, say Mark and Matthew,
Jesus *could not work any miracle there.* This is, as Mark
shows, one of the Semitic "relative absolutes": he did heal
a few sick people. Nazareth stands as typical of the barren-
ness of unbelief. Luke underlines this while showing its petti-
ness and pointlessness as well, possibly combining events
from yet other encounters of Jesus in this city. *Doctor, heal
yourself!* is perhaps a petulant and mocking retort inspired by
Is 61:1 which Jesus had cited. The Nazarethites apparently
reproached Jesus for making Capernaum rather than Nazareth the center of his ministry in Galilee. He replied by re-
minding them of *Elijah and the widow of Zarephath* (cf.
1 Kgs 17) and *Elisha and Naaman the Syrian:* great prophetic figures often rejected by their own people, whose great
works were expended not on Israel but on Gentiles with
whom they found faith. It is Luke, too, who relates—somewhat unusually for him—the violent reaction of Jesus' compatriots who tried, or at least strongly desired, to lynch him.

Mk 6:6b–13   It is necessary again to do con-
Lk 9:1–6   siderable violence to the order of
Mt 9:35, 10:7–11, 14   Matthew's Gospel simply to keep
                    it in parallel with the less com-
plicated disposition of Mark and Luke. The passage that we
have before us Matthew has incorporated into the second of
the major discourses which set forth the teaching of Jesus;
it is even necessary, therefore, to break up one of the cherished five instructions to maintain our parallel. The narrative
nucleus common to the three Gospels and occurring roughly

in the same "chronology" justifies this procedure, however, and we can extract it from the Matthaean heart of the discourse which we reserve for later treatment. This is admittedly not an ideal way to approach the several Gospels, but then again we have already settled for something less than the ideal.

The parallels in Matthew and Luke, who have worked from independent sources, help to explain the importance of this development in Mark. The crisis pointed up by the rejection at Nazareth continues. There is a strong note of urgency and of working against time in Jesus' tour of *all the towns and villages, teaching in their synagogues and proclaiming the good news of the kingdom, healing every disease and every sickness.* We have the impression that Jesus appreciates as never before the immensity of the task with which he is challenged and the odds against his succeeding.

It is in this light that we should understand his missioning of the Twelve. This was no long-range plan for providing a succession to himself, despite the fact that Matthew has made it the precedent for such an idea of the apostolate in his Gospel. Rather, it was a practical measure dictated by a present need. The Twelve could be his presence in many places at one time in proclaiming the kingdom here and now. Hence they were empowered to do precisely what he was doing: to preach, to heal, to exorcise—the signs of the advent of the kingdom of God.

In keeping with the urgency of their mission are the practical instructions given them for their conduct on the road. They should go *two by two*, says Mark; this was a Jewish custom (cf. Lk 7:18; Jn 1:37), not mentioned here by Matthew or Luke (but cf. Lk 10:1). They were, further, to live strictly off the land, like an invading army, and to carry with them, practically speaking, only the clothes on their backs. Some of the details here are spelt out differently by Mark (*take a staff, wear sandals*) and Matthew and Luke (*no staff, no sandals*), but the spirit is the same; it is doubtless impossible, and in any case inconsequential, to decide which version of the Lord's injunction is the more "primitive."

The mission of the Twelve constituted them what Jesus himself had become, an itinerant preacher of the kingdom. The urgency of their mission is also communicated in his instruction to *shake the dust from your feet* of any town or village that would not receive them. This expressive gesture was intended to be a sermon in itself, to indicate that the inhabitants were taking upon themselves the consequences of a spiritual attitude that marked their land as heathen and unclean.

Describing the beginning of the mission of the Twelve, Mark alone adds the detail that they were *anointing sick people with oil*. The use of oil in healing was contemporary practice (cf. Lk 10:34) and had a religious significance in the apostolic Church (cf. Jas 5:14). It is not impossible, therefore, that Mark both recalls a factual occurrence and insinuates an apostolic precedent for one of the rites of the Church with which he was familiar.

Mk 6:14–29   It is somewhat extraordinary that Mark,
Lk 9:7–9   usually so singleminded in his choice of ma-
Mt 14:1–12   terial to make up the Gospel of Jesus Christ,
                  should have devoted the attention that he
has to the story of the Baptist's execution, a story that involves Jesus neither directly nor indirectly. The explanation is partly that Mark, who is a stickler for detail, needed the story to supply the background for Herod's superstitious fear related by the evangelist in the verses that now constitute its prologue—verses which do involve Jesus very much. Also, the story provides an artificial time lag to separate the account of the mission of the Twelve from that of their return immediately after. Matthew has given one of his customary summaries of the story, placing it topically in relation to Jesus' rejection at Nazareth. Luke has retained only the prologue. The execution itself is the kind of motif that he avoids; besides, he had already said about it as much as he felt it necessary to say earlier in his own way (see above on Lk 3:18–20).

The tradition relates that *Herod the king* (Luke and Matthew more accurately refer to Antipas as *the tetrarch*) was disposed to credit the popular, and singularly uninformed, opinion that Jesus was *John the Baptist raised from the dead.* Apparently one amateur accounting for Jesus' miraculous powers was that they were the new manifestation of the famous preacher whose earlier ministry had not been accompanied by miraculous signs (cf. Jn 10:41). Herod's information doubtless came from his courtiers, lax Jews who had heard of Jesus with amused disinterest and followed his career by hearsay here and there. Herod had thought to rid himself of the troublesome Baptist, and now, here was the trouble all over again! Others were speaking of Jesus as *Elijah* or another *prophet like one of the prophets* of old (see above on Jn 1:19–24). Luke alone adds that Herod *kept seeking to see* Jesus, and later Luke alone will record the gratification of his wish (cf. Lk 23:8).

The story of the Baptist's execution by Herod Antipas is one of the few instances of a Gospel account which is paralleled in profane history (chiefly by Flavius Josephus in his *Antiquities* XVIII. 116–19). The two histories do not agree in all details but rather complement one another. Antipas *imprisoned John on account of Herodias, his brother Philip's wife.* In the Gospel the explanation of this is that the Baptist was denouncing the tetrarch for the violation of the Mosaic law (Lev 18:16, 20:21). Antipas had taken as his wife Herodias, his niece as well as his brother's wife, a woman of about thirty-five who had already borne her husband a daughter, the girl who figures in the Gospel story and whose name was Salome. Herodias had repudiated her husband by a divorce recognized in Rome but not in Jewish law. Salome, as it happened, later married her uncle, Antipas' brother, the tetrarch Philip. It may be that the Gospel has followed a tradition which had confused the names of Salome's husband and Herodias' (who is not otherwise known in profane history except as "Herod"); given this incestuous entanglement, confusion is hardly surprising.

To marry Herodias, Antipas had repudiated his first wife, the daughter of the Nabataean king Aretas, who in revenge

eventually gathered an army and defeated Antipas. It is in
this context that Josephus explains the Baptist's execution,
as a political measure taken by Antipas against a man whom
he feared as too popular with the masses and therefore a
potential leader of rebellion against his rule. Though Mark
says nothing of this and speaks instead of a *birthday banquet*
at which Antipas was persuaded to kill John, the military and
political background explains the presence of the *military
officers and leading men of Galilee* which he notes; the scene,
according to Josephus, was Antipas' palace at Machaerus in
Perea, on the Nabataean frontier. Neither Josephus nor the
Gospel provides us with any information on the time of this
event in relation to the ministry of Jesus.

Extrabiblical history contains nothing as interesting as the
Gospel story of Salome's dance, to say nothing of the Freud-
ian paraphrase by Oscar Wilde, who unfortunately erred in
several points of fact, including the timely demise of the cold-
blooded young murderess. The biblical tradition rings true,
however, in any number of details. The moral swampland
of the Herodian family has not been exaggerated, nor has
the complicated character of Antipas been caricatured, a
man who was hagridden in more than a single sense.

Mk 6:30–33   Only Matthew connects what follows with
Lk 9:10–11   the execution of the Baptist: Jesus' with-
Mt 14:13   drawal *by boat to a deserted place* was,
Jn 6:1–4   in his mind, a prudent removal from the
territory of Herod Antipas. Mark and Luke,
however, understand it as a retreat for the twelve *apostles*
(who, incidentally, are given this name in this passage) after
their arduous mission tour. Luke specifies the place to which
they withdrew as near the *city called Bethsaida* Julias, in the
territory of the tetrarch Philip, the birthplace of Peter and
Andrew (Jn 1:44). Mark explains that the crowds which,
despite Jesus' intentions, *assembled there before them* were
Galileans who had seen them depart and had followed them
by foot on the shore. John, whom at long last we rejoin
in these parallels, tells us nothing contrary to any of this; we

shall discuss the Johannine "chronology" later. He indicates
that the gathering was due to Jesus' reputation for miracles:
as both he and the Synoptics have shown many times, this
was not invariably a good sign. John locates the scene that
is about to ensue *on the mountain,* a determination that is
unparalleled here by the Synoptics (but paralleled in Mt
15:29); see on Mk 3:13–19; Lk 6:12–16; Mt 5:1 f. John
adds that *the Jewish feast of Passover was near.* He does this
for a theological purpose, since he has in mind the Christian
passover figured for him in the miracle of the loaves; however,
the Synoptic story also presupposes quite incidentally that
it was spring (cf. Mk 6:39).

Mk 6:34–44   The miracle of the loaves, the only miracle
Lk 9:12–17   story found in all four of the Gospels, raises
Mt 14:14–21   innumerable questions. The question that
Jn 6:5–15   most naturally comes to the mind of twen-
              tieth-century man, or at least of most twen-
tieth-century men, probably is: What actually happened?
This is not a question to divide the believer from the unbeliever, but one which the believer can also ask. We frequently speak of this event as a "multiplication of loaves,"
but the Gospels do not call it that. "Multiplication of loaves"
is an interpretation of the event—a rationalistic interpretation,
if you will—made by one who accepts it as a miracle. It
may be, and probably is, the correct interpretation, but an
interpretation it is in any case. If we ask, "How otherwise
could five thousand people be fed with five loaves and two
dried fish, and fragments be gathered into twelve baskets,
than by a miraculous multiplication of food?" we ask a legitimate question; but we imply the same rationalist principle
that accounts for the hundreds of alternative solutions that
have been proposed by those who believe that miracles do
not (not necessarily cannot) happen. Let us leave the matter
there. Everyone is free to speculate, but speculation begins
where the Gospel leaves off. It is sufficient for our purposes
simply to see what the Gospel has said. The Gospel has told
us what happened, but now how. It will have to be added,

however, that what happened, as the Gospels tell it, was
something indeed miraculous, and any explanation that does
not do justice to this fact is not faithful to the biblical record.

The next question may be easier to answer: What did the
miracle signify in the life of Jesus? Matthew and Mark tell
us explicitly that it was a work of *compassion*, because Jesus
saw that the people were *like sheep with no shepherd*. John
especially brings out the disparate character of the crowds
who witnessed and participated in the act of Jesus. Jesus'
solicitude was not simply for the people's material hunger,
but to represent to them the kingdom of God which could,
if they would allow it, assuage their often unfelt hunger for
the things of the spirit. For Jesus the miracle of the loaves
anticipates the eschatological messianic banquet (see below
on Lk 14:15–24; cf. Mk 14:25 and parallels; see also Apo
19:9). It is a parable in action of the kingdom, the merciful
dragnet of God drawing into itself things of every kind (see
above on Mt 13:47–50).

It is this significance which the Gospels develop in inter-
preting the miracle as a foreshadowing of the Eucharist,
the messianic banquet of the Church. The Synoptics describe
Jesus' actions in terms that are allusively liturgical: *he took
. . . looked up to heaven, blessed, and broke . . .* (cf. Acts
2:42). John does not have this much detail, but on the other
hand his word for "blessed" (*eucharistēsas*) is more suggestive than the Synoptics' (the same word is used in
1 Cor 11:23, in Paul's account of the institution of the
Eucharist, and by Mk 8:6 and Mt 15:36 in the doublet
narrative of the loaves which we shall consider later). While
the Synoptics say that Jesus gave the blessed food to the
disciples who in turn gave it to the people, a perfectly natural
detail when we think of the logistical problems involved in
feeding a crowd of five thousand people, John's omission
of the detail may well be deliberate in view of the circumstances of the Last Supper. In John the gathering (*synaxis*)
of the fragments, noted by all the Gospels, is given as a command of Christ. The Didache uses this term for the gathering
of the Eucharistic bread, and it likewise uses the same word
(*klasmata*) for the Eucharistic bread that is found in all four

Gospels to designate the fragments of the loaves of this story.

Mark and John especially have distinctive details to contribute that make this something quite different from a stylized tale of wonders. The somewhat querulous retort made by the disciples to the Lord's initial command to feed the people in Mark sounds like a conversation taken from life. In John it is turned into an interrogation to test Philip's faith made by a Master who is in complete control of the situation; it is likewise a continuation of the Mosaic theme (cf. Num 11:13, 22). The apostle Andrew in John's account emerges from the anonymity that generally surrounds most of the Twelve in the Gospels. He finds a boy, presumably a hawker of food, who provides the *five loaves*—John alone tells us they were *barley loaves*, the bread of the poor—and *two fish*—John alone tells us they were *dried fish*, though in any case we should doubtless have presumed this. Perhaps the most delightful descriptive detail of all is Mark's *they sat down, flower beds here and flower beds there, in hundreds and fifties*, which paints for us a vivid picture of the gay bright colors of Oriental dress clashing with the green of the hillslope.

A much more important contribution, from the standpoint of the Gospel history, is that made by John in his final two verses. In the sign which they have experienced the crowds recognize in Jesus the prophet-like-Moses of Deut 18:18 (see above on Jn 1:19–24). So much to the good. But their enthusiasm is deceived and misguided. John has the same view of this period of the Galilean ministry as do the Synoptics: in various ways, but in every genuine sense of his mission as he conceived it, Jesus is being rejected. *They were about to come and forcibly make him king*, their Jewish Messiah (see above on Lk 4:3–13 and parallel). Therefore *he fled back to the mountain alone*. The "alone" hangs impressively in the air. What of the faithful Twelve?

Mk 6:45–46 Mt 14:22–23a Jn 6:16–17a	The answer to this question seems to be given us by Matthew and Mark when they continue their chronicle stating that Jesus *forced his disciples to get into the boat*

and precede him to the other shore of the Sea of Galilee.
(Mark adds *toward Bethsaida,* precisely where, according to
Luke at least, they already were! All in all, it seems we
must conclude that for Mark Bethsaida, like Gerasa, was
merely a name he had heard, and that he had only the
vaguest notion of its situation. To imagine another Bethsaida
on the western shore is quite unnecessary.) Though the
Synoptic Gospels said nothing of the attempt of the crowds
to make Jesus king, they appear to know something of what
happened, and they appear to recognize that the Twelve
were also involved in it. It is really not surprising that the
disciples, too, should have caught the messianic fever of the
multitudes, and that Jesus quickly had to separate the one
group from the other and himself from both. How prudent
this was, would appear on the morrow.

At all events, Jesus was quite alone as he prayed in the
hills near Bethsaida that night after the miracle of the loaves.

12. THE BREAD OF LIFE

Mk 6:47–52   This chapter begins, as did the last, with
Mt 14:23b–33 a storm on the Sea of Galilee. The pas-
Jn 6:17b–21   sage before us, small though it is, has
              stirred up storms of its own. No other
miracle story of the Gospels has been more questioned than
this one. The issue is not the possibility of miracles: for those
for whom all miracles are alike impossible, this miracle story
is hardly different from any other. It is, rather, those who
are unembarrassed by miracles in principle and who believe
in the Gospel miracles specifically who experience difficulty
with this one. Many Christian commentators, some Catholics
included, prefer to understand this episode as a symbolic
narrative, a parable constructed in Christian tradition, rather
than as a record of sober historical fact. They would not
thereby necessarily insist that it is purely symbolic, that
there was no historical event at all that could underlie it.

Why is this story so much different from the other miracle
stories of the Gospel? For one thing, unlike Jesus' other
miracles, this one does not seem to go anywhere. Jesus did
not work miracles for their own sake, but to reveal himself
in response to faith, to proclaim the inbreaking of the kingdom of God over death and evil and sin, to save men. In this
instance Jesus did not save the disciples from any peril to

their life: the storm, which is hardly mentioned by John, was merely tossing them about a bit and delaying their progress. Secondly, what are we to make of Mark's statement that *he was going to pass them by?* This makes admirable sense as a narrative device to elicit a response from the disciples, but it is more difficult to explain historically. The same may be said of the disciples' mistaking Jesus for *a ghost* (Matthew and Mark), a detail consonant with a story of men seeing a figure *walking on the sea* from their boat far out on the water (*twenty-five or thirty stadia* from land, says John, or about two and a half miles) in the middle of the night *around the fourth watch* (after three in the morning). At all events, whether the story is to be taken as a parable or as factual reporting, there is no doubt that it is concerned with a miraculous power that is ascribed to Jesus and recognized as such. It is not a story that grew out of some misunderstanding or exaggeration—the disciples mistakenly observing Jesus wading in the water near the shore, for example. Such an interpretation would submit the Gospels to a childish rationalism of which they are undeserving.

The three evangelists who have reproduced this story have done so apparently for three distinct purposes. Mark's intention seems to be summed up in his final verse. *They were astounded,* he says, now that they had seen Jesus walking on the waters, *for they had not understood about the loaves; and the reason for this was that their minds were completely blinded.* Their blindness, Mark suggests, was not malicious, but due simply to a lack of sight that had not yet been awakened by faith. They had witnessed the miracle of the loaves with little more, if any, understanding than was evinced by the crowds of whom John spoke in 6:14 f. Mark does not necessarily say that Jesus' walking on the water helped them to a better understanding, merely that it added to their astonishment. Miracles, this seems to be the point, do not direct and determine faith, but rather they are defined and determined by it.

Matthew, for his part, introduces the story of Peter also walking upon the water, but only for a while and only to underscore the vast gulf that separates his human powers from those of the Master who sustains him. It is doubtless this spectacle above all that persuades the disciples, according to Matthew, to confess of Jesus, *Truly you are Son of God!* Strictly speaking, this is, of course the confession of full Christian faith. Whatever meaning Matthew intended it to have at this point, it is in some sense an anticipation of Peter's confession on behalf of the disciples in Mt 16:13–20. Correspondingly, this latter passage by no means has the climactic function that the parallel Mk 8:27–30 does for the Second Gospel.

According to John also the disciples confess Christ, but later (cf. 6:68 f. below). For John the walking on the water is one of Jesus' seven "signs," as was the miracle of the loaves (see above on 2:1–11), the full meaning of which is brought out in the lengthy discourse that follows. John undoubtedly sees a theophany in Jesus' appearance on the water and his identification of himself as *I am* (vs. 20, *egō eimi*: the ineffable name of Yahweh as translated by the Septuagint in Ex 3:14). The Synoptics have the same expression, but doubtless in the conventional meaning, "It is I." In the next verse John observes that the Lord thus revealed (cf. the imagery of Pss 29:3, 10, 46:2–4, etc.) the disciples *wanted therefore to take into the boat* (contrast the Synoptics).

Mk 6:53–56   We have been without the help of Luke
Mt 14:34–36   in the preceding passage, though we have
Jn 6:22–25   had and continue to have an unexpected parallel in John. The episode of Jesus' walking on the water marks the beginning of Luke's "great omission" of Marcan material (Mk 6:45–8:26 is without Lucan parallels), which is something of an anomaly when we take into consideration Luke's fairly consistent adherence to Mark both before and after the omission. From this fact some have theorized that the edition of Mark used by Luke did not contain the omitted portions, but this seems unlikely. Rather, it is probable that most of the "great omission" was made by

Luke on principle, together with some contiguous passages that went along as a matter of course. The story we have just concluded, for example, he probably left out for some of the reasons we noted on beginning this chapter. It is not Luke's way to introduce passages, or even verses, that could cause difficulty for his readers.

It is Matthew, Mark, and John, therefore, who now return us to Galilee. While the Synoptics offer a summary description of Jesus' healing ministry in the region of Gennesaret, however, John is busied with the crowds of yesterday, who eventually make their way to Capernaum. It is important to John that it should be those who witnessed the miracle of the loaves—not all five thousand, of course—who engage in the dialogue that ensues. Gennesaret is the fertile plain, only a few miles long, that borders the Sea of Galilee south of Capernaum.

There is no Synoptic parallel to the Johannine Eucharistic discourse that now begins. As we know by now, John's Gospel represents the ultimate development of a tendency, the opposite end of which is Mark with Matthew forming an intermediate stage, to portray the revelation of God in Christ less in action than in extended doctrine, the fruit of a long generation of Christian meditation and enlightenment in the Spirit. The present discourse is very much like the preceding ones in John. It begins with a question which is answered ironically in the development of the discourse: not how Jesus came to be in Capernaum is the vital issue, but whence he came to them as Bread of Life. The people address him as *Rabbi,* just as did Jesus' first disciples (Jn 1:38) and Nicodemus (Jn 3:2) at the beginnings of their encounters with him.

Jn 6:26–51a Their curiosity about the way of his coming to Capernaum is symptomatic of their material thinking. Just as the woman at the well could think first of all only of natural water (Jn 4:15), they have been thinking only of the material bread with which he has fed them. *Not because you have seen signs:* the signs (in the

Johannine sense) were there, but they have not recognized them. He therefore bids them raise their minds to higher things. Just as they must *labor* for their daily bread, so must they for *the food which endures unto eternal life*. The revelation of God as "bread" or "food" was a recognized Jewish figure.

Labor? What work must they do to perform *the works of God*? Their question seems to presuppose another misunderstanding: they are taking his meaning to be that there is something they can do which will provide them with a miraculously eternal bread. Jesus' reply is that the bread of which he speaks God gives to him who has *faith in him whom he sent*: the labor of which he has spoken involves the total submission of self to the Word of God in Christ. Persisting in their superficiality and understanding by faith merely human credibility, they ask, and not too politely, *what sign* he has to offer, at the same time minimizing the miracle of the loaves—the sign which yesterday had moved them to want to proclaim him king! Jesus, after all, had but fed them with earthly bread, whereas in the days of Moses *he gave them bread from heaven to eat* (Neh 9:15).

Not so, replies Jesus. First of all, it was not Moses but God who fed Israel with the manna. Secondly, the manna was heavenly bread only after a fashion. Only the Father now gives *true* bread from heaven (see above on Jn 1:9-13). This bread, which truly *comes down from heaven*, does not merely sustain life but *gives life to the world*. At this point the people reiterate the petition of the woman at the well (Jn 4:15); they recognize, at least, that he is speaking of something of which he alone is the source. This bread he now identifies with himself: *I am the bread of life*. This is the first of a series in John's Gospel (cf. also 8:12, 10:7, 9, 10:11, 14, 11:25, 14:6, 15:1, 5) in which Jesus employs the "I am" of Old Testament revelation (cf. especially Is 43:10, 46:4, 51:12) in connection with the New Testament kingdom as realized in himself. We have already seen the Synoptic Gospels' view of the miracle of the loaves as an enacted "parable of the kingdom" (see above on Mk 6:34-44 and parallels). In John's Gospel, which contains no parables, various of the themes of the parables of the kingdom are personified in Christ, who is for the evangelist the glorified Christ identical with his Church. *You have seen me,* Jesus continues, *yet you have not believed.* Their unbelief is culpable and evidence that they have not received and acted on the grace of God. Christ has come into the world precisely to be the instrument of God's grace, to do his will, that men might have eternal life and rise with the just *on the last day.*

The hostility of the crowds, latent up to this point, from verse 41 on becomes overt. Perhaps for this reason John now refers to them *as the Jews,* the term which he so often uses for the unbelieving Palestinian "world" of Jesus' own time (see above on Jn 1:9–13). Like their ancestors of the time of Moses, they *grumbled* at what they had received (cf. Ex 16:2, 8 f.). They reject Jesus' prophetic word for the same reason alleged by the Synoptic Gospels in relation to the incident at Nazareth seen in our last chapter: this is the Johannine parallel to Mk 6:1–6a and parallels above. Jesus' response to this challenge is mainly to reiterate what he has said previously, in addition to quoting Is 54:13. *Not that anyone has ever seen the Father:* see above on Jn 1:18.

Jn 6:51b–59   This little section forms the properly Eucharistic part of Jesus' discourse: *The bread which I shall give is my flesh for the life of the world.* Up to this point it has been a question of a bread of life=Christ which God gives=reveals to men; now it is Christ who gives this bread=his flesh=himself. The change of direction as well as of intent legitimately raises the question whether these verses are original to the discourse or are an insertion into it. There is no reason at all, however, to doubt that they are original to John's Gospel. This discourse, like others in the Gospel, has been composed of parallel strands of Jesus' teaching in the Johannine tradition; the composition was not necessarily made all at one time. The Eucharistic doctrine itself is perfectly in keeping with John's other sacramental interests. Here the Eucharist is connected with the redemptive life and death of Jesus as Eucharist is connected with the redemptive life and death of Jesus as is done later by the Synoptic Gospels and also by Paul (cf. 1 Cor 11:24).

John's Eucharistic word is "flesh" (*sarx*), whereas in Paul and the Synoptic Gospels it is the "body" (*sōma*) of Christ; in the early patristic Church both terms were used indifferently. The Johannine formula is probably closer to the Semitic expression employed by Jesus. For the significance of "flesh," see above on Jn 1:14 in Chapter 2.

The interchange between Jesus and his listeners continues in the Johannine pattern. Like Nicodemus (Jn 3:4) and the woman at the well (Jn 4:11), the Jews tend to take Jesus' statement in a crudely material sense. They would not have been encouraged to understand it merely as a figure of speech: in Hebrew "to eat someone's flesh"="to slander," "backbite" (so in Ps 27:2; a similar expression is found in Aramaic in Dan 3:8). Neither is Jesus' meaning figurative, though it is spiritual. Six times over he repeats his previous assertion, that to have eternal life it is necessary to eat his flesh and drink his blood. "Flesh and blood" is the common Semitic way of referring to the whole person. Through the Eucharist the Christian is made to share in the life of Christ, which is in turn the life which the Son shares with the Father. *I live because of the Father:* as usual, the divine life of Christ is not considered as isolated in itself apart from the economy of salvation, in which *the living Father sent* the Son into the world. *This is the bread:* thus the connection is made with the preceding part of the discourse. It is part of the technique of John's Gospel, therefore, that the bread which is Christ of the preceding verses could have been intended in a twofold sense all along, referring also to the Eucharistic bread in which Christ is present to the Church.

These things he said in a synagogue instruction at Capernaum. Inserted at this point, perhaps this is a further indication of the composite character of the discourse. The notation probably applies more to verses 26–51a, however, than to this present section which sounds like an instruction to a relatively restricted group of disciples (cf. the following verses). For the Capernaum setting, cf. verses 24 f. above.

Jn 6:60–66   *Many of his disciples* is the final designation of the crowd–in a synagogue instruction no more than a few hundred could have been involved–which just a moment ago were called "the Jews." Again we are persuaded that the discourse is composite. Furthermore, in the original intent of the passage it would appear that the *hard saying* which they refuse to hear was that uttered in the first part of the discourse rather than in that pertaining to the Eucharist. This makes relevant Jesus' question in verse 62 which corresponds to his dialogue with Nathanael (Jn 1:50 f.) and Nicodemus (Jn 3:12): the Eucharist is precisely one of those mysteries which they could not be expected to understand who were incapable of believing the "lesser" truth that Jesus is the bread of life come down from heaven (vs. 41). As he had once before to Nicodemus (cf. Jn 3:6–8), Jesus insists on the grace of God and the need of the Spirit's presence for the realization of spiritual things. *The flesh is of no value:* this is not a reference to his own flesh of which he spoke in the Eucharistic section, but to the incapacity of unaided human understanding (cf. Jn 1:14, 3:6); here we have a Johannine parallel to Mt 16:17 (see below). This rejection of Christ by those who had first been his disciples anticipates the summary statement of Jn 12:37 ff., and corresponds to the Synoptic evaluation of the Galilean ministry found in Mt 11:20–24 and parallel.

Jn 6:67–71   The confession made by Peter in the name of the Twelve, here in contrast to the rejection of Jesus by many of his disciples, is the equivalent in John's Gospel of the Synoptic scene in Mk 8:27–30 and parallels. This is the first time that John has taken explicit note of the Twelve.

Jesus asks if they, too, *want* to leave him: there is doubt-

less a deliberate allusion to the conclusion of the story in
Jn 6:17b–21 seen above. Peter's confession of Jesus as the
one who has *the words of eternal life* and whom they have
come to know as *God's Holy One,* therefore, points to the
walking on the water as a Johannine "sign" just as the preceding discourse pointed to the miracle of the loaves. In both
these works Jesus revealed his glory, the saving presence of
God. Jesus repeats (cf. vss. 37, 44, 63, 65) that their faith,
by which they can truly see what was in the signs, has
been made possible by divine election (cf. again Mt 16:17).
But one of you is a devil: here the reference is interpreted by
the evangelist as made to Judas Iscariot, the betrayer (cf. Jn
13:2). In the aftermath of Peter's confession in the Synoptic
version (Mk 8:31–33 and parallels), it is Peter himself who
was called "Satan" by the Lord, though in a quite different
sense.

Jn 5:1   The fifth chapter of John's Gospel describes a
            visit by Jesus to Jerusalem (ignored, as usual, by
the Synoptic tradition) which interrupted the Galilean ministry, the second such visit recorded by the evangelist (cf.
2:13 ff.). The visit took place on the occasion of *a Jewish
feast.* It would be most convenient were John's fifth and sixth
chapters reversed—the order, indeed, in which we are treat-
ing them here!—for then it would be easy to identify the feast
with the Passover (the second Passover brought into connection with Jesus' public life by John) which according
to Jn 6:4 above was "near." Unfortunately, there is no
textual evidence to indicate that these chapters were ever in
any order other than the one in which they now appear.
In any case, it is extremely doubtful that a chronological
concern of this kind would have mattered much to John.
He has not determined the feast in this instance (the scribes
of various manuscripts determined it in differing ways,
however) because the precise occasion was irrelevant to his
purpose. Neither has he bothered to insert this chapter into
any satisfactory sequential framework whether geographical
or temporal. In Jn 6:1, as we have already seen, Jesus is

presumed to be in Galilee, yet 5:47 leaves him in Jerusalem;
furthermore, while chapter 4 is wholly taken up with Jesus'
departure from Judea and journey to Galilee, 5:1 returns
him immediately to Jerusalem. In exactly the same way, Jn
6:71 concludes in Capernaum, but the very next verse beginning chapter 7 appears to be at pains to explain Jesus'
presence in Galilee rather than Judea.

Since John has not much cared where this story should
be set within the Gospel chronicle, it is of no great consequence that we should reverse the order of his chapters here.
This we do simply for the convenience of our treatment in
this book, the more readily to bring John into harmony with
the Synoptic order. Nothing further than this is implied
or intended. For John and for us it is the story itself that
matters. Its purpose is to set forth another of Jesus' "signs."

Jn 5:2-15   *In Jerusalem,* says John, *there is at the Sheep*
                  [Gate] a pool. It is well to note that, how-
ever potentially symbolic John may have found this story, it
is also filled with quite factual and even prosaic details.
The Sheep Gate (cf. Neh 3:1, 12:39), to the northeast of
the temple area, was unused in Jesus' time, but it had given
its name to the area even as names like the Bowery and
Bowling Green linger on today. The pool, if it is to be
identified with the large double cistern beneath the present-
day Church of St. Anne in Jerusalem, did indeed as John goes
on to say have *five porches.* As archaeological exploration
has verified, four of the porches surrounded it in a rectangle
and it was bisected by a fifth. If the setting of this story is
matter-of-fact, so also are the persons who figure in it. The
unnamed man who is healed by the Lord appears to have
been taken from a rather ordinary and routine life and
hardly made to order for the occasion.

The pool was *called in Hebrew* (read "Aramaic") *Bethesda*
(other manuscript readings are "Bethsaida," "Beth-zatha,"
etc.). The name "Bethesda" may have found confirmation
in the nomenclature recorded on a copper scroll discovered
in the third cave at Qumran. Whatever its name was, John's

purpose in citing its "Hebrew" connections was doubtless to
characterize the pool as the "water of Judaism" (as before in
Jn 2:6, 4:12). Once again a salvation that Judaism had been
powerless to effect will become reality merely through the
word of Christ.

Curative powers, at least in the popular estimation, were
attached to the water of this pool: the idea that the waters
of certain regions are medicinal for bathing or drinking is
still widespread today and is zealously encouraged by
local chambers of commerce, with or without the support
of medical opinion. In this instance, the water was thought
to be efficacious when it *bubbled* (vs. 7); presumably what
is meant is the periodical refreshing of the pool from the
ground drainage or the spring which fed it. It may well
have been that in the popular mind this phenomenon was
ascribed to supernatural activity, as is asserted in the addition
to the text found in verses 3b–4: ". . . waiting for the
moving of the water. For an angel of the Lord went down
into the pool from time to time and stirred up the water;
and whoever was first to step in after the stirring of the
water was healed, no matter what disease he had." These
verses, un-Johannine in language, are missing in the best
Greek manuscripts and undoubtedly are an explanatory gloss
inserted by an imaginative scribe at some early time. We are
left to imagine the impact that would have been made on
history had there really been a pool with such powers,
performing miracles by the clock day in and day out year
after year.

The authentic text does not assert that anyone was actually
healed at the pool, only that it was thought to have healing
power. This gives added significance to Jesus' question: *Do
you want to get well?* In place of a faint hope, perhaps
grounded on scanty evidence if any at all, he offers an
immediate certainty. The man's reply indicates that only a
few, or perhaps only one person, could enter the pool at the
time of the water's bubbling. The limitation may have been
imposed by the smallness of the area, but more likely it was

a rule established for the sake of preserving order at the pool.

Now that day was a Sabbath. Jesus' healing activity provokes a controversy over the Sabbath law, as in the Synoptic Gospels (see above on Mk 3:1–5 and parallels). The immediate issue was the man's carrying his pallet, against which specifically there was a rabbinical prohibition. The Gospel story supposes that in ordinary circumstances he would have followed rabbinical interpretation of the Law as a matter of course, but he argues reasonably enough that if Jesus was powerful enough to heal him his authority must also extend to determining what was lawful for the Sabbath. The man's character does not clearly emerge from this story. Seemingly he was little affected by what had been done to him. His reporting of Jesus to *the Jews* was probably not malicious but neither did it show great awareness of what was happening round him in Jerusalem. Jesus had to seek him out *in the temple* area on a later occasion, and there is no indication that his identification of *the man who made me well* was ever pursued on any more personal basis than this casual encounter in a public place. *Sin no more:* Jesus did not make a direct correlation between sickness and personal sin (cf. Jn 9:3); he was warning the man against the *worse thing* than physical illness that could befall him, namely the judgment of God.

Jn 5:16–30 John does not insinuate that the discourse which he has attached to the preceding story is all of one piece or that it was uttered on any single occasion. It is incident to *such things* as Jesus *was doing on the Sabbath,* for which cause *the Jews were persecuting* him: the imperfect tense in both verbs points to a repeated and continued activity. The Sabbath controversy is soon left behind in a development of majestic themes that mark this as one of the most important of the Johannine discourses.

My Father is still working, and I work as well. The implications of this pregnant assertion are immediately drawn out in the following verse. What Jesus was saying, first of all,

was the truism accepted by all, that despite the anthro-
pomorphism of Gen 2:2 f. by which the Sabbath law was
motivated in the Priestly creation story, the activity of God
was never at an end and never interrupted: how else could
new life come into being and the world continue to exist? But
Jesus' invocation of the divine example as precedent for his
own action together with his persistent and exclusive reference to God as "my" Father (cf. vs. 18: *he called God his
own father*) certainly did imply that he was *making himself
the equal of God*. In the Synoptic Gospels also there are
various indications that Jesus spoke of himself as Son of God
in a unique sense and addressed the Father with an intimacy
that others would not dare to use (for example, see below
on Lk 10:21 f. and parallel). The present Johannine passage
is, therefore, the equivalent of the Synoptic teaching of the
Son of Man as Lord of the Sabbath (see above on Mk
2:23–28 and parallels).

Neither do the following verses mitigate this claim, though
they might appear to on the surface. *The Son can do nothing
on his own* is not said to imply the inferiority of one person
to another but to express a functional relationship of persons
in regard to their common work. Not only does the Son work
as the Father works, he also works *what* the Father works:
their work is one and the same. The work in question is that
of the divine economy of salvation. In this economy the
function of the Son is to perform the will of the Father
(cf. Jn 4:34 above). Doing the will of the Father, Jesus
shows forth a community of divine action and of divine *love*,
of which he is God's revelation to the world (cf. Jn 3:16,
35 above).

Two works in particular which are distinctively God's are
exercised by the Son in his ministry, and by the Christ
who continues to live in his Church: these are the *greater*
works which Jesus will show, greater, for example, than the
healing of the man at the pool. First, *he gives life*, he raises
the dead to life. Secondly, he judges man, for *the Father
. . . has given all judgment to the Son*. While the eschatological resurrection and judgment are not ignored, it is on the

here-and-now realization of what eschatology has in store
that the emphasis is laid, for *the hour is* not only *coming, it
now is.* By faith in Christ, the Word of God in the world,
man passes from death to life eternal—the life of grace which
is the earnest and principle of the life of glory—and is
acquitted of the judgment of God. It is in Christ that man
finds God and in him alone. The divine life which the Father
has in himself he has given to man through the *Son of Man,*
by sending him into the world as its life-giver and judge.
Jesus' part in this work of God, and the guarantee of its
efficacy, is the perfect harmony of his will with the Father's.

Jn 5:31–47   John concludes this discourse by reverting to a
                   favorite theme, that of *witness* (see above on
Jn 1:6–8 and 1:19–24). Jesus recognizes in connection with
the claims he has been making the validity of the universally
accepted legal principle that a man's testimony in his own
interest *is not true,* that is, it is juridically valueless without
corroboration. But he does have his corroborating witnesses.
There is, first of all, *John* the Baptist, to whom the Jews had
sent (cf. Jn 1:19–24). As the Baptist had witnessed to
him, so Jesus witnesses to the Baptist (cf. Lk 7:24–35 and
parallel above). *He was a lamp* (cf. Ps 132:17) shining
before the true Light (cf. Jn 1:6–8), and by the Jews themselves he had been received as a prophet. Therefore his
witness should be relevant in the present case. For his own
part, however, Jesus needs no *testimony of man,* for he has
a testimony greater than John's.

The ultimate witness to which Jesus appeals to testify that
he does the works of God are *the works* themselves! The
argument, however, is not circular, for he does not mean by
"works" merely the verifiable deeds that he has performed,
but rather experienced events in which God speaks and
appears to him who has the ears and eyes of faith. His reproach to the Jews is that *you have neither heard his voice
nor seen his form* (an echo of Num 12:8). Because of their
unwillingness to believe, to be open to the voice of God, they
do not have *his word* (*logon*) *abiding* (*menonta*) in them:

unlike Jesus' true disciples who from the beginning took up
their abode with the Word (Jn 1:39: *emeinan*) and who
continually abide in him as he does in them (Jn 15:4:
menēte). Deaf as they are to Jesus' prophetic word, they are
equally deaf to the prophetic word of *Moses* in *the scriptures,*
Moses *who wrote of me* (probably Deut 18:18 is meant; see
above on Jn 1:19–24), whose teaching they fondly believe
they are following. Therefore Moses will witness against
them before God.

In these final verses the Gospel adverts to the specific
question of Jewish unbelief, a posture and a fact to which
the early Church was quite sensitive (cf. Rom 9–11). Despite
his habitual references to "the Jews," John is not really as
often concerned with this question as might appear. Frequently enough he is thinking in broader terms, of the unbelieving world of his own as well as of Jesus' times to which
the Word of the Gospel continues to come in vain (Jn
1:10 f.), and it is only because of the historical circumstances of Jesus' life that he identifies this world as "the
Jews." Here, however, the Jewish rejection of Jesus is contrasted with the acceptance of *another who comes in his own
name:* doubtless a reference to the series of political mes-
siahs (cf. Acts 5:35–37) whose leadership eventually led to
rebellion against Rome and Roman vengeance on Palestine
(cf. also Mk 13:6, 22 and parallels below). John's verdict
on Jewish incredulity is essentially the same as the more
general verdict he has passed on the unbelieving world at the
end of his "book of signs" (see on Jn 12:37–50 below).
St. Paul has dealt with the same question with somewhat
greater sympathy and with a broader outlook on the providential designs of God.

Jn 7:1   Jesus' discourse ended, John has no further
Mk 7:1–13   interest in the situation that gave rise to it.
Mt 15:1–9   Whatever is to be said of the sequence of the
               text according to the evangelist's intention,
however, the first verse of Jn 7 provides a logical sequel to
what we have just seen above (cf. Jn 5:18). This verse takes

us back to Galilee, where we rejoin the Synoptic tradition according to Mark and Matthew. The section before us is part of Luke's "great omission." The Jewishness of its subject matter, which Mark is at some pains to elucidate for his Gentile readers, may offer a sufficient explanation why Luke left it out. There is something similar, though not the same, in Lk 11:37–41.

We have here a typical conflict story which could have taken place at any time in the Lord's ministry. Jesus' adversaries in this instance seem to have been some local *Pharisees* of Galilee apparently egged on by *certain scribes who came from Jerusalem* (Matthew's summary makes both scribes and Pharisees Jerusalemites). The issue this time was not the interpretation and practice of the Law itself but *the tradition of the ancients,* the extension of the Law by custom to analogous observances which were sometimes regarded as having greater binding force than the written Law. Jewish practice was much divided concerning these observances. The professional Pharisee followed them as a matter of principle. The Sadducees firmly rejected them on the same principle. The ordinary Jew probably kept as many of them as he conveniently could, and the Judeans were in all likelihood more scrupulous on the point than the Galileans.

Jesus' attitude was also one of principle, neither mere acquiescence nor casual disregard. In respect to traditionary interpretation of the Law he agreed with the Pharisees: only in such an acceptation could the Law remain a living word and not become a fossilized letter. But the tradition had to get at the heart and spirit of the Law and serve these if it was to have any genuine religious significance. If, on the contrary, it became a law unto itself subject to no further interpretation it could easily end by destroying the Law it professed to explain (see above on Mk 2:23–28 and parallels). It was then only the *precepts of men* about which Is 29:13 had spoken, human observances which were no help but a positive hindrance to the true service of God.

So it was with the many Jewish purifications (cf. Jn 2:6), originally rites connected with the sacrificial liturgy

which had now been extended by custom to the circumstances of everyday life, sometimes occasioning much hard-
ship by disregarding the realities of existence in water-shy
Palestine. It was not that the washings were a bad thing;
religiously they were indifferent. What was bad was the en-
couragement given by such formal practices to the notion that
they did, indeed, constitute a man's religion. They could so
easily get in the way of his real religious duties. Just as it has
not been unknown for a Christian to be more readily identified by his Friday diet than by his attention to the Sermon on
the Mount, it was easier for a Jew to verify that he had
indeed washed his hands to the elbow than that he had
loved the Lord his God with his whole heart and his
neighbor as himself.

It is under this aspect that Jesus speaks harshly of the
Pharisaical traditions. Too easily could they *nullify God's
word*. A particularly flagrant example of this he finds in the
extension of *korban* permitted by some rabbis as a legal sub-
terfuge by which a man might evade sacred duties, all in the
name of piety. *Korban* was everything consecrated to God,
which could not be put to profane use (in Mt 27:6 the temple
treasury is called the *korbanas*). Mean-spirited men could
release themselves from their natural obligations to support
even their parents by declaring all their goods *korban*.
Whether or not the "consecrated" wealth actually ever made
its way into the coffers of religion might, of course, be
another question. Whether or not it did was immaterial to
Jesus. That this kind of shoddy transaction could be con-
doned by the same persons who professed shock at unwashed hands, this was the insufferable hypocrisy which
revolted him.

Mk 7:14–23   The pronouncements that follow may have
Mt 15:10–20   originally belonged to other contexts. Their
                  use here, however, helps explain the interest
taken by the early Church in stories like the one we have
just read. The Church had to be concerned from the very
beginning with the twin perils that are the standing temp-

tation offered to every religion and every religious person: to conceive of righteousness as a legalistic science, and to confuse religion with its externals. That Judaism had sometimes given in to the temptation was a cautionary example to Christians, an example, of course, which Christians have not always heeded.

Jesus' teaching is now addressed to the Galilean *crowd* rather than to the scribes and Pharisees. He had, as we know, no illusions about these people, who were as capable as any others of closing their minds to truth. According to Matthew, who reports the disciples' concern over the disgruntlement of the Pharisees, in this very passage Jesus speaks of the Galileans as *blind men* led by these *blind guides* (the parable found in Lk 6:39 above). Whatever their shortcomings, however, in this as in other matters they deserved better leaders than they had had. As for the Pharisees, Jesus denies that they are God's *planting* of which Is 60:21 had prophesied and insists that they *shall be rooted up*: a word whose fulfillment Matthew recognized in the supplanting of the Synagogue by the Church.

The Pharisees were scandalized because Jesus told the Galileans that *nothing that enters a man from outside can make him unclean; it is what comes from out of a man that makes him unclean*. It is not hard to see why they took offense, for this little statement is one of the most revolutionary utterances ascribed to Jesus in the context of contemporary Judaism. It is not merely that he is teaching the priority of the interior over the exterior in religion: the prophets of the Old Testament, the Law itself, as well as rabbinical Judaism had already affirmed this principle. He addresses himself, rather, to the source of uncleanness, whether moral or otherwise, and finds that it is entirely internal to man and in no wise brought to him by things or persons from without. Radically, this principle struck at the very existence of the legal and ritual purity inculcated by the Mosaic law (especially the laws codified in the "Law of Holiness," Lev 17–26, but also other precepts scattered throughout the Pentateuch, as Lev 11 and Deut 14:1–21).

Foods that from time immemorial had been avoided for
various reasons the Law classified as "unclean" in order to
give visual expression to the true and spiritual purity that
should characterize a people consecrated to God. There was,
therefore, no fetishism involved in the kosher laws, nor
did the best rabbinic teaching fail to bring this out. Nevertheless, until Jesus no rabbi had yet suggested the provisional character of the laws as such, as far as the letter of
their observance was concerned. It is precisely this that
Jesus did suggest, as the evangelists make quite clear.

Under other historical circumstances, it might have been
that Judaism itself would have arrived at a similar conclusion, as some modern Judaism has done. There was from
ancient times a strong prophetic tradition that pointed in that
direction. Nevertheless, all the influences brought to bear
on postexilic Judaism had determined it otherwise, inter-
preting the laws more rather than less rigidly and adding
to them all kinds of extensions. Even Jesus, as far as we can
tell, never carried out his own principle to the extent of
actually disregarding the letter of the ancient laws. He did,
as we know, interpret them more liberally than suited the
taste of other rabbis. He refused to accept the traditions
that had enlarged their compass and rigidified them. He did
many things and consorted with many people that a narrower view of the Law called "unclean." It was the precedent
of his life and his teaching alike that eventually led the
Church, not without agonized hesitations (cf. Acts 10:9–16,
28, 15:1–21, 21:20–26; Gal 2, etc.) to follow his principle
to its inevitable conclusions under the guidance of his Spirit.

These conclusions are presupposed by the evangelists when
they report Jesus' explanation of his saying—actually, he
paraphrases it with another parable—given to *his disciples*
(in Matthew, Peter asks the question) privately *in the house*
(cf. Mk 4:34). That the conclusions have been drawn is
more obvious in Mark than it is in Matthew: Matthew's stand
on the Mosaic law has been made quite definite in the
Sermon on the Mount. In Mark, the last three words of verse
18 f. are almost certainly to be read as the evangelist's com-

mentary: *He said to them, ". . . ," cleansing all foods.*
What remained obscure to the disciples in Jesus' lifetime was
now clear to the Church of the Gospels. The impressive list
of vices that concludes the passage is Pauline in vocabulary
and technique, and confirms what we have already judged
to be the fact, that we have been reading a catechesis of
the apostolic Church.

13. UPON THIS ROCK

Mk 7:24–30 For all practical purposes Mark has now
Mt 15:21–28 ended his story of the Galilean ministry as
he takes the Lord up into the land of
Phoenicia, the pagan *district of Tyre and Sidon* that bordered
on Palestine. Even though he will show Jesus re-entering
Galilee once or twice, there will hardly be any more question
of a "ministry" there. The proclamation of the kingdom,
Mark seems to be saying, has now been made, and for
better or for worse the Galileans have heard the word
preached to them. Later on (see on Lk 10:13–16 and
parallel below) the other Synoptic Gospels will offer a more
dramatic judgment on the Galilean ministry (Matthew has,
in fact, already anticipated it in his Gospel). From now on
Jesus is seen more and more in the intimate company of his
chosen disciples, secluded from the public gaze or at least
seeking seclusion, forming and instructing the little band that
had heeded his call. Though we know that too great a point
is not to be made of the kerygmatic outline of the Gospels,
there is no reason to think that this phase of it does not
correspond to an historical reality in Jesus' life.

Such a development also suits the purposes of Matthew,
who is preparing for Jesus' discourse on the community life
of the Church in chapter 18. The present story is obviously

much to his liking, insinuating, as it does, that the mission of salvation to the Gentiles began in the Lord's own life. At the same time, the passage strikes the "Jewish" tone that we so often hear in the First Gospel: the woman's prayer is heard only after she has acknowledged the priority and privileges of Israel. It may be for this reason that Luke, who has co-ordinated his ecumenism better than either Mark or Matthew, has seen fit to omit the story.

Jesus' fame had crossed the border ahead of him into Phoenicia. Mark sets the scene in *a house,* but Matthew, who appears to have drawn on an additional source, has the woman following Jesus about the countryside. Matthew calls her by the ancient Semitic term *Canaanite,* while to Mark she is a *Syrophoenician,* the word used by Greek writers to distinguish the Phoenicians of the Syrian coast from those of northern Africa, the Carthaginians. The parable which provides the basis for the interchange between Jesus and the woman, and which the latter cleverly turns to her advantage, probably makes an allusion to the eschatological messianic banquet (cf. Lk 14:15), but the main point is the distinction made between *the children* for whom the meal has been prepared, that is, the Jews, and *the dogs* which at best are present on sufferance. Gentiles were sometimes called "dogs" by the Jews (see above on Mt 7:6); the Gospel softens the expression somewhat by using a diminutive form, thus "whelps" rather than the rangy curs that one would kick aside in the Near Eastern bazaars. The woman's witty solution, that even the dogs may expect the table scraps, somewhat resembles Paul's idea expressed by another figure in Rom 11:17.

The vivid personality of the woman in the story, along with some of its details which a Gentile Church could assimilate without finding altogether palatable, argue alike for its antiquity and its dependence on authentic recollection.

Mk 7:31–37   A glance at the map of northern Palestine
Mt 15:29–31   should convince the reader that in verse 31
              Mark is either displaying his quite vague

grasp of the regional geography, something we have had reason to suspect before, or he is describing a most circuitous route—New York to Washington, say, by way of Montreal and St. Louis—which Jesus took for some undisclosed reason. Matthew passes over the route, but along with Mark brings Jesus *to the sea of Galilee*. Both evangelists seem to suppose that the locale was outside of Galilee, somewhere in the pagan territory on the eastern shore (cf. vs. 31 in Matthew: the people *glorified the God of Israel* whom they have had revealed to them for the first time, presumably). Matthew also notes that *he went up on the mountain* (see on Mk 3:13–19; Lk 6:12–16; Mt 5:1 f.), making a point of it probably in view of the story that he is to tell next.

While Matthew contents himself here with a summary statement on Jesus' healing, Mark describes in some detail the cure of *a man who was deaf and had an impediment in his speech*. The sacramental gestures of the Lord on this occasion were not lost on the Church, which at a very early time incorporated them into its ritual of baptism, the sacrament by which the Christian's senses are opened to the word of God. Mark also has it that Jesus *groaned* preparatory to effecting the man's cure: quite likely this corresponds to other of his expressions of emotion on similar occasions (see above on Mk 1:40–45). In verse 36 the imposition of the "messianic secret" (see above on Mk 1:22–28) should not really have applied in this pagan land. It is possible that by now such conclusions to Jesus' miracle stories have become reflex and somewhat stereotyped for Mark. It is also possible that the story originally had a setting elsewhere in the Galilean ministry.

Mk 8:1–10   There seems to be no really convincing al-
Mt 15:32–39 ternative to the prevailing scholarly view,
             that the story of the feeding of the four
thousand is a doublet, that is, a variant form in the tradition, of the story of the feeding of the five thousand which we saw in Chapter 11 (see above on Mk 6:34–44 and parallels).

There are, it is true, various differences of detail between the two stories—without these, doublets could hardly arise—but they are all of such a kind as naturally develop in oral transmission. In every essential, on the other hand, the two stories are the same. Mark, followed by Matthew, has repeated in another setting what was originally the same account of the miracle of the loaves. John has only the former story, though in any case it is by exception that he parallels the Synoptic Gospels. Neither has Luke repeated it. Even did it not figure in his "great omission" (see above on Mk 6:53–56 and parallels), he would doubtless have followed his usual practice of omitting even apparent repetitions.

The message of the two narratives, trivial emphases apart, appears to be identical. Why, then, did Mark and Matthew retell the story, since they were as well aware as we of its repetitive character? For one thing, the event had come down to them in two variant forms, and they respected all the material that tradition had given them. Doublets are a commonplace in Old Testament history, and they posed few problems to biblical writers who were little bothered with questions of relative chronology and statistical detail. Matthew in particular repeats himself more than once: in just a moment we shall see another instance of this. Secondly, this story was especially prized because of its sacramental overtones which we have already noted. Finally, it is likely that the evangelists were pleased at the chance to relate in a Gentile setting such a work as had once been performed on behalf of the Jews of Galilee.

The ending of the story poses a geographical problem that still awaits solution. Both Matthew and Mark presuppose Galilee as the scene of the next brief episode. Mark says that Jesus *got into the boat with his disciples and went to the district of Dalmanutha*. No such place is known, unfortunately. If Mark is something less than an expert on Galilean nomenclature, however, in this instance Matthew, who revises him, affords us no better help. It was *the region of Magadan*, he says. Magadan is equally unknown.

Mk 8:11–12   Back in Galilee—again, from the standpoint
Mt 16:1–4   of any genuine chronology, this passage
Lk 12:54–56   must be timeless—Jesus is asked by the Jewish leaders for *a sign from heaven* (cf. Jn
6:30). Mark says that the Pharisees made this demand,
while Matthew says it was the Pharisees and Sadducees. The
combination of Pharisees and Sadducees acting in concert
is historically unlikely, and it is probable that for Matthew in
this context these are little more than traditional names. In
the parallel Lk 11:16 which we shall see later it was simply
"some of the people" who asked for the sign.

The sign for which Jesus was asked was the very thing
he could not and would not give. His miracles were not
available on call, but were true signs of the inbreaking of the
kingdom as he had proclaimed it. Such witness as he could
give was palpable only to a genuine faith (see above on
Jn 5:31–47). They were not asking for a sign of the kingdom
but for a sign that would confirm their own aspirations for
the kingdom, their attempt to dictate to God the terms on
which they would accept his dispensation. Before *this* unbelieving *generation* Jesus *groaned in spirit* (see above on
Mk 7:31–37). To it *no sign will be given*.

Except the sign of Jonah, Matthew adds in eloquent
paraphrase. Jonah, an historical prophet (2 Kgs 14:25)
known, however, only from the seriocomic story in the Old
Testament book that bears his name, in a sense epitomizes
all prophecy. Jonah of the paradoxes, a nationalistic prophet
sent to preach to Gentiles, cast away by men and brought
back from death to proclaim a doom that proved in reality
to be the salvation of a great city, who fled from the very
word of God with which he was charged and who understood its fulfillment last of all men—Jonah stands as a sign of
God's mysterious ways that confound the wisdom of men.
A generation that is *evil and adulterous*, that is, faithless, unbelieving (cf. Is 57:3; Ezek 23:27, etc.), could understand
Jesus no more than it could Jonah.

In verses 2b–3 Matthew, or someone who has expanded
his text, has inserted a proverb which in a variant form Luke

also has in a similar context. The proverb builds on the idea of "heavenly" signs and contrasts the ability of those who can read *the signs of the times* in a banal sense with their complete blindness to them in the one sense that ultimately matters.

Mk 12:38–42   *The sign of Jonah the prophet* has already
Lk 11:29–32   appeared in Matthew's Gospel, practically in the same words, offered in response to a challenge of *certain of the scribes and Pharisees;* in Luke's parallel, it is again *the crowds* who are addressed.

Here there is an expansion on the figure of Jonah as a type of Christ. *Just as Jonah was in the belly of the sea monster three days and three nights* (cf. Jon 2:1), *so the Son of Man will be in the heart of the earth three days and three nights.* This seems to refer to the mortal peril in which Jesus must carry out his prophetic witness, similar to that of Jonah, and even to the death that he will eventually undergo: all the evangelists testify that Jesus prophesied his death. Does it also allude to his resurrection? This may be. Luke's parallel is: *As Jonah became a sign to the men of Nineveh, so will the Son of Man be to this generation.* Jonah did, it is true, come before the men of Nineveh as one who had been brought back from certain death, yet it was not precisely in this fashion that he was a "sign" to them. Luke does not necessarily mean to say more than that Jesus comes before his generation as Jonah came before his, as a prophet, equipped with no further credentials than the word of God. Neither, therefore, does Matthew necessarily see in Jonah a prefigurement of the resurrection. The primitive Christian formula for the resurrection is habitually "on the third day" (Mt 16:21, 17:23, 20:19, 27:64; Lk 9:22, 18:23, 24:7, 21, 46; Jn 2:1 [!]; Acts 10:40; 1 Cor 15:4) or, more rarely, "after three days" (Mt 9:31; Mk 14:58, etc.), neither of which expressions is really the equivalent of "three days and three nights."

Whether or not Jonah's deliverance figured in the thought of Jesus or of the New Testament as a type of the resurrec-

tion, it may be as well to observe at this point that no change
is thereby affected in our judgment of the Book of Jonah,
which is a work of didactic fiction. The New Testament use
of Old Testament types is theological and symbolical, not
historico-critical.

Both Matthew and Luke exploit a further detail from the
Jonah story: the conversion of Nineveh—Gentiles!—at the
preaching of an Israelite prophet (Jon 3:5–10), an object
lesson to this unbelieving generation that has heard and
not heeded a prophet *greater than Jonah*. In like manner,
the Queen of Sheba who once traveled from far-off Arabia
to seek the wisdom of God incarnated in Solomon (1 Kgs
10:1–10) is a rebuke from Israel's history to those Israelites
who have now spurned *one greater than Solomon*.

Mk 8:13–21   Rejoining Mark's chronicle, which is still be-
Mt 16:5–12   ing followed by Matthew, we find the Lord
Lk 12:1   and his disciples once again in their boat, de-
              parting from Galilee almost as soon as they
had come. Luke does not parallel this story, but he has reproduced its key statement in another context where he has
gathered various sayings of Jesus.

As Mark and Matthew tell the story, it takes on some of the
elements of a Johannine discourse. The disciples react with
surprising obtuseness when Jesus warns them against *the
leaven of the Pharisees, which is hypocrisy,* Luke explains.
Matthew has *the leaven of the Pharisees and Sadducees*
(cf. Mt 16:1 above), while Mark adds *and the leaven of
Herod,* doubtless with reference to the land of Dalmanutha/
Magadan which they had just quitted. Leaven or yeast as a
figure for doctrine, whether good or bad, fermenting in men's
minds and determining their whole being and action, was
well established in Jewish symbolic thought (see above on
Mt 13:33). Nevertheless, according to Mark the Lord was
forced to apply to his disciples on this occasion the same
words he had previously spoken of the unheeding crowds
who stood disbelieving before his parables (see above on
Mk 4:10–12 and parallels).

In this story the evangelists seem to be making a catechetical point that transcends the saying about leaven. Even Jesus'
disciples did not always comprehend the real meaning of
his signs, a fact the Gospels themselves can obscure for us
simply because they have been written in the light of a later
Penecostal faith. This point the story makes well by showing the disciples entirely consumed by trivialities while Jesus
must patiently catechize them concerning the superficial details of the miracle of the loaves, which they had not understood (cf. Mk 6:52). The story in its present form presupposes the separation of the two versions of the miracle story
in the tradition. This lesson was a useful one for the Church
of the Gospels, which also counted members who did not
properly appreciate the enduring Christian mysteries to which
such miracles had testified (cf. 1 Cor 11:20–22, 27–29).

Mk 8:22–26 It is probably not by accident that Mark
locates this next event, omitted this time
even by Matthew, at *Bethsaida,* the site of the first miracle
of the loaves. Blindness, he tells us, however hopeless it may
appear is always curable. The story has some resemblance
to the one found above in Mk 7:31–37, but its right to a
place of its own in the tradition is assured. In particular,
the man's comparison of the people whom he sees, apparently
for the first time, to *walking trees* sounds like the uncontrived
detail of a remembered and moving experience. On the other
hand, Jesus' elaborate efforts to preserve secrecy may indicate
an original setting in the Galilean ministry.

Mk 8:27–30   This next passage is a watershed dividing
Mt 16:13–20 the flow of Mark's Gospel. With the con-
Lk 9:18–21   fession of Peter a climax is reached, the
"messianic secret" is broken once for all,
and from now on the Gospel prepares us for Jesus' passion
and death. Matthew, for whom the event does not have
precisely the same significance, nevertheless has made an
even greater thing of it in his own way for the special ends
of his Gospel. Even Luke breaks his silence at this point to

rejoin the kerygmatic outline of Mark. John, as we have seen, has his own version of a Petrine confession of Jesus (see above on Jn 6:67–71).

From Bethsaida, Mark supposes that Jesus and the disciples journeyed north, following the Jordan to its sources in *the environs* (Mark: *the villages*) *of Caesarea Philippi.* Caesarea Philippi, so called to distinguish it from the Caesarea of Palestine which was the residence of the Roman governor of Judea, had been recently rebuilt by the tetrarch Philip and named for the Roman emperor. Situated in the southern foothills of snow-covered Mount Hermon which rose majestically before them, it was and is a place of great natural beauty. It was undoubtedly for solitude and retreat that Jesus had brought his disciples here, and it is unlikely that they entered the pagan city itself. Luke says nothing about the place (the last event that he described was the miracle of the loaves at Bethsaida), but he notes, as he often does, that the Lord was at prayer before the important interchange that was to follow.

It was *while they were on the way* that Jesus for the first time put to them the question, *Who do men* (Luke: *the crowds*) *say that I am?* Their answers fairly correspond to the rumors and popular reports noted already on another occasion (see above on Mk 6:14–29 and parallels). Matthew alone has the name of *Jeremiah,* possibly because of the many late Jewish legends that surrounded the life of this great prophet (cf. 2 Macc 2:1–8, 15:13–16; however, 4 Ezra [2 Esdras] 2:17 ff. is a Christian interpolation inspired by Mt 16:14), possibly because the resemblance between the two prophetic figures was already remarked in Jesus' lifetime. It is initially surprising that no mention is made of the title Messiah, though this had most certainly been connected with Jesus on more than one occasion. Apparently the disciples withhold this word deliberately in order not to mingle popular ideas with their own belief, recognizing what the Lord was about to ask of them.

In all three Gospels *Peter* speaks, in his own name and that of the Twelve, the conviction at which they had arrived through reflection and observation. *You are the Messiah* is doubtless the primitive form of the confession, as found in Mark. Luke's *the Messiah of God* is synonymous with this. Matthew's addition *the Son of the living God* contributes a certain verbal solemnity but does not alter the sense. "Sons of the living God" was a title used by the prophet Hosea (2:1) for the eschatological Israel, a text quoted by Paul in Rom 9:26; its use here is doubtless in the same sense, that is, applicable pre-eminently to the Messiah of Israel. Messiah meant a variety of particular things to many people, for as we have seen the Jewish messianic expectation was complex and nuanced. What Peter may have meant by it we do not know in details, but it is evident that by using the title at all he intended to sum up in Jesus the realization of Israel's salvation-hope.

Did Jesus accept this designation as an accurate description of his role in salvation history? From Matthew (vs. 20) it would appear that he did, but Mark and Luke by no means permit us to give such a univocal answer. In these Gospels Jesus neither accepts nor rejects Peter's words, but immediately *ordered them not to tell anyone about him.* Furthermore, though we have described this passage as the ending of Mark's "messianic secret," it might be more accurate to say that it is the beginning of the process by which Jesus himself reveals a concept of messiahship that had not been grasped by Peter (see on Mk 8:31–33 and parallels below). It is impossible, therefore, to give a simple answer of yes or not to the question. It would seem that Jesus did accept the title in the spirit in which it was offered, but with some important reservations. This may become clearer from an examination of Matthew's major addition to the text, Jesus' conferring on Peter of primacy in his Church.

We call this an addition not to imply that Matthew made it up, but to acknowledge that it originally pertained to another historical context. Matthew's is not the only Gospel in which a primacy is ascribed to Peter. Luke has something very similar, which, however, he has placed amidst the events of the Lord's passion (Lk 22:31 f.); in John's

Gospel it is by the resurrected Christ that Peter is singled out as the shepherd of his brethren (Jn 21:15–19). The variety and independence of the Gospel testimony persuade us of its objectivity. Most scholars would have no difficulty in accepting the fact that Jesus once said to Peter what we read in Mt 16:17–19, or something very like it. But not, apparently, on this precise occasion. Matthew, as he has done so often, has arranged his material topically, joining his tradition of Petrine primacy to the Marcan story of Peter's confession just as he has also chosen to narrate at this point the change of Peter's name, another development brought into various contexts by the other Gospels (cf. Mk 3:16; Lk 6:14; Jn 1:42).

When we recognize the nature of Matthew's parallel to the story of Peter's confession, its individual parts fall into place and make sense. We may recall that he has already shown the disciples confessing Jesus with a title more significant than that of Peter's "Messiah" (see on Mt 14:23b–33 above). Similarly, in Matthew's Gospel alone the Lord asks his disciples on this occasion, "Who do men say that *the Son of Man* is?," again already implying something more exalted than the comparatively prosaic "Messiah" elicited in the confession. While he has not verbally altered the terms of Peter's confession, therefore, not even by adding "the Son of the living God," be undoubtedly expects us to see in it not the still obscure affirmation of the disciples' pre-resurrection experience of Jesus, but the fullness of meaning which Peter, the disciples, and the entire Church later attached to the title *Christ* when confessing their resurrected Lord and Savior (cf. Acts 2:36).

It is for this reason that in Matthew's Gospel Peter's confession is ascribed to divine revelation: *flesh and blood have not revealed this to you, but my heavenly Father.* It is this confession of Christian faith which evokes Jesus' reciprocal testimony to Peter, for it is only within the ambit of Christian faith that Peter can exercise the role which Jesus assigns to him. *Therefore I say to you:* Peter has named Christ, and now Christ names Peter. If Matthew had written as Mark does, he would now have: *You are Cephas, which means Peter,* or, *which means Rock.* There is no doubt whatever that Jesus gave to his disciple Simon bar Jona ("son of John," according to Jn 1:42) the Aramaic name *kêphā* (see above on Jn 1:35–42), the name by which he was commonly known in the apostolic Church (cf. 1 Cor 1:12, 3:22, 9:5, 15:5; Gal 1:18, 2:9, 11, 14). The Greek *petros,* whence our "Peter," is a translation of this word, which means "rock." The word provides Jesus with the figure by which he designates Peter as the foundation of his messianic community: *upon this rock I shall build my Church.* The verb is in the future tense, for the Church comes into being only in the apostolic age following the resurrection and the gift of the Spirit. How Peter served as the rock of the apostolic community has been portrayed best of all by Luke in the first part of his Acts of the Apostles.

Only once again, and again by Matthew (18:17), is the word "church" (*ekklēsia*) used in the Gospels. Statistically in the New Testament it is eminently a Pauline word, and therefore many scholars have doubted that it or its Aramaic equivalent could actually have been used by Jesus. There appears to be no reason, however, why Jesus could not have said precisely what Matthew reports him as saying. In the Septuagint Old Testament *ekklēsia* is a common word, ordinarily the translation of the Hebrew *qāhāl,* the term which designates Israel as the congregation or community of the Lord (Deut 23:2, etc.). "The *qāhāl* of God" is one of the titles by which the eschatological Jewish community of Qumran identified itself. That Jesus, who had already begun to gather about him the messianic community which accepted his proclamation of the kingdom, should have provided for its continuance in the Church that would survive his death, is altogether reasonable. The occasion of this action, however, as we have already suggested, was probably more intimately connected with the time of his passion, death, and resurrection than this relatively remote period of Caesarea Philippi.

Against this Church, Jesus adds, *the gates of hell shall not prevail.* "Hell" here is not *gehenna* but *hadēs*, ordinarily the equivalent of the Hebrew *sheol*=death in a purely "neutral" sense as opposed to life (cf. Apo 1:18, 6:8, 20:13 f.), not the place of punishment of the evil dead (though in Lk 16:23 *hadēs* is represented as a place of torment, as is *sheol* in the Psalms of Solomon, a Jewish apocryphal work of the first century B.C.). Death is figured here as a city with gates, just as the Church is, "built" on a rock. The gates of an ancient city were its stronghold both for defence and offence. Death and the Church are thus seen as two warring cities, and victory is assured to the Church. In the biblical view death was never something merely natural as the inevitable lot of man—the pagan idea—but as evidence of the power of Satan (cf. Heb 2:14), the reign of sin and evil inimical to life and truth (cf. 1 Cor 15:26; Apo 6:8, 20:13 f.). Against all of this the power of the Church will be proof.

Still using the same figure, Jesus promises to Peter *the keys of the kingdom of heaven.* He who had the keys of a city controlled it as its head and ruler (cf. Is 22:22). The effect of Peter's rule will be to give men access to God's kingdom, in contrast to the teaching of the scribes and Pharisees (cf. Mt 23:13). How this rule will be exercised is expressed in the terms *binding and loosing.* This was a rabbinical legal formula meaning to declare with authority what was or was not of obligation. Peter's decisions as ruler over the Church of God will be ratified by God himself. The early Church was conscious that it survived as a result of these decisions, living by the teaching of the apostles under the headship of Peter (cf. Acts 2:42). In Mt 18:18 (the Johannine parallel is Jn 20:22 f.) this power of binding and loosing, shared by all the apostles, is more specifically defined in the jurisdiction of the Church over the forgiveness of sin.

Mk 8:31-33   It is important to recognize how closely in
Mt 16:21-23 the mind of the evangelists the following
Lk 9:22   passage is connected with Peter's confession. Even Luke, who delicately omits in this instance the continued interchange between Jesus and

Peter, brings out the connection by making verse 22 a part of the same sentence as verse 21. The disciples had confessed, in the person of Peter, Jesus' messiahship, but now Jesus himself completes the confession by defining the terms of his messiahship as known only to him and the Father. Accordingly, he applies to himself the title *Son of Man* (Matthew has already used it above) which he preferred to any other as most accurately defining his character. This is the first of three Synoptic passages in which the Lord unequivocally speaks of his suffering, death, and resurrection. The Son of Man *must* undergo these things by the divine decree; the *elders, chief priests, and scribes* designate the three divisions of the Sanhedrin. As already noted (above on Mt 12:38–42 and parallel), that Jesus foresaw his death and even his resurrection, which in Jewish concepts would be an inevitable corollary, as entailed in the messianic destiny he had been given to perform, is part of the consistent testimony of the Gospels and is by no means hard to credit. Accounts such as the present one, however, which have been written in the light of subsequent fulfillment, have almost certainly made explicit what was at the time understood far more obscurely by men who had not yet taken in the theology of the cross. Otherwise, much of what appears in the ensuing pages of the Gospel would be incomprehensible.

Peter's reaction to the Lord's words shows, in fact, how little as yet the fullness of Jesus' messiahship was appreciated by his own disciples. He *took him aside:* Peter's attitude is one of genial condescension, an attempt to raise the sagging spirits of his Master who is taking a far too pessimistic view of his prospects. Jesus' reaction in turn was a violent one: *he turned on* Peter in the presence of the other disciples. Without realizing it, Peter was playing the part of *Satan* (see above on Lk 4:3–13 and parallel), tempting him to follow the easy, human path of an earthly messiah rather than to adhere to the lonely course on which he had set himself, the course of total sacrifice of self. How little

Peter still knew of his Master, and to what he had committed himself in becoming his disciple!

Mk 8:34–9:1 It is about the consequences of discipleship
Mt 16:24–28 that Jesus now begins to speak, in a series of
Lk 9:23–27   sayings which have been assembled doubtless from various periods in his life and
appropriately attached to this context in which the doctrine
of the cross has been broached for the first time. Evidences
of editorial work are not lacking, including Mark's curious
reference to *the crowd,* which is out of place here and
obviously earlier belonged to another context.

The first saying has a greater immediacy to the life of
Jesus as it appears in Matthew and Mark than in its Lucan
version. *Take up his cross* Jesus probably intended to be
understood most literally. It is by no means necessary to suppose that the Gospel tradition has paraphrased his original
utterance in view of its knowledge of his crucifixion. It is
probably safe to say that everyone of his hearers had seen
more than once the terrible sight of a convicted criminal
being driven along by whips, naked and covered with blood,
a beam of wood lashed to his shoulders, on his way to the
place of his execution. The Romans had made crucifixion a
familiar occurrence in Palestine. If Jesus foresaw that his
course was leading to his death, he would naturally have
thought of a death by crucifixion. And this was what they
must also expect who would heed his invitation to *follow me.*
On the other hand, *take up his cross daily* in Luke indicates
an adaptation of the saying to the continued perils and
sacrifices of Christian living (cf. 1 Cor 15:31) rather than
an immediate summons to martyrdom.

The second saying, which Matthew and Luke repeat here
in Mark's version, they also have reproduced elsewhere (along
with a variant version of the first saying) from the source
they share that is independent of Mark (cf. Mt 10:38 f.;
Lk 14:27, 17:33); it is also found in Jn 12:25 where we
shall see it later in context. It is therefore, certainly one of
the best attested of Jesus' teachings. In context it continues

the thought of following Jesus in the face of death and plays on the multiple sense of the word *psychē* (the Hebrew *nephesh*), that is, the soul or self as it refers simply to sentient existence on the one hand, and as it is destined for eternal life on the other. A man may refuse Jesus' call to follow him thinking thereby to save his life, yet by that very concern for self-preservation he may lose his share in the only life that counts. To be willing to throw one's life away, paradoxically, is the way into eternal life. *What would be man's profit,* the Gospel adds, *were he to gain even the whole world, yet forfeit his life?* When the Son of Man comes into his eschatological kingdom, it will be made apparent who has really preserved his life and who has in reality thrown it away.

The passage concludes with a final saying that has little to do with the context but has been brought in because of its topical connection with *the kingdom of God.* It is one of the most perplexing and debated of the sayings ascribed to Jesus in the Synoptic Gospels—and, because of its difficulties, doubtless one of the most authentic. Because in it Jesus appears to entertain an eschatological view that did not correspond with the subsequent development of the Church, it has raised all sorts of questions concerning the limitations placed on his knowledge of such events (see below on Mk 13:28–32 and parallels). *Those standing here* would almost certainly have understood him to be speaking of the final judgment of God and the consummation of this order. The Gospel tradition has interpreted such sayings of Jesus in various ways, all of them, as we shall see, having some foundation in his other words and teaching. At least a provisional fulfillment of the coming of the kingdom they have seen in the story of the transfiguration that immediately follows.

Mk 9:2–10   If the preceding saying is perplexing to the
Mt 17:1–9   commentator, even more perplexing is the
Lk 9:28–36   story that follows it. The story of the transfiguration fits so strangely into the picture of

Jesus' public life and is filled with so many symbolic details, by many it has been thought to be either a displaced resurrection-narrative or a parabolic protrayal of the spiritual realities which were hidden by the incarnation and perceptible only to the eyes of faith (cf. Jn 1:14). It may be doubted, however, whether either of these explanations completely accounts for the story of the transfiguration, which was assumed by the apostolic Church to have historical value in its own right (cf. 2 Pt 1:16–18). Whatever may have been the exact circumstances of the event, however, there is no doubt that as the story appears in the Gospels it has an artistic relationship to its surrounding context. It is, for one thing, the completion of the story of Peter's confession. This is the reason for the chronological indication, *after six days* in Matthew and Mark, *about eight days* in Luke, or as we would say, "a week later"—a virtually unprecedented agreement among authors who are usually notoriously indifferent to such matters. Peter's confession and its sequel, Jesus' prediction of his passion and its consequences for his disciples, form a unit with the transfiguration to set forth in all its fullness what the Synoptic Gospels want to say of the historical Jesus as the Christ.

Jesus takes with him the favored disciples *Peter, James, and John,* the same three who will witness his agony in the garden (see below on Mk 14:32b–42 and parallels); in several ways the Gospels associate these two episodes in which such seemingly conflicting sides of Jesus' person became manifest. Matthew and Mark locate the scene on *a high mountain,* while Luke says that *he went up on the mountain to pray.* It is Luke's practice to mention the Savior's prayer on important occasions; here, however, he makes a point of the prayer as part of the event itself, for it was *as he was praying* that Jesus was transfigured. Luke follows an independent source in his description of the transfiguration, and it is likely that this detail has something to say as regards the historicity of the event, that it may have been the consequence of ecstatic prayer. Luke alone also recounts that the disciples shook themselves awake from a heavy sleep as the vision opened before them (vs. 32), a thing which might suggest a psychological conditioning for this spiritual experience. Because of the connection of this story with Caesarea Philippi, it has often been suggested that the high mountain was nearby Hermon. The next events described by the Gospels, however, occurred in Galilee (cf. Mk 9:30), and therefore most early commentators identified the site with Mount Tabor. It should be evident, in any case, that it is impossible to extract a geography of the transfiguration from the Gospels.

The transfiguration, according to the Gospels, consisted in a change of Jesus' bodily appearance and an accompanying resplendence of his clothing. The verb used by Matthew and Mark which we translate "transfigure" (*metamorphoō*) is found elsewhere in the New Testament only in Rom 12:2 and 2 Cor 3:18 where it designates the spiritual transformation of the Christian through grace. The connection of these passages is more than verbal. The transfiguration was a visible anticipation of the eschatological *glory* (the word used by Luke in vss. 31 f. and by Paul in 2 Cor 3:18) of the Son of Man (cf. Mk 8:38 and parallels), even as the life of grace is an invisible anticipation of the eschatological glory of the children of God. In keeping with this understanding of the event is the appearance of *Moses and Elijah*. As we know (see above on Jn 1:19–24), in Jewish eyes these were eschatological messianic figures: in a sense they sum up all of Old Testament expectation, the Law and the Prophets. Matthew and Mark leave us to imagine about what they were *conversing with Jesus*. Luke, however, says that they *spoke of his departure* (*exodos*) *which he was about to accomplish in Jerusalem*. The glorification of the Son of Man is to be achieved through the willing obedience of the Servant of the Lord, not through the triumphant messianism of popular and nationalistic thought.

This message, too, is brought out in what follows. Of Peter's excited proposal that they build *three tents*, Mark observes that *he did not know what to say*. This can be taken two ways. Peter was understandably confused, and therefore his words need not be taken too seriously. On the other hand, it was the wrong thing that he said, for he was seeking to prolong the present glory by ignoring the means by which it was to be made possible, just as he had at the time of his confession of Jesus' messiahship. Doubtless there is an allusion to the eschatological Feast of Booths (Tabernacles or Tents): this joyous feast, in which ancient Israel had celebrated the kingship of Yahweh, in late Jewish prophecy had come to signify the consummation of the messianic age (cf. Zech 14:16–19), and thus its annual observance was particularly a time of messianic excitement (cf. Jn 7:2 ff.). Rather than with Peter's tents, however, the three eschatological figures are covered with a *cloud* of theophany (cf. Ex 24:15, 40:35; Num 9:18), and as before at Jesus' baptism the heavenly voice proclaims him Servant of the Lord (see above on Lk 3:21–22 and parallels). Matthew and Mark have, as in the story of the baptism, *my beloved Son*. The best manuscripts of Luke read *my chosen Son,* which contains an additional allusion to Is 42:1. *Hear him* is new: it undoubtedly refers to the injunction of Deut 18:15.

Jesus' command that they should say nothing of this vision *until the Son of Man had risen from the dead* underlines the anticipatory character of the transfiguration. Mark also takes the occasion to note the puzzlement of the disciples over the very idea of resurrection, another reminder that we are viewing the Gospel story through the refracted light of post-resurrection faith and understanding.

Mk 9:11–13   Mark and Matthew conclude the story of the
Mt 17:10–13   transfiguration with a conversation between
                  Jesus and the disciples concerning the rabbinical opinion that Elijah would return, according to the prophecy in Mal 3:23 f., to prepare the way for the Messiah; Luke, who likes to think of Jesus as himself taking the role of Elijah the reconciler, has omitted this passage.

Elijah had just been seen together with Jesus. How, then, could it be said that *Elijah must come first?* Jesus' reply is that

Elijah has, indeed, come first, in the person of John the Baptist. More importantly, he came as a real prefiguration of the Messiah revealed in Jesus, for just as *it is written of the Son of Man*/Servant of the Lord that he *must suffer many things and be despised,* so it had been with the Baptist. The Baptist, too, *they treated as they willed, as it was written of* Elijah long ago (cf. 1 Kgs 19:2, 10).

14. YET A LITTLE WHILE

Mk 9:14–29   The episode with which we begin appears
Mt 17:14–21   to presuppose the Galilean ministry, es-
Lk 9:37–43a   pecially if by *scribes* Mark means here
              what he usually does. The *amazement* of
the crowd at the sight of Jesus does not necessarily look
back to the transfiguration, as though it saw some traces of
what the three disciples had seen on the mountain, but
can be explained by the tension and excitement that had
built up before his sudden and unexpected appearance. The
failure of Jesus' disciples to cure the afflicted boy had provoked a heated controversy, doubtless over Jesus himself, who
now arrived at the psychological moment. The atmosphere
of skepticism and unbelief which surrounds the scene, and
which Jesus sees as typical of a whole *unbelieving generation,*
stands in sharp contrast to the vision of glory so recently
described in the Gospels.

In their accounts of the unfortunate boy's affliction the
Gospels seem to be describing the symptoms of epilepsy,
which was popularly equated with insanity and the possession of an evil spirit. Jesus' lament over the general lack of
faith is the more understandable as it becomes evident
that the disciples, too, were unbelieving. This, at least, is

Matthew's explanation of their inability to exercise the power Jesus had given them (see above on Mk 3:13–19 and parallels): he cites in this connection a well-known saying of the Lord (cf. Mt 21:21; Mk 11:23; Lk 17:6), here to imply that their faith is not even as great as *a mustard seed* (see above on Mt 13:31 f. and parallels). Even the distraught father mingles incredulity with his humble cry for help— *if you can.* Jesus' retort is an exasperated echo, the reaction of a weary Master who has done so much with such little effect. *"If you can"! For one who believes, everything is "can"!* The man's response in the consciousness of an awakening faith remains an inspiration to the Christian surrounded by a world of doubt: *I do believe; help my weak faith!*

Mark ascribes the failure of the disciples to heal the boy not so much to their lack of faith as to their complacent exercise of a committed power without due recognition of its source: *This kind cannot be cast out except by prayer.* Most of our Greek manuscripts add here "and by fasting," but the critical evidence leaves us in no doubt that this is an early expansion of the text. The text thus expanded served as a model for another early scribe who inserted what appears as verse 21 in the standard version of Matthew's Gospel.

Mk 9:30–32   At this point the evangelists have placed the
Mt 17:22–23 second of Jesus' predictions of his coming
Lk 9:43b–45 passion and death (see above on Mk 8:31–33
                 and parallels). The terms are somewhat less precise than those used on the former occasion, which has led some to suppose that in this passage we may have a more primitive form of the same tradition. The Gospels feature here the disciples' uneasiness over what Jesus has said and their fear at enquiring more deeply into his meaning; this is undoubtedly an accurate portrayal of the state of mind of men who are only beginning to realize the implications of the commitments which they have made.

Mt 17:24-27 The story of the paying of the temple tax is told only by Matthew. Matthew's interest in Peter partly explains his use of the story, but probably even more important to him was its subject matter, which involved a problem that was of deep concern to all the evangelists and the early Church (see below on Mt 22:15-22 and parallels).

The *didrachma* or double drachma was a Greek coin worth upwards of a half dollar in our money, though of course in those times its purchasing power would have been far greater. It was considered to be the equivalent of the half shekel which according to the Law (cf. Ex 30:11-16) was to be paid by every Israelite each year for the support of the temple; under Roman domination the Jews were not allowed to coin their own money, except for small pieces of little value. Paying the temple tax was both a duty and an honor. Priests were exempted, but all other males subject to the Law, even the Levites, were expected to render it. On the contrary, it was not accepted from Samaritans and others whose title to Jewish orthodoxy was rejected.

The question whether Jesus would pay the tax was doubtless asked without ulterior motive. The tax was collected locally, in this case by citizens of Capernaum, and then sent to Jerusalem by means of the pilgrim caravans. Peter's affirmative answer was probably based on his experience of Jesus as well as presumption. The payment of the tax is never at issue; the point of the story, however, is that it was paid freely and to avoid disedification, not as of obligation. The little parable suggests that Jesus—and with him, Peter—are *the sons* of whom *the kings of the earth* do not expect tribute. Jesus, in view of his unique relationship to his Father, did not recognize the temple tax as required of him. Presumably Matthew implies to his Christian readers that they are somewhat in the same position as regards the taxes imposed upon them by the law of Rome. As children of the Father of all law and authority *they are free,* but other serious considerations should persuade them to pay. Their

Master had given them no precedent for rebellion or anarchy.

The miracle story which concludes the episode—actually, not so much the story of a miracle as the promise of one—is not open to the objection that miracles are not to be expected where natural means will do. It is consistent with Jesus' insistence that he, and Peter because of him, are free of the tax, and that if he submits himself to it he does so entirely on his own terms. The Roman silver *stater* had the value of four drachmas.

Mk 9:33–37   The three Synoptic Gospels now continue
Mt 18:1–5   with a story that admirably suits their in-
Lk 9:46–48   tention of characterizing this present stage
of Jesus' career as one of the education of his disciples. Essentially, the story is the same in all three Gospels. It must be observed, however, that in this instance it is Matthew who has made the most of it, he has depended here on another source besides Mark.

In the context of Jesus' reiterated pronouncements concerning the true nature of his kingdom and his messiahship, there is something ironical in the spectacle of the disciples' dispute over their relative dignity in the messianic realm-to-be. Mark has the Lord first (vs. 35) make a pronouncement which we find later in a somewhat ampler form (see below on Mk 10:43 f. and parallel). Then he preaches to them a parable in action. It is easy to imagine the scene, bearing in mind once more the informality of Palestinian life. Into the group of men sitting on the rush-strewn floor in earnest conversation had wandered one of the village children. Jesus places the child in their midst, holds it in his arms, and tells them that such they must become if they are to have any part in his kingdom. The saying that makes the point of the parable is Matthew's contribution: *unless you change and become like little children, you shall not enter the kingdom of heaven.*

The sense of this saying has often been misunderstood. The Oriental loves children, sometimes to excess, but he has no sentimental illusions about them. The Lord is not extolling here any supposed childlike virtues of humility or simplicity, virtues which many parents would be surprised to learn are proper to children. *Whoever considers himself of little account like this little child* means exactly what it says. The child was without rights to consideration in society, totally dependent upon the good will of his elders, an "it" rather than a "he." By deliberate choice, Jesus says, his disciples must become what the child is by necessity. This is the only greatness allowable in the kingdom of him who came to be the servant of all.

The other saying which concludes this passage is independent of the foregoing (cf. Jn 13:20), but related to it conceptually. To *receive a child such as this*—to succor the needy, the helpless, the abandoned—*in my name*, is truly to take in Christ and his revelation of the God of love and mercy (cf. 25:31 ff.). This is likewise the teaching of 1 Jn 4:19–21.

Mk 9:38–41   The "in my name" of the immediately pre-
Lk 9:49–50   ceding verse has led Mark and Luke to
Mt 10:40–42   insert here the case of "the strange exorcist."
Acts 19:13–16 tells of certain Jewish exorcists who invoked Jesus' name as a kind of magical formula, and a well-known exorcism papyrus now in the National Library of Paris, written about A.D. 300, includes among the efficacious names to be used that of "Jesu, the god of the Hebrews." The situation called to Jesus' attention by *John*, the son of Zebedee, does not seem to have been of such a character. Though unauthorized and unknown to the rest of the disciples, the man appears to have been successfully appealing to God with some kind of true faith in the person of Jesus. Jesus' argument is based on his exercise of a power for good, and it is rightly cited as a principle of tolerance. If the man was healing in Jesus' name he could hardly be counted as an enemy, *for he who is not against us is for us*. Obviously, this is not Jesus' only word on the often com-

plicated issue of others' relationship to him and his teaching.

Matthew has omitted these verses, possibly because he was afraid that they might be misunderstood (cf. Mt 7:22 f.). In the context of his "missionary discourse" of Jesus, however, he has applied to the disciples a lengthier expression of the sentiment which Mark ascribes to the Lord in verse 41. Acceptance of Christ's followers and representatives is the measure of accepting Christ himself. Good works done in their behalf will be rewarded as having been done to the Lord. Such ideas were precious to the Church of the Gospels.

Mk 9:42–48
Mt 18:6–9
Lk 17:1–2
Building again on a verbal connection with the preceding context, this time with the "child" of verse 37, Mark, followed by Matthew, attaches a saying of Jesus on the scandal of the weak: *Whoever causes one of these little ones who believe to commit sin.* There is also a connection of ideas: if we are to be rewarded for doing good to God's children, we shall certainly be punished for doing them evil, and there is no greater evil we can do them than to cause them to sin against the faith by which they are saved. *Better for him if a millstone were hung from his neck and he were thrown in the sea.* The millstone of which Jesus speaks is the *mylos onikos,* "donkey mill," a huge stone three or four feet in diameter and weighing several hundred pounds, turned on a pivot by oxen or asses.

Scandals must come, Matthew adds. In this world, constituted as it is, they are inevitable. Yet no one is thereby excused from guilt in being the occasion whereby evil finds an outlet in the world. Thus far there is a Lucan parallel to what Mark and Matthew have in this place, but put in another context which we shall understand better later on.

Mark and Matthew continue with a transition from the objective to the subjective aspect of scandal, that is, from the consideration of man as an occasion of sin to others to the consideration of how he can be a danger to himself.

Basically, Matthew repeats here what he has already included in the Sermon on the Mount (see above on Mt 5:27–30). Mark's version is substantively the same, but in speaking of *gehenna* and its *unquenchable fire* he cites the final graphic verse of the Book of Isaiah (66:24), which originally referred quite literally to the rotting corpses and smouldering refuse of the Valley of Hinnom.

Mk 9:49–50
Lk 14:34–35
It is this citation which leads Mark into his final verses which deal with "salt"—the connection, however, is difficult to see at best. *Everyone will be salted with fire:* apparently the association is purely verbal, leading to the enunciation of a new thought. Fire—now the fire of eschatological judgment and purification rather than the fire of destruction of the preceding verse—will preserve the people of God as salt preserves food. Mark now brings in the little parable on salt as a quality of the Christian character which Matthew used earlier in the Sermon on the Mount (see above on Mt 5:13–16) and which Luke has also placed in a context of the demands of discipleship, where it appears, however, as a grim warning against apostasy. *Have salt in yourselves,* Mark concludes. Salt is also figurative of the astringent qualities of practical wisdom and prudence required for social living: *thus you will be at peace with one another.*

Mt 18:10–14
Lk 15:3–7
During the past several passages we have lost contact with Luke's continuity, as now we do with Mark's as well. Shortly we shall rejoin these two evangelists to see how they continue the Gospel story. For the moment it is Matthew who provides the best unity. He has made the immediately preceding passages the beginning of his fourth major discourse into which he has gathered the Lord's teaching on the nature of the community life of the Church, and it is this that he now continues with the present parable of the lost sheep, which Luke has put in another context for a somewhat different purpose.

As Matthew tells the parable, it builds on the theme of the concern due to *the little ones* of the Church and is an exhortation to apostolic zeal; *their angels in heaven continually look on my heavenly Father's face* underlines the divine solicitude for even the least deserving and most erring of God's children, a solicitude which should serve as a model for that of the Church. The parable itself is quite clear and requires little explanation. Luke makes a more dramatic story of it: in his context it is told in rebuke of the Pharisaical scandal taken at the Lord's association with sinners.

Mt 18:15–18   Consideration of the erring brother leads Matthew to follow the parable of the lost sheep with these words of Jesus on fraternal correction and the discipline of the forgiveness of sin. The Gospel is speaking of real sin, not just social offenses: *if your brother sins* is the reading of the best manuscripts, and "against you" is recognized to be an addition to the text. Previously we have seen Jesus vindicate to himself as Son of Man authority on earth to forgive sins, and we also noted the Church's recognition that this authority continued as its own (see above on Mk 2:1–12 and parallels). This is one of the several Gospel passages in which Jesus' transmission of his power to his apostles is explicitly affirmed (cf. also Mt 16:19; Lk 17:3; Jn 20:23).

The exercise of this power must be above all pastoral. Private fraternal correction may suffice to bring the sinner to the repentance that is required for his forgiveness. *But if he will not listen, take one or two others:* the invocation of the legal precedent of Deut 19:15 indicates that a serious and public matter is in question. If even this does not suffice, the case should be referred *to the church,* to the entire community. Only when contumacy is proof against all these measures of suasion should the person be excommunicated from Christian society, declared to be, in Jewish terms, *like the heathen and the publican* (cf. Mt 5:46f.). In verse 18 the same judicial power is affirmed for the Church through the apostles which in Mt 16:19 was ascribed to Peter.

Mt 18:19–20   The following two verses appear to interrupt the continuity of thought, for verse 21 takes up again the idea of forgiveness, but actually the connection is quite close and logical. Jesus has not been talking about fraternal correction on a private and individual level, but of a power over sin and its forgiveness exercised by the Church, a power that it can exercise only because *I am in their midst.* It is the same presence of Christ which guarantees a special dignity and efficacy to the prayer of the assembled Church. Previously Jesus described the proper spirit of prayer as one in which a man retires into the privacy of his room and asks God in secret for what he wants (see above on Mt 6:5–8). This was not a condemnation of public prayer, but his way of rebuking ostentation and insincerity. The public prayer of the Church does not depend simply on the fervor of the individual Christian who prays, but it partakes of the efficacy of the prayer of Christ himself living in his Church gathered together *in my name.*

Mt 18:21–22   From the public sin with which the Church is to deal with pastoral charity the discourse passes to the question of fraternal charity in regard to personal offenses. *Peter* asks how often he is obliged to pardon someone who has offended him: *up to seven times?* Apparently the rabbis taught that no one could be expected to forgive an offender beyond three or at the most four times, and Peter doubtless thought he had seized the spirit of Jesus' generous interpretation of the Law when he had raised the number to seven. But the Lord's answer is that there is no law to regulate charity. As often as offense has been given, so often is there need to forgive (cf. Lk 17:4); the *seventy times seven* of verse 22 is a conscious reversal of Lamech's song of vengeance in Gen 4:24. Unrestricted vengeance had been banished by the Law of Moses, but for him who loves as a Christian should there is no need of law (see above on Mt 5:21–26).

Mt 18:23–35   Appropriately Matthew ends Jesus' discourse with another well-known parable, which forms a kind of commentary on the petition of the Lord's Prayer, "forgive us our debts as we forgive our debtors" (see below on Mt 6:9–15 and parallel). Far more importantly, however, it gives the motivation for the extraordinary spirit of forgivingness which is expected of Christians and which has just been commended to Peter: they must forgive their brothers their trifling offenses because of the far greater offense which God has freely forgiven them.

The parable in this instance takes almost the shape of a fairy tale. Most of the details are somewhat fabulous. The *king*—more properly, "a kingly person"—is an Oriental potentate who disposes of a debt of *ten thousand talents* —twenty million dollars might suggest the sum—as casually as the next man might cast an alms to a beggar. The exaggerations are all calculated. In contrast, the second debt of *a hundred denarii* was paltry indeed. Though such details help to make the point of the story, we must as usual resist the temptation to allegorize it. The lesson of the parable is in verse 33 (positively) and in verse 35 (negatively), not in the intervening verse that rounds out the story. The parable, in other words, does not teach that God will take back a pardon he has once given or deliver anyone over to a debtors' prison. Its message is that of 1 Jn 4:11.

Mt 19:1–2   Matthew concludes Jesus' discourse with his
Mk 10:1   usual formula (see above on Mt 7:28 f.) and
Lk 9:51   takes us immediately *to the district of Judea beyond the Jordan.* Here he is following Mark, who now begins what is sometimes called the story of the "Perean ministry." Each in his own way, the Synoptists are doing much the same thing. They have at last brought the Galilean ministry to a definitive close and now set the Lord

on his way toward Jerusalem for the last act of the drama
of our salvation in his passion, death, and resurrection.

Luke, who has made the most of this section in his Gospel,
deserves the greatest attention. He has long been waiting
for this moment, and now he announces it in the tones of
a triumphant exordium. Up to this point, though we may not
have always noticed it, he has been quietly preparing for this
climactic turn of events. In the other Gospels it has been
made evident that Jesus has left Galilee more than once;
in Luke's it has not. Even in describing something as important as Peter's confession of the Lord at Caesarea Philippi
(see above on Mk 8:27–30 and parallels), Luke carefully re-
frained from identifying the place, thus not to anticipate
this instant when he departed his Galilean homeland and
set his face to go up to Jerusalem. For the same reason, from
now on he will suppress any geographical reference that
would detract from the theme of Jesus' journey toward his
destiny.

Luke designates this moment as *when the days had been
fulfilled for him to be taken up.* This "being taken up," an
expression which Luke uses for the Lord's ascension in Acts
1:2, 11, 22, employs the language which the Greek Old
Testament applied to such events as the assumption of
Elijah (2 Kgs 2:9–11; Sir 48:9; 1 Macc 2:58) and of Enoch
(Sir 49:14), the latter a figure which was of intense interest
for the later Judaism of New Testament times. Luke means
by this term the summation of Jesus' atoning life in his suffering, death, resurrection, and ascension to the Father, the
complex of events which have made possible the coming of
the Spirit into the Church. The term is, therefore, analogous
to John's speaking of Christ as "raised up" or "glorified" (see
above on Jn 3:14–21).

Lk 9:52–56   Only Luke has recorded this episode of the
hostile Samaritans: the last time we saw Jesus
in Samaria, he had a more hospitable reception (cf.
Jn 4:4 ff.). As we know, the animosity between Jews and
Samaritans was always intense and reciprocal. It was apt to

flare up into bloodshed at the times of the pilgrimages to
Jerusalem for the great feasts, when religious differences
became underlined and accentuated. Sometimes it was worth
the life of a Jew to venture through Samaritan territory, and
this fact made it all the more inconvenient for those who
had to come from Galilee. Jesus ran into this kind of situation. Having prudently *sent messengers before him* to feel
out the sentiment, he learnt that he would not be welcome
in this place *because his face was set toward Jerusalem,* and
therefore he directed his way *to another village* where there
would be no trouble.

James and John (as "sons of thunder"? cf. Mk 3:17) ask
the Lord if he would have them *call down fire from heaven
to consume them.* The evangelist is thinking of the event in
the life of Elijah according to 2 Kgs 1:10–12. But while
Jesus is the great prophetic figure of the New Testament,
his prophetic word did not take such a form at all; hence *he
turned and rebuked them.* "The Son of Man did not come to
destroy the lives of men but to save them," found in a great
number of manuscripts, is doubtless a gloss on the text, but
an accurate reading of its meaning. On the other hand, what
appears in some manuscripts as verse 55b, "He said to them,
'You do not know what spirit you are,'" is probably a
Marcionite interpolation. Marcion, a strange second-century
heretic who accepted for his Scriptures only a corrupted form
of Luke's Gospel and some of the Pauline epistles, taught
that the main work of Jesus, the God of mercy of the New
Testament, was to undo all that had been done by the God
of justice of the Old Testament.

Jn 7:2–13   We shall interrupt the Lucan "journey" narrative at this point, however, to consider the
continuation of the Johannine version of Jesus' public life.
John, of course, has not built up his Gospel to show one
climactic appearance of Jesus in Jerusalem; he has, as a
matter of fact, centered the story of Jesus in Jerusalem
rather than Galilee. This present passage concerns a pilgrimage to Jerusalem on the occasion of *the Jewish feast of*

Tabernacles, the importance of which we noted when commenting on the story of the transfiguration (see above on Mk 9:2–10 and parallels). The section conforms to the Johannine pattern: the feast serves as the occasion for a discourse in which Jesus is revealed as the sign of God's glory replacing Jewish prefigurements (see above on Jn 2:1–11, 2:13–17, etc.), here the light of life shining in the darkness of an unbelieving world (Jn 1:4 f.).

Jesus' *brothers* in the sense of his family relations (see above on Mk 3:31–35 and parallels) appear only here in the Fourth Gospel (in Jn 2:12 and 20:17 Jesus' brothers=his disciples). For John they represent unbelievers of the type encountered in Jn 2:23–25, 6:15—that is, those who misinterpreted Jesus' *works,* seeing in them a fulfillment of their own aspirations rather than a revelation of God for their acceptance, and whose incipient faith led therefore ultimately to a rejection of his word. Here they ask him to *go up to* Jerusalem, to make the solemn pilgrimage entry into the Holy City, taking advantage of the nationalistic overtones of the feast of Tabernacles to *manifest* himself *to the world* as they thought he should. Jesus' answer is that the time for his manifestation has not yet come; and when it does come, it will be of a vastly different kind, which can be perceived only through the eyes of true faith. Therefore he will not go up to Jerusalem in their sense, but only in his own way. The world has, as a matter of fact, already seen and rejected him (see above on Jn 3:14–21). His brothers themselves belong to this world.

Jn 7:14–39 When Jesus does come up to Jerusalem *secretly* and *when the feast was already half over,* he finds the usual situation of controversy about his person, varying degrees of interest both idle and serious, dominated by the hostility of *the Jews,* here quite obviously the Jewish leadership which is distinguished from the crowds who are more confused than inimical. He begins to teach *in the temple* courts thronged with pilgrims to the feast and all *marveled* at this (here we have the Johannine parallel to Mk 6:2; Mt 13:54; Lk 4:22a). To the implied criticism that he is self-taught, Jesus replies that he teaches a doctrine that is from God, which would be recognized as such by anyone who was truly trying to do God's will. His argument strikingly parallels that of Jn 5:31–47 (see above).

He now addresses himself to the previous controversy of Jn 5:16–30 (see above), employing new arguments. In the name of the Law they condemn his supposed violation of the Sabbath, *yet not one of you observes the Law:* the Law, of course, forbade the taking of an innocent man's life, and they were seeking to kill him (cf. Jn 5:18, 7:1). Doubtless the protestation of many in the crowd was sincere: *Who is seeking to kill you?;* however, verse 25 shows that the intentions of Jesus' enemies were not entirely secret. *One work I did* refers back to the miracle of Jn 5:2–15 (see above). Jesus' argument here on the "breaking" of the Sabbath parallels such Synoptic passages as Mk 2:27; Mt 12:11; Lk 13:15. The principle that circumcision was to be administered on the eighth day (Lev 12:3, etc.) even though it might coincide with the Sabbath was commonly accepted by the rabbis. But if the Sabbath can be set aside in favor of one member of the body, why *are you angry with me because I made a whole man well on the Sabbath?*

The next stage of the discourse plays on the theme of another popular misunderstanding. *Some of the Jerusalemites,* who knew full well what Jesus' enemies had in mind for him, were impressed by his boldness and the reasonableness of what he had to say. They noted that their leaders had fallen silent. Was it because they had become convinced and were ready to acknowledge him as Messiah? Doubtless they knew better than that; but still, silence gives consent, and perhaps the leaders had been convinced even against their wills. Yet *we know where this man comes from; but the Messiah, when he comes, no one will know where he comes from.* One popular notion of the Messiah was that his origins would be unknown before his sudden manifestation to Israel. Here, however, was Jesus, whose career the crowds had long watched, and whose relatives were even now standing about.

The passage is fraught with Johannine irony. They know him, yes, but only in the most superficial way possible. As regards everything that is essential they do not know him at all. They cannot know him because they do not know God, the one who has sent him. Had they known God, they would have recognized his messenger. It is probably in the same ironic vein that John refers in verse 31 to the *many in the crowd* who *believed in him:* their faith depended on miraculous *signs*, the real significance of which they had not perceived (see above on Jn 2:23–25). Even this passing interest, however, provoked *the Pharisees and chief priests* to try to take further measures against him. Thus Jesus is inspired to his final utterances to this people. *Yet a little while I am with you:* nothing that his enemies can do will determine his coming and going, but only his free decision as the agent of the Father. *I go back to him who sent me:* even when it will seem that his enemies have prevailed, in reality Jesus will have fulfilled the mission of salvation for which he is in the world. *You will see me . . . you cannot come:* the finality of this sentence contrasts with the promise to the disciples in Jn 13:33–36. As usual, his words are taken in a superficial sense. *Does he intend to go into the Diaspora?* The question is intended sarcastically: since Jesus has gained no hearing with his own people, perhaps he will now try his luck with the Gentiles. But John sees its ironic implications: Christ in the Christian Church has indeed passed irrevocably from Palestinian Judaism into the Gentile world.

Jesus' closing statement is somewhat obscure, especially since for some reason the passing of several days is presupposed. The theme of Christ as living water is familiar (see above on Jn 4:4–19), and has probably been introduced here in view of the extensive libations proper to *the last day* of Tabernacles. *As the Scripture says:* we have to do with a paraphrase rather than a quotation, the identification of which is the more difficult since it is not clear whether it is to be referred to Christ or to the believer in Christ. Some passage like Ex 17:6 (cf. 1 Cor 10:4), Zech 14:8 (cf. Ezek 47:1–12), or Is 58:11 are probably in the evangelist's mind.

At all events, it is clear that Jesus spoke of the outpouring of *the Spirit* which would be consequent on his glorification.

Jn 7:40–52   The variety of messianic expectations is again made evident in the discussion incident to Jesus' discourse. On *the prophet,* see above on Jn 1:19–24. Here the objection to recognizing in Jesus *the Messiah* is based on the standard doctrine of a Davidic Messiah of Judean origin: in John as in the Synoptic Gospels Jesus is commonly regarded as "the Galilean" (see above on Jn 4:43–45). The evangelist doubtless presupposes the Synoptic information on Jesus' Judean birth and therefore finds in the crowds' remarks a further indication of how little they know in comparison to what they pretend to know (vs. 27).

Jesus remains in control of his situation, as he had implied (vs. 33); no one as yet dared *lay hands on him.* Even the temple police sent to harass him (vs. 32) returned to their masters somewhat dazed from having heard Jesus (we are dealing here with the Johannine parallel to Mk 1:22; Lk 4:32; Mt 7:28 f.). The Pharisees' reaction to this accurately reflects some scribal opinion on the condition of the ordinary Jew who was no professional student of the Law: *this crowd which does not know the Law is accursed.* This time, however, they had overstepped themselves and invited a rebuke from one of their own. *None of the Pharises has believed in him,* they say. Out steps a Pharisee—and a Pharisee of Pharisees, for he is a member of the Sanhedrin—who does believe in him. They did not know that he was a follower of Christ, and with his characteristic timidity *Nicodemus* (see above on Jn 3:1–13) did not dare to make more than an indirect defense of Jesus, but it was enough to show that they had gone too far and enough, therefore, to enrage them further. *Are you also from Galilee?* they ask with a sneer. This was hardly to address themselves to the serious question of law—the very Law that they pretended to reverence—that Nicodemus had raised. Their final statement is likewise bluster. *From Galilee a prophet* (some important manuscripts have *the prophet*) *does not arise* interposes regional prejudice between themselves and the word of God.

Jn 7:53–8:11   There seems to be no doubt that the beautiful little story that now follows and which interrupts Jesus' Tabernacles discourse did not originally belong to the Gospel of John. It is lacking in practically all of the best Greek manuscripts of John, but there is some good reason to think that it has been dislodged from the Gospel of Luke, whose language and viewpoints it suits much better (in some manuscripts it appears at the conclusion of Lk 21). It is possible that in early times it was transferred to this location in the Gospels as a kind of commentary on Jn 8:15 below. At any rate, it is part of the Gospel which deserves consideration in its own right, regardless of its context.

A situation is supposed like that of the Synoptic account of Passion week, when Jesus was spending the nights on *the Mount of Olives,* the hill that overlooks Jerusalem on the east, separated from the Holy City by the narrow Kidron Valley (cf. Lk 21:37 f.). *In the early morning* he has returned *to the temple* and, as before, the people gather to hear him while he sits on the ground before them in the manner of Oriental teachers. Through the courtyard passes a group of *scribes and Pharisees,* dragging with them a woman accused of adultery. They are taking her to trial. Then they see Jesus and quickly they form a plan to use the woman to hurt him in the eyes of the people.

Jesus' foes present him with a dilemma not unlike others in the Synoptic Gospels (see below on Mt 22:15–22). If he says that she should be condemned to stoning as the Law directed (Deut 22:23 f.)—or was he being challenged to specify stoning where the Law was silent as to the method of punishment? (cf. Lev 20:10; Deut 22:22)—then what would be thought now of his gentle teaching, of his principles of love and mercy that had already made him suspect in their eyes of defying the Law? If, on the other hand, he asks for her release, is not this another clearcut proof of his disregard for the Law of Moses and God?

The text says that *Jesus bent down and wrote with his finger on the ground.* Since only here in the Gospels is Jesus ever said to have written anything, commentators have enjoyed speculating over the centuries as to what he wrote. Probably he wrote nothing, but merely traced idle lines in the dirt to show his lack of interest in their simulated concern over his opinion. This seems to be indicated by what follows. *As they continued to ask him,* he finally stood and gave them his answer in a seemingly careless way, as though he had been distracted from something more important, for he immediately returned to his tracings in the earth.

His answer was adequate to the situation, but by no means should it be extended beyond the situation nor sentimentalized to produce the portrait of a Christ indifferent to sin. He asked the woman's accusers to examine their own consciences before inflicting punishment on others, and here they were, prepared to exploit a wretched person's shame and humiliation simply to face down one of their adversaries. Though he himself judges no one, his very presence is judgment against them and their unworthy motives (cf. Jn 8:15). He likewise stands as a merciful judge of the woman, who is told to go and *sin no more.* Forgiveness of sin does not condone sin, but looks toward its eradication in the sinner.

Jn 8:12–20   After the interpolated story of the woman taken in adultery, Jesus' Tabernacles discourse continues with another theme suggested by the rites of the feast, this time the illumination of the temple area to symbolize the light of truth. *I am the light of the world* (see above on Jn 1:3b–5) and *the light of life* identify with Jesus concepts which the Old Testament (cf. Is 51:4), rabbinical Judaism, and the Qumran literature would use to describe the revelation of God in the Mosaic law.

Immediately there is a controversy. Previously (see above on Jn 5:31–47) Jesus had conceded the legal principle that a man testifying in his own behalf needs corroborating witnesses. Now, however, his approach is somewhat different:

Even if I am my own witness, my testimony is true. The reason for this is that *I know where I came from and where I am going* (cf. Jn 7:14–39 above) while they clearly do not: the only testimony that is valid in his case only he can give, and they are incapable of receiving it. In this situation, since his testimony is at the same time that of *the Father who sent me*, the requirement of the two witnesses (Deut 17:6, 19:5) is met by the only two witnesses competent to testify. Jesus says *it is written in your Law:* the "your" is eloquent of the evangelist's idea of the separation from Judaism of the Christ of the Church. The Pharisees demand that Jesus produce his second witness, *your Father,* a puerile request which is their self-condemnation, confirmed by Jesus' reply, that they know neither God nor his Word.

Judgment is the other theme of this interchange. Jesus says *I judge no one* (as we saw, it may be this statement that occasioned the insertion of the preceding story). This does not really conflict with Jn 5:16–30 (see above), where Jesus defines his character as judge in that his presence in the world works judgment in the face of unbelief. Here he is contrasting his oneness of spirit with the Father with the superficial judgments of the Pharisees, *according to the flesh* (cf. Jn 7:24).

These words he spoke in the treasury while teaching in the temple. Jesus was probably standing at the door of the strong room adjoining the court of the women, the most public of the temple courtyards. If, as is likely, a crowd was assembled during this dispute, it would sufficiently explain why *no one arrested him.* The evangelist probably sees a further irony in the fact that it was in the temple that he spoke, and went unrecognized, who was to replace the temple (see above on Jn 2:18–22).

Jn 8:21–29   *Again* (on another occasion?) Jesus speaks to *them* (vs. 22: *the Jews*) in language that is strongly reminiscent of what we have already read above (see on Jn 7:14–39). As in Jn 7:33 f., Jesus tells them that he is *going away* and that they will seek him in vain; this time he adds that *you will die in your sins.* Putting the idea of death together with his assertion that *where I go you cannot come,* they arrive at an even more foolish conclusion than in Jn 7:35. He is going to commit suicide, thus go to hell and be out of reach of all righteous men! John's irony is found, of course, in the half-truth they have unwittingly stumbled on: Jesus will, indeed, lay down his life, and as a result he will be beyond their grasp forever.

Jesus has introduced the theme of their sin. They belong to the order that is *below* and *of this world,* which can lead only to death. He has come *from above* to bring them life. But the condition of this life is faith, and thus their unbelief proves that they will die in their sin. *You do not believe that I am* (see above on Jn 6:17b–21).

The Jews recognize Jesus' "I am" to be a title. But what does it mean? *Who are you?* they ask. The Greek of his reply is not too clear, but probably it should be translated: *From the beginning the same that I am now telling you.* All his words and deeds up to this point, in other words, have been consistent with his present assertion. They have not understood the one because they have not understood the others. It is, therefore, pointless for him to continue to speak to them, his words judging them the while. His testimony he continues to offer only because it was for this that he was sent into the world. The final testimony is coming, irrefutable for all who believe; though it, too, will be wasted on them. *When you have raised up the Son of Man* (see above on Jn 3:14–21), *then you will know that I am he.*

Jn 8:30–36   It is surprising to find in the midst of these polemical passages the notation that *while he was saying these things many believed in him,* and even more surprising to learn that Jesus spoke the words that follow *to the Jews who had come to believe him*—who speedily demonstrate that they do not believe him at all and who end by trying to kill him! However, we have by now seen it suggested more than once that his lengthy Tabernacles discourse is an artificial literary unity made up of elements in part disparate, in part duplicated elsewhere in the Johannine discourse material. Hence, we should not attach too much historical importance to the present editorial transition. It may serve as a reminder, nevertheless, even though it is little relevant to this context, that Jesus' sermons did not always fall on deaf ears and that there was a variety of dispositions among his hearers.

Jesus' initial statement could very well, as a matter of fact, have been directed to his disciples or to those who would be his disciples (vss. 31 f.). The reaction to it, however, is not that of believers but of the willfully obtuse. *The truth shall make you free*, he had said. This man is offering them freedom? Freedom to *the seed of Abraham*? The Jews had been subjected to foreign conquerors for centuries—to Assyrians, Babylonians, Syrians, Egyptians, Persians, Greeks of divers degrees, and lately to Romans. Yet in a sense they had never surrendered. Secure in the conviction that the God of Israel was their truth, they had stubbornly preserved their national and religious identity despite all the odds, while other religions and other peoples, including many of their oppressors, had now been lost in time. There was a great deal of truth in their proud retort: *We have never been enslaved to anybody!*

A great deal of truth, but also more than a little of the wrongheadedness that made them deaf to the word of life. They were assuming that the freedom of which Jesus spoke was theirs by birthright as Jews. But as another great Jew would write: "The true Jew is not he who is such outwardly . . . the true Jew is he who is such inwardly" (Rom 2:28 f.). Jews, too, can commit sin, and *everyone who commits sin is a slave of sin*. Thus, Jesus implies, they are really slaves after all, and as slaves they have no abiding home in the household of God along with his sons who have received their freedom at the hands of his one Son (cf. Jn 1:12 f.).

Jn 8:37–47 If they are in reality slaves, he goes on, in what sense can they claim to be the *seed of*

Abraham? He repeats the charge, *you are seeking to kill me* (cf. Jn 7:19). Does this mark them as children of Abraham, inspired by Abraham's example? Just as Jesus' words and deeds manifest him as the Son of his Father, so do their actions show them to be children of another father, who is certainly not Abraham.

Twice Jesus has managed to suggest that his adversaries are children of a father other than the one they claim. At first they indignantly exclaimed, *Abraham is our father.* Now they cry, *We were not born out of wedlock*—implying that Jesus had been?—*we have one Father, who is God.* But, replies Jesus, just as their works prove that Abraham is not their father, their lack of love for God's Son shows that neither can he be their Father. If God were their Father they would recognize his Son. Their ears would be attuned to a message that clearly speaks the words of God. They have heard him speak, but it has only been sounds to them. This proves that they have no part with God.

Must he tell them who their real father is? It is *the devil*, and what they are doing is this father's will. Do they want proof? Very well, he has already convicted them of two things, that they are seeking to murder him and that they prefer falsehood to truth. Are not these the works of the devil? The devil *was a murderer from the beginning*: it was he who introduced death into the world (cf. Gen 3:3 f.; Wis 2:24). It is the devil whose very nature it is to lie. This, then, is why they will not listen to Jesus' word: they hate the truth. Jesus has proved his devotion to the truth, for there is none of them who can convict him of any sin. He therefore concludes his argument as he began it: if they were God's children they would hear his word; that they refuse shows that they have no part with God.

Jn 8:48–59   The discourse ends in recriminations and the threat of violence. In calling Jesus *a Samaritan* the crowd doubtless intended nothing more than a term of deep contempt (cf. Sir 50:25 f.); that he possessed *a demon*, that is, was insane, demented, had been suggested before (cf. Jn 7:20). From their point of view, they were merely paying Jesus back in his own coin. Had he not said that their father was the devil?

Jesus leaves to God the judgment of the issue between them. This is also a warning to his traducers. That he has nothing in common with the devil is proved by the honor he gives to God and his promise to all who receive his word that they will *never see death*, the death which is the very province of Satan. This assertion affords the Jews the occasion to bring in Abraham a final time. *Not taste death?* Abraham, whose patronage Jesus has tried to deny them, great as he was, died like any man. Is he making himself something greater than Abraham? He has spoken of his word that gives life. But *the prophets*, the men of the word, they too are dead. Is he greater than the prophets?

Jesus' answer is twofold. They have asked, *Whom do you make yourself?* He has said nothing for his own self-glorification; he has merely revealed the word of the Father. Is he greater than Abraham? Yes, since Abraham *rejoiced that he would see my day:* Abraham recognized that he was not the terminus of God's promises, but the beginning of a blessing that was to come (cf. Gen 12:3, 18:18; Gal 3:8 f.). *When he saw it, he was glad:* probably the reference is to Gen 17:17, understanding Abraham's laughter as a sign of his joy over the birth of Isaac, the earnest of the fulfillment of God's promises; this was the ordinary Jewish interpretation of the passage.

This last bald statement not unnaturally provokes the ire of this hostile audience. *You are not yet fifty years old*, still a young man, *and you have seen Abraham?*: the reversal of subject and object (Jesus had said that Abraham saw him, or rather, his day) is doubtless to heighten the supposed absurdity. Jesus' response combines the "I am" of verses 24 and 28 with the significant variation in tenses used in the Prologue to distinguish contingent being from the divine endurance (see above on Jn 1:1 f.): *Before Abraham came to be, I am* (cf. also Ps 90:2); on the historicity of what is implied in such an assertion, see below on Lk 10:21 f. and parallel. At this apparent blasphemy the Jews begin to look about for means to stone Jesus, who therefore quickly departs from the scene.

OTHER IMAGE BOOKS

OTHER IMAGE BOOKS

OTHER IMAGE BOOKS

OTHER IMAGE BOOKS

S42